BLACK MOSAIC

Benjamin Quarles

BLACK MOSAIC

Essays in Afro-American History and Historiography

Introduction by August Meier

THE UNIVERSITY OF MASSACHUSETTS PRESS

AMHERST

Library of Congress Cataloging-in-Publication Data

Quarles, Benjamin.
  Black Mosaic.

    1. Afro-Americans—History. 2. Afro-Americans—
Historiography. 3. United States—Race relations. I. Title.
E185.Q19 1988   973'.0496073   87–13929
ISBN 0–87023–605–9 (pbk. : alk. paper)

British Library Cataloguing in Publication data are available

Chapters in this book were previously published in
journals and collections. Their earlier appearances and
permissions to reprint are listed on the last printed
page of this book.

To my grandsons, James and Jonathan

Contents

BLACK MOSAIC

August Meier

Introduction: Benjamin Quarles and the Historiography of Black America

I T HAS BEEN nearly half a century since Benjamin Quarles published his first scholarly article in the field of Afro-American history.[1] With the appearance of his biography of Frederick Douglass in 1948, Quarles became a major contributor to the history of the black experience from the Revolutionary War through the Civil War. His leading works include the standard volumes on the role of Negroes in both of those conflicts, pioneering studies on black participation in the abolitionist movement, and two monographs on the interrelation between blacks and major white antislavery figures. Given the collective importance of this corpus of work, including the essays reprinted herein, this seems an appropriate time to assess his contribution.

As a scholar, Quarles was a "late bloomer," and in fact his achievement was accomplished under considerable odds. He was born in 1904, one of five children of a Boston subway porter. After finishing high school he worked for several years as a passenger steamship porter and Florida hotel bellhop,[2] and did not enter college until he was twenty-three. It was as a sophomore at Shaw University in Raleigh, North Carolina, that Quarles was first introduced to Negro history by an inspiring white woman teacher. Subsequently a Social Science Research Council fellowship enabled him to start graduate work at the University of Wisconsin in 1931. Members of the University of Wisconsin history faculty at the time assumed that blacks could not write "objectively" about their past. Even Quarles's liberal and supportive M.A. advisor, Carl Russell Fish, who at this time, just before his death, was rounding out ten years of service as a member of the council of the Association for

---

[1]Quarles, "The Breach Between Douglass and Garrison," *Journal of Negro History* (April 1938): 144–54.
[2]Interview with Quarles, Nov. 17, 1958; Hollie I. West, "A Sense of Self Out of the Past," *Washington Post*, June 18, 1976.

3

the Study of Negro Life and History, leaned toward this view and doubted that enough source material survived to make black history anything more than a marginal specialty. Nevertheless, William B. Hesseltine, under whom Quarles took his Ph.D., was at that time working on his biography of Grant. Because of an interest in Frederick Douglass's role in the politics of the Grant administration, Hesseltine was led to make "an exception" in Quarles's case, permitting him to write his dissertation on the famous black abolitionist's public career.[3]

Quarles, who received his doctorate in 1940, had meanwhile been on the faculty at Shaw and Dillard universities, and his scholarly career, already delayed, was further postponed by his duties as dean at the latter institution. Thus publication of his first book did not come out until 1948, when Quarles was forty-four. For the rest of his career—at Dillard and then as department chairman at Morgan State College—Quarles spent much of his time in administrative tasks. It was a mark of his discipline and skill at budgeting time that he emerged as a scholar of considerable productivity, bringing out *The Negro in the Civil War* in 1953, *The Negro in the American Revolution* in 1961, *Lincoln and the Negro* in 1962, *The Negro on the Making of America* in 1964, *Black Abolitionists* in 1968, and *Allies for Freedom: Blacks and John Brown* in 1974. Meanwhile his two essays in the *Mississippi Valley Historical Review*, "Sources of Abolitionist Income" (1945) and "The Colonial Militia and Negro Manpower" (1959), both reprinted here, had been the first articles by a Negro scholar to appear in the pages of that major mainstream journal of American history. The Frederick Douglass biography, which set the tone for Quarles's future work, reflected two diverse, if not contradictory, influences: the noted reformer Frederick Douglass himself and the skeptical Hesseltine, who distrusted reformers' motives. On the one hand, the book displayed the meticulous scholarship and emphasis on narrative writing that Hesseltine instilled in his students.[4] On the other hand, there was

---

[3]Interview with Quarles.

[4]Interview with Quarles. I am indebted to Sherman Merrill of Morgan State University for raising the question with me of Hesseltine's possible influence on Quarles, and to three former students of Hesseltine—Frank Byrne of Kent State University, Richard N. Current of the University of North Carolina at Greensboro, and T. Harry Williams of Louisiana State University—for helpful insights on Hesseltine and his relations with his students in general and with Quarles in particular. Hesseltine of course was a complex person and, while skeptical of the motivations of reformers, personally was involved in certain reform causes himself. Conversations with Merrill, Nov. 18, 1978, and with Byrne, Nov. 22, 1978; telephone interviews with Current and Williams, Jan. 5, 1979.

Quarles's fascination with Douglass, Quarles himself believing that his own interpretation of the black experience was unconsciously shaped by his encounter with the great reformer. Douglass, as Quarles points out, was a man simultaneously critical of American society and nearly always hopeful about the ultimate fulfillment of its democratic promise. This can be seen in his famous July 4 oration of 1852, which opens with a striking statement of black alienation but closes with a eulogy of America and its institutions. Quarles's publications have been imbued with a similar kind of optimism. Moreover, as he told me when I interviewed him in preparation for this paper, Douglass's "writings always reflected that blacks belonged in America, and that blacks shaped America consciously and unconsciously. Frederick Douglass showed that blacks had earned the right to participate in American society, and he regarded it as inevitable that the Negro would be a mainstream figure."[5] Then, too, Douglass's interest in women's rights was to find a parallel in the attention that Quarles, in nearly all his books, has paid to the role of black women.[6] And finally, Douglass served, again perhaps unconsciously, as a prototype for Quarles's consistent theme that blacks, rather than being passive objects of white actions, were themselves major actors in the struggle for their own freedom and influential shapers of American history.

Yet it appears impossible at this date to separate Douglass's influence on Quarles from the possibility that Quarles found Douglass so fascinating just because the black abolitionist's views were in accord with his own perceptions. Douglass, after all, expressed an ideology that has been at the mainstream of black thinking for most of the last two centuries. Negro spokesmen and leaders from Richard Allen to the present have appealed to the democratic values expressed in the Declaration of Independence; and as Quarles himself puts it, blacks "internalized the Declaration," taking it quite literally in a way that the white majority did not.[7] Moreover, Quarles came to intellectual maturity during the crisis of the 1930s, an era that was characterized not only by much disillusionment with the American system among many intellectuals, but also by a renewed faith in the possibilities inherent in that system for appro-

---

[5]Interview with Quarles. For text of Douglass's July 1852 oration, see Philip S. Foner, ed., *Life and Writings of Frederick Douglass* (New York, 1950), vol.2, pp. 181–204.

[6]See, for example, the opening chapter of *Lincoln and the Negro* (New York, 1962), entitled "Charlotte Scott's Mite"; *The Negro in the Civil War* (Boston, 1953), pp. 246–47; *Black Abolitionists* (New York, 1969).

[7]Interview with Quarles.

priate and humane reforms. Black leaders and intellectuals shared in this hopeful, reformist outlook. In addition the Depression decade witnessed the maturation of two major schools of black scholarship, both of which had begun back during World War I. These were the Negro sociologists, principally disciples of the University of Chicago's Robert E. Park, and the historians inspired by Carter G. Woodson, who founded the Association for the Study of Negro Life and History and the *Journal of Negro History* in 1915–16. Both groups, hopeful that white America could be brought to implement its professed democratic ideology, believed that an important function of their scholarship was to educate the white majority and thus gain acceptance for blacks in the American mainstream. Woodson, though possessing a strong nationalistic tinge, entitled his widely used textbook *The Negro in Our History*. Interestingly enough, Quarles, unlike most of his contemporaries and professors at Wisconsin, was not a Beardian. He did not share their stress on class conflict and economic causation, but, coming out of an essentially black tradition and conceptualization of American history, he has consistently stressed the moral dynamic as influencing the course of American history. On the other hand, this faith that Quarles and his fellow black scholars had in the moral dynamic inherent in the American value system dovetailed very neatly with the theory for social change explicated in Gunnar Myrdal's *An American Dilemma* (1944), in which form it was highly acclaimed by influential sectors in the American white intellectual community.[8]

The 1940s marked a new departure in Afro-American history, with the rise to prominence not only of Quarles but of John Hope Franklin, whose first monograph appeared in 1943 and whose *From Slavery to Freedom* was published just the year before Quarles's *Douglass*. Yet both men owed a significant debt to Carter Woodson and the black historians associated with him who had dominated the field for thirty years. The latter had propagandized for the study of Negro history, seeking to build race pride and self-esteem among blacks and simultaneously to break down the prejudices of whites. The *Journal* had provided an important vehicle for both black scholars and the few whites who were interested, and Woodson had

[8]It was the late T. Harry Williams who suggested to me the Beardian orientation of most of the people with whom Quarles interacted at Wisconsin. Quarles himself, quite correctly, does not perceive that Myrdal had any influence on his own thinking; he recalls that at the time he aptly thought that while Myrdal had "detailed the dilemma very well," few white Americans were actually aware of it. Interviews with Williams and Quarles.

encouraged a group of disciples who produced several truly important monographs. It is true that Woodson and his colleagues were engaged first and foremost in fact-gathering; Woodson's own specialized monographs were unsatisfying compilations of facts, and his general texts were little more than catalogues of black achievers. Yet Woodson's followers included a handful of men who made important scholarly contributions, most notably A. A. Taylor's early state studies on Reconstruction and Lorenzo Greene's authoritative *The Negro in Colonial New England.*[9]

The relationship between Woodson and his circle and the work of Quarles and Franklin was undoubtedly complex. Just as those of us who came to maturity and did out first work in Afro-American history during the 1950s and 1960s were so greatly indebted to Franklin's synthesis in *From Slavery to Freedom,* so also Franklin and Quarles, emerging in the 1940s, had built upon the edifice that Woodson had created. Yet where Woodson's work reads like a catalogue of facts and achievements, devoid of analysis, Quarles and Franklin gave Afro-American history a more coherent narrative thrust and turned away from focusing on outstanding individuals to stressing the collective experience of blacks in America.

Quarles is well aware both of his own debt to Woodson and of his differences from the older man. Although Quarles had used Woodson's textbook as a student and as a teacher, the two men did not meet until after the younger historian had completed his doctorate. There was, therefore, no direct connection between Quarles and Woodson, even though Quarles's first published work had earlier appeared in the *Journal of Negro History.* Quarles regarded Woodson as the great pioneer and recognized that he and Woodson were similar in important ways: in their respect for scholarship and in their belief that, with the role of blacks having been consistently underplayed by white historians, the collection and publication of facts would help build black self-esteem and change white attitudes. As Quarles has said, "We felt that this would strengthen interracial understanding; at the same time our purpose was to restore the race to its rightful place."[10] Yet Quarles is also aware that his narrative thrust sets him apart from Woodson, and that in his writing he has tried, as he says in the preface to *The*

---

[9]Alrutheus A. Taylor, *The Negro in South Carolina During Reconstruction* (Washington, 1924), and *The Negro in the Reconstruction of Virginia* (Washington, 1926); Lorenzo J. Greene, *The Negro in Colonial New England* (New York, 1942).
[10]Interview with Quarles.

Negro in the American Revolution, "to present a group portrait rather than a study of individuals."[11] Actually, in both respects, Quarles's departure from Woodson's style was not unprecedented, for Greene's and Taylor's specialized studies did much to anticipate the nature of the monographs that Quarles would produce. The scholarly works of all three men, possessed though they were of a deep commitment to studying the Negro's past, lacked Woodson's overt stress on building race pride, and were written with a detachment and fairness toward whites that stood in marked contrast to the racism pervading what most white historians wrote about blacks before midcentury. Nevertheless, Quarles—like Franklin—went beyond the whole Woodson circle in an important respect; both men were far more successful at placing blacks at the center of the American historical stage than any of their predecessors had ever been.

The role of Quarles and Franklin is all the more important because they were the last two black scholars of distinction to emerge until the early 1970s. While among whites only a small group of radicals and liberals had been doing significant research in Afro-American history, by midcentury the situation was changing dramatically. In fact, the work of Quarles's middle period—the volumes on the Civil War, Lincoln, and the Revolution, and three important articles reprinted here[12]—was published in a milieu characterized by a growing interest in black history among white historians, some of them quite prominent.[13] In fact, except for Franklin, Quarles, and Raymond W. Logan, whites would actually dominate the field during the 1950s and 1960s. Only after the tumultuous events of the civil rights movement and the emergence of a new sense of racial identity and heightened interest in the race's past did additional black scholars become important in the field. Quarles's latest books on the black abolitionists and John Brown were done against the backdrop of the rise of these new black scholars and of a whole new paradigm of black history. Interestingly enough, however, Quarles's scholarship and point of view were

[11]Interview with Quarles; *The Negro in the American Revolution* (Chapel Hill, 1961), p. xi.

[12]"The Colonial Militia and Negro Manpower," "Lord Dunmore as Liberator," and "The Abduction of 'The Planter.'"

[13]Prominent white historians of the 1950s who developed an interest in black history would include Kenneth Stampp and C. Vann Woodward. In addition, at the end of the decade Stanley Elkins made a splash with his provocative book on slavery and slave personality.

affected to only a minor extent by these rapid and profound changes in the field of Afro-American history.

Quarles has not made a major synthesis of black history,[14] but has produced a series of monographs characterized by careful scholarship and a balanced, though not entirely detached, perspective. In terms of subject matter he plowed new ground. He wrote the first scholarly biography of Douglass; created the first book length synthesis on Negroes in the Civil War and abolitionist movement; examined with revealing insight the relationship between blacks and the two whites who became heroes to Negroes (Lincoln and Brown); and produced the only thoroughly researched account of the Negro in the Revolution. Quarles in these monographs—even more explicitly than Franklin in *From Slavery to Freedom*—placed blacks on the center stage of major events and movements in American history. Moreover, Quarles has been quite original in the way he has focused on the interaction between blacks and whites—both in his treatment of pivotal events like the Revolution and the Civil War, and also in his accounts of the abolitionist movement and white antislavery figures. The view that blacks were not passive in the struggle for their freedom was far from novel. But Quarles's unique contribution lay in the way he analyzed the blacks' impact upon those whites who—either voluntarily, or pressed by the force of events—became the Negroes' sympathizers and allies.

The corpus of Quarles's work is suffused with the dual view that white treatment of blacks was a central theme in American history that violated the ethical norms upon which the nation was founded, and that at the same time blacks were key actors in the struggle to secure the fulfillment of these values. Quarles himself feels that his writings "always reflect that blacks belonged to America, and that blacks shaped America consciously and unconsciously. . . . There is scarcely any aspect of the American experience that you cannot trace the presence of blacks in; every major crisis involved the status of black men." Blacks were central even in a psychological sense— their very presence was important in a negative way for the forging of the white American's identity, since as Quarles puts it, "The American quest for self-identity was forged around the black man as an outsider."[15]

This theme of the centrality of blacks to the American ethos and

[14]Quarles, *The Negro in the Making of America* (New York, 1964), was a brief survey intended for undergraduate and high school classes.
[15]Interview with Quarles.

its fulfillment, along with the optimistic view that in the end the spirit of the Declaration of Independence would be fulfilled, are explicitly expressed in nearly all of Quarles's works. Thus in *Black Abolitionists* he wrote, "Freedom is and has always been America's root concern, a concern that found dramatic expression in...the most important and revolutionary movement in our country's past," that is, the abolitionist movement.[16] In his volume on the Revolution he argued that "the humanitarian impulse which inspired the Revolution" was helpful, along with the more potent manpower shortage, in bringing Negroes into the war effort. Even though "the cause of liberty had lost momentum" in the postwar years, Quarles nevertheless believed that late eighteenth-century Negroes were encouraged "by the conviction that the Revolutionary era...had marked out an irreversible path toward freedom...."[17] John Brown's significance lay largely in the fact that, "however flawed," he represented "a new peaking in a continuous process—that of a nation coming to grips with its conscience."[18] Like the Revolution, the Civil War "succeeded significantly in enlarging the compass of American democracy...However halting her antislavery action during the course of the war, America, as the land of the free, inevitably moved in the direction of her high calling."[19] That the Civil War was "a rendezvous with the created-equal doctrine of the Declaration of Independence," became "crystal clear to Lincoln...To say, therefore, that Lincoln lives in history is to say that he met head-on the greatest challenge to his country as the land of the free—the challenge of the Negro."[20]

Thus a consistent thread throughout Quarles's writings—implicit where not explicitly stated—is the dual function of blacks in major episodes of our history as both symbol and participant. This is most clearly stated perhaps in *The Negro in the American Revolution:* "In the Revolutionary War the American Negro was a participant and a symbol. He was active on the battlefronts and behind the lines; in his expectations and in the gains he registered during the war, he personified that goal of freedom in whose name the struggle was waged."[21] In the abolitionist movement the Negro, of course, "constituted a symbol of the struggle," but in addition, "More than

[16]*Black Abolitionists*, p. vii.
[17]*The Negro in the American Revolution*, pp. ix–x.
[18]Quarles, ed., *Blacks on John Brown* (Urbana, Ill., 1972), p. xiv; the same thought is expressed in *Allies for Freedom*, pp. 197–98.
[19]*The Negro in the Civil War*, pp. ix–x.   [20]*Lincoln and the Negro*, Foreword.
[21]*The Negro in the American Revolution*, p. vii.

fp an unhappy pawn, he had known that he must work to forge his own freedom. . . . To the extent that America had a revolutionary tradition, he was its protagonist no less than its symbol."[22] Similarly, during the Civil War, the black functioned as a central symbol, for in spite of all the debate on the causes of that conflict historians agree that without slavery there would have been no resort to arms. "Hence the slave was the key factor in the war. But the Negro's Tale was not merely a passive one; he did not tarry in the wings, hands folded. He was an active member of the cast, prominent in the dramatis personae."[23] Nowhere is this point more clearly seen than in Quarles's discussion of the black abolitionists. The theme is epitomized by the phrase "a different drummer," which he has employed to describe this distinctiveness of the Negro antislavery vanguard. In *Black Abolitionists* he writes that "the black abolitionist phalanx was not just another group of camp followers. The Negro, in essence, was abolition's 'different drummer.' "[24] Black abolitionists had what today would be called their own agenda, which differed from that of white abolitionists. Thus they were in the vanguard of anticolonization, in the forefront of the early vigilance committees that helped fugitive slaves, and far ahead of white abolitionists in efforts to advance the rights of northern free blacks—not to mention their frequent unhappiness with the way in which whites tended to dominate the major antislavery organizations.

This view of the black man as "a different drummer" is also implicit in Quarles's writings on the Revolution and the Civil War. Thus he pictures Negroes during the Revolution as being actuated by different motives than whites, being committed not to independence from England but to the pursuit of freedom: "The Negro's role in the Revolution can best be understood by realizing that his major loyalty was not to a place nor to a people, but to a principle. Insofar as he had freedom of choice, he was likely to join the side that made him the quickest and best offer in terms of those 'unalienable rights' of which Mr. Jefferson had spoken. Whoever evoked the image of liberty, be he American or British, could count on a ready response." (Indeed, one of the notable contributions made by Quarles's book is the detailed attention given to black

---

[22]*Black Abolitionists*, pp. viii, 248–49. [23]*The Negro in the Civil War*, pp. x–xi.
[24]Quarles, "Abolition's Different Drummer: Frederick Douglass," in Martin Duberman, ed., *The Antislavery Vanguard* (Princeton, 1965), pp. 123–34; *Black Abolitionists*, p. viii.

participation in the British military effort as well as in the colonial armed forces.) Quarles's conception of what the Revolution meant to blacks is similarly reflected in the recent essay reprinted here, "The Revolutionary War as a Black Declaration of Independence." Similarly, in his Civil War volume, Quarles emphasizes how blacks were in the vanguard of those who saw the conflict as a struggle for black and human freedom, not only well in advance of Lincoln but—when it came to making blacks fully equal in American society—ahead of many white abolitionists as well.[25]

One of the striking, persistent themes in Quarles's work—extending from his first published article on "The Breach Between Douglass and Garrison"[26] through his volumes on the black abolitionists and Lincoln to his most recent works dealing with John Brown—is his abiding concern with the interrelations between blacks and those whites who became their allies. Thus it is not without significance that the opening chapter of *The Negro in the Civil War,* where Quarles begins *in medias res* with an account of the assault on Fort Wagner, not only demonstrates the extraordinary heroism of the black soldiers, but actually has as its central figure and hero a white officer, Colonel Robert Gould Shaw. Quarles's interest in this theme of the black man's white allies has been quite conscious. These figures, he feels, "deserve their place as established heroes among blacks." Canonized by Negroes who were either unaware of—or preferred to ignore—their complexities, these individuals provided an important source of black optimism about the future of American society. Negroes actually viewed them "as role models for other whites—who would show other whites the right thing to do." Today, of course, there is more skepticism about these white allies. But to Quarles "the question is how were these white men regarded by blacks in the context of their own day?"[27]

In his treatment of these white allies one sees the dualism so characteristic of Quarles's monographs—a profound concern for what blacks were doing and how they shaped the course of events, and a deep interest in the white actors whom he treats with profound understanding. I especially like the duality in his books on Lincoln and Brown, with their coordinated focus on the actions of these men regarding Negroes and on the blacks' views of the two whites. Particularly impressive is Quarles's thesis that the blacks' enthusi-

---

[25]*The Negro in the American Revolution,* p. vii; *The Negro in the Civil War.*
[26]"The Breach Between Douglass and Garrison."
[27]Interview with Quarles.

asm for Lincoln actually helped shape that president's evolving beliefs about them and their place in American society.

The evenhandedness and even empathy with which Quarles treats the diverse allies acquired by the blacks in the course of their struggle for freedom is a striking feature of all his writings. His discussion of the break between Garrison and Douglass is more than fair to the white antislavery leader. Of course, in his later works, Quarles takes into account the recent scholarship which has demonstrated the prevalence of paternalism and often racism among white abolitionists, but his treatment of Garrison—as well as of Brown—is essentially cast in heroic terms. This is so even though Quarles explicitly makes clear the limitations and weaknesses of both men. Garrison is pictured as no paternalist but as a hero to blacks, as unswervingly dedicated to racial equality, and as the first important white abolitionist to listen to what blacks were saying—as evidenced by the reversal of his stand on colonization.[28] Brown is viewed as an even more genuine egalitarian than Garrison, as a man who was outstanding if not unique in his attitude toward blacks. "Unlike the overwhelming majority of white abolitionists, Brown did not share the almost universal belief in black inferiority.... Brown was of a different mold, feeling no strain in the presence of blacks on a peer basis."[29]

Garrison never achieved the status that blacks accorded the martyred Brown and Lincoln. As Quarles has said, "Blacks revered both of these men," and their limitations and weaknesses proved irrelevant to their symbolic significance in Afro-American history.[30] Admittedly, Brown was dictatorial and secretive, but this did not bother blacks, who "tended...to ignore or gloss over any of his shortcomings—his assertive self-righteousness, his unwillingness to give praise or credit to others, and his dictatorial type of leadership. Brown was also reticent to the point of secrecy, but this trait hardly mattered to his black followers. They realized that if one were engaged in work considered seditious...secrecy must be the order of the day."[31] Quarles concedes that Brown's behavior in the Pottawatomie incident was "unpardonable," yet observes, "To his black supporters no blame attached to his conduct.... With a perception born of an oppressed minority...they viewed the incident from a wider perspective of aberrant behavior in their country,

[28]"The Breach Between Douglass and Garrison"; *Black Abolitionists*, pp. 19–22.
[29]*Allies for Freedom*, pp. 13–14; see also *Blacks on John Brown*, pp. ix–x.
[30]Interview with Quarles.
[31]*Blacks on John Brown*, p. xiii; see also *Allies for Freedom*, p. x.

13

from a greater familiarity with the climate of violence . . . in the land of their birth."[32] Even the most militant black leaders, like Douglass and Henry Highland Garnet, regarded Brown's insurrectionary plot as hopelessly unrealistic; they "knew Brown misled them—but they felt his heart was in the right place."[33] And so, after the debacle at Harpers Ferry, "on one thing . . . all blacks seem to have been in agreement—their single-minded negative attitude to the charge that he was mentally unbalanced. . . . Blacks held that society, rather than John Brown was deranged."[34]

As in the case of Brown, so also in the case of the very different Abraham Lincoln; blacks, glossing over his imperfections, created a heroic figure, even a messianic deliverer. As David Potter pointed out in his review of *Lincoln and the Negro*, Quarles treats the president with extraordinary evenhandedness: "Professor Quarles handles his ambiguous theme with candor, realism, and excellent balance. He takes the evidence as he finds it, and without apparent dismay pictures a Lincoln who cracked Negro jokes. . . . He does not shrink from showing that Lincoln invariably put military success ahead of the question of slavery. . . . Yet he makes an impressive showing of Lincoln's concern for the welfare of Negroes."[35] In the end, what is important in Quarles's view is not Lincoln's obvious deficiencies but how blacks came to view him as a martyr in the battle for their freedom. "They viewed him as a humanitarian, one whose love for his fellows embraced all sorts and conditions of men. Doubtless the Negro's attitude toward Lincoln was tinged by wish-fulfillment. . . . Yet the Negroes of his day saw him as a man growing in knowledge and wisdom, and to them he was emancipator, benefactor, friend, and leader." "Some Negroes thought of him as a Moses."[36]

Implicit in Quarles's discussion is a distinct contrast in the way that blacks interacted with Brown and Lincoln. Brown, the genuine egalitarian, was self-propelled in his ideology, and while treating blacks as peers misread their readiness to engage in open rebellion and went his own way unfazed by their realistic objections to his plans. Lincoln, the mild antislavery advocate who harbored race prejudice and who long favored colonization, was paradoxically

---

[32]*Allies for Freedom*, pp. 34–35. [33]Interview with Quarles.
[34]*Allies for Freedom*, p. 119.
[35]David Potter, review of *Lincoln and the Negro* in *New York Herald Tribune Book Review*, May 27, 1962.
[36]*Lincoln and the Negro*, Foreword, p. 209.

the one in the end who was more sensitive to black opinion and grew immeasurably as a result of the Negroes' largely unwarranted faith in him. Especially impressive is the way in which Quarles, analyzing the cross-pressures to which Lincoln was subjected, suggests how blacks by their admiration for Lincoln during the latter part of the war led him to rise to the occasion and begin to play the role of benefactor and "great emancipator" that Negroes had laid out for him. "True enough, Lincoln had originally conceived of the proclamation as a measure for self-preservation, rather than for the regeneration of America. But the proclamation, almost in spite of its creator, changed the whole tone and character of the war. Negroes sensed this more quickly than did Lincoln." For his part the astute president "was not slow in sensing the new dimensions his proclamation had taken on. The more abiding meaning of the edict became ever clearer to him," until in February 1865, not long before he was assassinated, he could assert that "as affairs have turned, it is the central act of my administration, and the greatest event of the nineteenth century." "Lincoln," Quarles adds, "came to believe that his chief claim to fame would rest upon the proclamation."[37]

Finally, in regard to both Brown and Lincoln, Quarles—exploring the implications of his thesis that blacks were more committed to American democratic values than were whites—makes the significant point that it was Negroes who first made the two men symbols of American freedom, and thus played an important part in creating the Brown and Lincoln of popular myth and legend. Negroes "were instrumental in creating the image of the proclamation that was to become the historic image"; assuming the role that "Negroes had given it at the outset," the edict was "destined to...take on the evocative power reserved only for the half-dozen great charter expressions of human liberty in the entire western tradition." "The black concept of Lincoln," he concludes, "is the one that lives.... Blacks immediately canonized him; the rest of the country came around to that interpretation."[38] Similarly, "the John Brown that lived in history is the legendary John Brown, a black creation."[39]

Although Quarles's principal interests have been in Afro-American history between the Revolutionary Era and the Civil War, he possessed a solid grasp of the entire history of black Americans.

[37]Ibid., pp. 150, 151.   [38]Ibid., p. 150.
[39]Interview with Quarles; see also similar wording in *Allies for Freedom*, pp. x–xi.

This is evident not only in his brief textual survey, *The Negro in the Making of America,* but in certain of his later essays, two of which are reprinted here, most notably "A. Philip Randolph: Labor Leader at Large."

Crucial though Quarles's publications have been to the growth of Afro-American history over the past three decades, he has not been at the center of any significant historiographical controversy. Not that Quarles is lacking in freshness of interpretation. As I have just indicated, for example, his analysis of the blacks' part in shaping the evolution of Lincoln's position is an original and perceptive contribution. His discussion of Lord Dunmore's noted proclamation undermined traditional assumptions in two ways: by demonstrating that manpower shortages rather than the threat of Dunmore's edict led to the reversal of the colonists' policy regarding the recruitment of Negro troops, and by showing how blacks, rather than being passive, took an active role in British military operations in response to Dunmore's offer. Similarly, the book on the black abolitionists is sprinkled with fresh insights. Thus, in contrast to those who have stressed the racism prevalent among the white Garrisonians, Quarles makes the sound point that the Garrisonian movement of the 1830s was a marked departure from the earlier antislavery movement in part because blacks could join and be named to leadership positions and because the philosophy of the new and more radical abolitionism was partly shaped by black ideas.[40] Then, too, he makes the suggestive observation that it was the split in the abolitionist ranks in 1839–40 "that tended to make Negroes more outspoken toward their fellow crusaders." For with so much dirty linen being washed in public, blacks grasped the opportunity to air their objections to the shortcomings of their white colleagues in the movement.[41] Again, there is the very skillful presentation of the development of the underground railroad and fugitive rescue work and of how what had at first been mainly a black enterprise became a genuine interracial effort.[42]

Nevertheless, Quarles has been a paradoxical figure—a seminal contributor to the history of black America and author of what is probably a definitive account of Negroes and the American Revolution, and yet a scholar whose works have spawned no heated debates. I think there are several reasons for this. First, Quarles is a careful scholar and even where, as in his volumes on the Civil

[40]*Black Abolitionists,* chapter 1, passim. [41]Ibid., pp. 46–47.
[42]Ibid., chapter 7 and pp. 200–215.

War and the black abolitionists, he has not sought to be definitive in his research, he has produced solid volumes with which it is difficult to quarrel. Then, too, he consistently treats with extraordinary fairness both his subjects and his fellow historians. Thus only by a close reading of *Allies for Freedom* does one sense Quarles's profound disagreement with David Potter's analysis of Brown's leadership role in the black community. Actually Quarles emphatically feels that historians like Potter "misread Brown completely," and miss the essential point that while Brown was indeed dictatorial, there was nothing racially paternalistic about this, because he behaved in exactly the same way toward whites.[43] Again Quarles, while not propounding the viewpoint of the black nationalist historians who loomed so prominently in the 1970s, has regarded their perspectives as important and treated them with genuine respect, as two of the essays in this volume—"Black History Unbound" and "Black History's Diversified Clientele"—suggest.

Moreover, certain of Quarles's books, most notably *The Negro in the Civil War* and *The Negro in the Making of America,* are clearly intended for a fairly broad audience. It is true that Quarles, as his meticulous scholarship indicates, had consciously addressed himself chiefly to the academic community, black and white. Yet, within a world of academic historians Quarles, as he himself puts it, is essentially a "narrative" rather than a "conceptual" historian.[44] This characteristic of his work, while revealing a good deal of the influence of Hesseltine's seminar teaching, also accords with Quarles's personal bent and talents. His emphasis on narrative has, of course, tended both to make his works less controversial and to strengthen his appeal to a wide audience. On the other hand, this very emphasis on a strong narrative line, combined with Quarles's careful research, has produced important syntheses and pioneering monographs that have stood the test of time and made possible what I have called "the freshness of interpretation"—the subtleties of analysis—that often appears in his books.

By virtue of his tendency to focus on what blacks as a group have felt about the events and persons he describes, Quarles, as Arvarh Strickland has observed, has expressed the consensus of what Negroes have thought about their past.[45] Some sense in Quarles's latest work a "more militant and urgent" tone, as if he

---

[43]*Allies for Freedom,* p. 81; interview with Quarles.
[44]Interview with Quarles.
[45]Discussion with Arvarh Strickland, Nov. 11, 1978.

had consciously or unconsciously shifted over time as sentiment among blacks changed.[46] John Bracey, for example, regards *Black Abolitionists* as the most "nationalist" in tone of all Quarles's volumes.[47] Quarles himself believes that during his early years as a scholar, he was trying to win an audience among white historians ignorant of, where not hostile toward, the fact that blacks had a history worth studying. But by the 1970s, with Afro-American history generally recognized as an important part of American history, and with a militant group of younger black historians to his left, Quarles was writing with a somewhat different voice. He concedes that he would not today write certain of the passages in *The Negro in the Civil War*, as where, for example, he writes sentimentally of how the freedman "showed no vindictiveness toward his former master; there was no hatred in his heart."[48] I suspect also that the effort to win an audience goes a long way toward explaining why in his first book Quarles took considerable pains to disassociate Douglass from the Radical Republicans, then in such bad repute among most historians of the period.[49] Yet to me such changes in the tone of Quarles's work seem marginal when set against the essential continuity of viewpoint that pervades his books.

Although Quarles has not been more than peripherally involved in any historiographical controversies, I do not mean to say that he has entirely escaped criticism. Reviewers have sometimes faulted him for undue optimism or for a tendency to romanticize the black man's role. Thus both George Tindall and Dudley Cornish, in reviewing *The Negro in the Civil War*, warmly praised this "solid addition to literature" (Cornish), but felt that "it tended toward "apologetics" (Tindall). As Cornish wrote, "In his commendable effort 'to set the record straight' he has gone too far in the other direction with the result that his study is short on critical analysis and all too long on praise for the Negro, whether loyal slave at the South, contraband with Ben Butler in Virginia, soldier or sailor in the Union ranks." A decade later James McPherson, in his study of abolitionists during the Civil War and Reconstruction, observed that *Lincoln and the Negro* "glosses over some of the anti-Lincoln sentiment among radical Negroes."[50] About the same time, review-

---

[46]Interview with Quarles.
[47]Telephone conversation with John H. Bracey, Jr., Sept. 18, 1978.
[48]Interview with Quarles; *The Negro in the Civil War*, pp. xii–xiii.
[49]*Frederick Douglass* (Washington, 1948), pp. 195–96, 222–25.
[50]Review by George Tindall, *Mississippi Valley Historical Review* 40 (December 1953): 540–41; review by Dudley Cornish in *Journal of Negro History* 38 (October

ers Jack Greene and Winthrop Jordan praised the research (Greene) of Quarles's "thoroughly judicious" (Jordan) volume on the Revolution, but questioned the optimistic view that the gains made by the blacks in that period represented any irreversible commitment of the new nation to liberty and equality for the Negro.[51]

More recently the view of black history as a march from oppression toward equality in fulfillment of the promise inherent in the Declaration of Independence—a view shared by the older generation of black historians and one that Quarles expressed especially well—has come under attack from another quarter. I am referring to a segment of the new generation of black historians, persons like Vincent Harding and Sterling Stuckey, who see white society and culture as hopelessly corrupted by the evil of racism.[52] One cannot, of course, make any sweeping generalizations about the perspective and outlook of the new generation of black historians. Yet it would be accurate to say that given Quarles's focus on the contribution Negroes have made to the mainstream of American history, his interest in black-white interaction and the Negro's white allies, and the minimal attention he gives to the themes of black nationalism[53] or the development of black culture and institutions, one can clearly distinguish his work from what can be called the new paradigm of black history. This paradigm, which emerged nearly two decades ago, and is now so prominent in the writing of both black and white scholars, carries further than Quarles and Franklin the emphasis upon the collective group experience. More important, it is interested less in the contribution of blacks to American society than in the distinctive black institutions and culture that slaves and free Afro-Americans have maintained in the face of white prejudice and discrimination. It focuses on the blacks' success in coping with

1953): 440–41; bibliographical essay in James M. McPherson, *The Struggle for Equality* (Princeton, 1964), p. 447.

[51]Review by Winthrop Jordan in *New England Quarterly* 35 (September 1962): 424–25; review by Jack P. Greene in *American Historical Review* 68 (January 1963): 474–75.

[52]Vincent Harding, "Beyond Chaos: Black History and the Search for the New Land," *Amistad I* (New York, 1970), pp. 267–92, passim; Sterling Stuckey, "Twilight of Our Past: Reflections on the Origins of Black History," *Amistad II* (New York, 1971), pp. 261–95, passim.

[53]The treatment of black nationalist tendencies in the thinking of men like Douglass and Martin Delany is downplayed where not ignored in *Frederick Douglass;* there is no reference to the subject in the index to *The Negro in the Making of America* (although there is a three-page discussion of the Garvey movement in the volume, for example). The most extensive treatment of emigration and collective self-help efforts is to be found in *Black Abolitionists*, though even here the emphasis is rather less than other scholars would now be likely to give.

their hostile environment and their resilience in maintaining a sense of group identity in their own distinctive culture and community. This model has had an enormous impact and is exemplified not only in the writings of black scholars like John Blassingame, but also in major works by white historians like Eugene Genovese, Peter Wood, Herbert Gutman, and Lawrence Levine.[54] There are of course differences in viewpoint among such scholars. Yet I think that despite these differences—the often acrimonious debates that cropped up between these gentlemen—the new paradigm quite effectively separates the current generation of scholarship in black history from the scholarship of the older generation that matured during the 1940s and 1950s.

I do not mean to say that elements of the new paradigm are entirely absent from the work of Quarles or others of the older generation. Quarles himself, from an early date, not only stressed black activism but recognized the Negro antislavery crusader as "a different drummer." His *Black Abolitionists* devotes considerable attention to the role of the Negro antislavery leaders in the development of black community institutions, and to the way in which so many of them had their roots as leaders in an institution like the black church.[55] Moreover, as indicated above, Quarles has been exceedingly open to the new perspective. In "Black History Unbound" in particular, he maintained that it would be a mistake—even perilous—to ignore the views of individuals like Stuckey and Harding.[56]

Finally, no matter how much Quarles's view differs from the new paradigm, it is clear that all of us in the field are greatly in his debt. Like Franklin he has served as a model to a whole generation of scholars in Afro-American history, white and black alike. His syntheses of Civil War and abolition, his authoritative book and articles on the Revolution, his sensitive analysis of Lincoln and the

---

[54]John Blassingame, *The Slave Community* (New York, 1972); Peter Wood, *Black Majority* (New York, 1974); Eugene Genovese, *Roll, Jordan, Roll* (New York, 1974); Herbert Gutman, *The Black Family in Slavery and Freedom, 1750–1925* (New York, 1976); Lawrence Levine, *Black Culture and Black Consciousness* (New York, 1977). Paradoxically, Stuckey and Harding, among the most enthusiastic proponents of the new paradigm, which in their view includes the unredeemable racism of white society as well as the positive emphasis on black culture and black consciousness, have not produced much in the way of empirical research themselves. Yet their thinking has had considerable impact on the writings of certain leading white historians.

[55]*Black Abolitionists*, chapters 4 and 5, passim.

[56]Quarles, "Black History Unbound," *Daedalus* 102 (Spring 1974): 167. Reprinted in this volume.

blacks are all works that remain unequalled or unsurpassed. Even his pioneering *Frederick Douglass* remains a solid and highly respected monograph. The present and the next generation of historians are, and will be, writing from a later perspective and addressing themselves to different questions, but Quarles's works not only plowed new ground; they will live as standard treatments of topics for years to come.

Blacks in the Revolutionary Period

1. The Colonial Militia and Negro Manpower

N THE MAINLAND colonies of British America there existed no homogeneous militia system, operating under a central command. Instead, each colony maintained and controlled its own independent militia force. Yet on one point, the use of the Negro for military service, policy became uniform throughout the colonies. Slave or free, Negroes were excluded from the militia, save as noncombatants or in unusual emergencies. This policy of semiexclusion became so prevalent as to constitute a basic tenet of American military tradition.

Since most of the Negroes were slaves, one of the major reasons for their exemption from military service was the concept that the servant's duty to his master superseded any obligation owed as a citizen to the colony or local community. Provincial legislatures, sensitive to the property rights of the master, were impressed by claims that tampering with his labor supply struck at the roots of colonial prosperity.[1] Hence legislation to enlist nonfreemen for the militia usually stipulated that the consent of the master must first be obtained.

[1]This feeling was also demonstrated in the difficulties encountered by crown officials in trying to recruit indentured servants for the royal army. Governor Horatio Sharpe, for example, informed William Shirley in February, 1756, that unless recruiting officers stopped signing up apprentices and servants in Maryland, "an insurrection of the people is likely to ensue." William H. Browne et al., eds., *Archives of Maryland*, 66 vols. (Baltimore, 1883–), 6:342. A similar letter came from the governor of Pennsylvania. Robert Hunter Morris to William Shirley, February 16, 1756, Charles H. Lincoln, ed., *Correspondence of William Shirley*, 2 vols. (New York, 1912), 2:391–92. "I did give private orders," wrote a New Jersey governor, "to be very cautious of inlisting servants." Lewis Morris to William Gooch, July 14, 1740, *The Papers of Lewis Morris* (Newark, 1852), p. 96. This "cautious" attitude toward the enlistment of servants in the provincial armies is dealt with in Cheesman A. Herrick, *White Servitude in Pennsylvania* (Philadelphia, 1926), pp. 233–53; Abbot E. Smith, *Colonists in Bondage* (Chapel Hill, 1947), pp. 278–84; and Richard B. Morris, *Government and Labor in Early America* (New York, 1946), pp. 282–90.

A second important reason for this limited use of the Negro was an understandable reluctance to put a gun in his hands. Furnishing military "accoutrements" to a slave and training him as a potential soldier was thought to be asking for trouble. Going through military evolutions on training day, a musket in his hands, might arouse notions of revolt in the slave. Furthermore, in time of actual warfare a bondman might disappear,[2] or even show up in the ranks of the enemy—French, Spanish, or Indian. In the military use of Negroes, "there must be great caution used," wrote a group of Carolina patentees, "lest our slaves when armed might become our masters."[3]

To prevent Negro enlistments, statute law lent its weight to custom. As might be expected, Virginia's enactments were earlier and more numerous than those of her sister colonies. In January 1639 came the first prohibitory law: "All persons except negroes" were to be provided with arms and ammunition.[4] In the 1690s a Council order enjoined militia officers from enlisting "Physicians, Chirurgeons, Readers, Clerks, Ferrymen, Negroes."[5] Other enactments at the turn of the century forbade Negroes from holding any military office and slaves from serving "in horse or foot."[6]

Fear of slave uprisings subsided with time in the colony and the legislature eased somewhat the limitations on nonwhites. Under a law of 1723 free Negroes, mulattoes,[7] and Indians might be enlisted as drummers or trumpeters. Moreover, in case of invasion, insurrection, or rebellion, these groups would be required to march with the militia and do "the duty of pioneers, or such other servile labour as they shall be directed to perform."[8] But Virginia went no further. By subsequent militia acts these Negroes and Indians, although

---

[2] "If any servant upon pretence of going to the wars against the enemy do run away from his master's service," warned the New York legislature in 1684, "he shall if taken be greviously punished at the direction of the Governor and Council." *The Colonial Laws of New York*, 5 vols. (Albany, 1894–1896), 1:161–62.

[3] "Agent for Carolina and Merchants Trading Thither" to Board of Trade, July 18, 1715, William L. Saunders, ed., *Colonial Records of North Carolina*, 10 vols. (Raleigh, 1886–1890), 2:197.

[4] William W. Hening, ed., *The Statutes at Large: Being a Collection of All the Laws of Virginia*, 13 vols. (Philadelphia and New York, 1810–1823), 1:226.

[5] Henry R. McIlwaine, ed., *Executive Journals of the Council of Colonial Virginia, 1680–1739*, 4 vols. (Richmond, 1925–1930), 1:526; also "The Randolph Manuscript," *Virginia Magazine of History and Biography* 20 (April 1912): 117.

[6] Hening, *Statutes at Large*, 3:251, 336.

[7] Virginia defined a mulatto as the "child of an Indian and the child, grand child, or great grand child, of a negro." Ibid., 252.

[8] Ibid., 4:119.

eligible to summons, were prohibited from carrying arms.[9] Furthermore, any exempted Negro who presumed to show up at a muster was to be fined 100 pounds of tobacco, "and shall immediately give security to the . . . commanding officer, for paiment of the same."[10]

Similar policies evolved above the Potomac. As early as 1643, Plymouth, having joined the New England Confederation and deeming it necessary to establish a militia, stipulated that no one should be permitted to enlist "but such as are of honest and good report, & freemen."[11] But it was Massachusetts, New England's oldest and strongest permanent colony, that set the pattern of military policy in that region. Shortage of manpower in early Massachusetts fostered widespread encouragement of militia training, and even the parents of children from ages ten to sixteen were urged to permit them to take instruction in the handling of small arms.[12] An enactment followed in 1652 specifying that militia enlistments were to include "all Scotsmen, Negers and Indians inhabiting with or servants to the English."[13] This measure was of short duration. Four years later the legislature prohibited the mustering in of Negroes or Indians, explaining the step as necessary in the interests of "the better ordering and settling of severall cases in the military companyes."[14]

Henceforth, despite the perennial difficulties of procuring militiamen,[15] Massachusetts officially held to this policy of exclusion. Governor Simon Bradstreet, writing to his superiors in England in 1680, indicated that enlistment in the militia was nonselective, "except Negroes and slaves whom wee arme not."[16] In 1693 a reaffirmation came from the General Court: Negroes were included among those "exempted from all trainings."[17]

Exclusionary legislation of the Virginia and Massachusetts type

[9]Act of 1738, ibid., 5:17; Act of 1755, ibid., 6:533; Act of 1757, ibid., 7:95.
[10]Ibid., 4:119.
[11]Nathaniel B. Shurtleff et al., eds., *Records of the Colony of New Plymouth in New England*, 12 vols. (Boston, 1855–1861), 2:61.
[12]Nathaniel B. Shurtleff, ed., *Records of the Governor and Company of the Massachusetts Bay in New England*, 5 vols. (Boston, 1853–1854), 2:99.
[13]Ibid., 3:268. [14]Ibid., 397.
[15]For these difficulties see Jack S. Radabaugh, "The Militia of Colonial Massachusetts," *Military Affairs* 18 (Spring 1954): 10–11.
[16]Simon Bradstreet to Privy Council, May 18, 1680, James Savage, ed., "Gleanings from New England History," *Collections of the Massachusetts Historical Society*, 3rd series, 8 (Boston, 1843):336.
[17]*Acts and Laws of the General Court of Massachusetts, 1692 to 1719* (London, 1724), p. 51.

soon became standard practice. Connecticut in 1660 forbade Negroes from serving in the watch or train bands.[18] Twenty years later the Maryland assembly ordered that "all negroes and slaves whatsoever shall be exempted the duty of trayning or any other millitary service," a prohibition that was reenacted in 1715.[19] New Hampshire in 1718 exempted Negroes from training,[20] and New Jersey in 1760 ruled against the enlistment of slaves without the written permission of the masters.[21] In Philadelphia as late as the opening of the Revolutionary War, the Committee of Safety ordered to the workhouse one David Owen, "a person suspected of enlisting Negroes."[22]

The exemption of Negroes from militia duty seemed to put them in a privileged class with clergymen, public officials, and other notables. Hence Massachusetts devised the practice of labor service. A law of 1707, after pointing out that Negroes shared the benefit of military protection without bearing a commensurate responsibility, stipulated that they should "do service equivalent to trainings." This was spelled out as "so many day's work yearly" in street cleaning, highway maintenance, and other service for the common benefit. Moreover, in times of peril, Negroes were required "to make their appearance at parade" and, once there, to do as directed. Failure to report was finable at five shillings for each day's neglect of duty; the penalty for not showing up in time of danger was twenty shillings or eight days' labor.[23]

Watch service, rather than labor, was preferred in Rhode Island. Here in 1676 the legislature decreed that "a negro man capable of watch...shall be lyable to that service."[24] This step was in line

[18]James H. Trumbull and Charles J. Hoadly, eds., *Public Records of the Colony of Connecticut*, 15 vols. (Hartford, 1850–1890), 1:349. For the relationship between military defense and slave legislation in the Puritan colonies see Lorenzo J. Greene, *The Negro in Colonial New England, 1620–1776* (New York, 1942), pp. 126–27.

[19]*Archives of Maryland*, 7:56; *Laws of Maryland* (Annapolis, 1744), p. 143.

[20]*Acts and Laws of His Majesty's Province of New-Hampshire in New-England* (Portsmouth, 1771), p. 95.

[21]Samuel Nevill, ed., *The Acts of the General Assembly of the Province of New Jersey*, 2 vols. (Woodbridge, 1752–1761), 2:267.

[22]*Colonial Records of Pennsylvania, 1683–1790*, 16 vols. (Philadelphia, 1852–1853), 10:427.

[23]*Acts and Laws of Massachusetts, 1692 to 1719*, p. 242. During the first year after the law was passed thirty-three Negroes in Boston spent a total of 218 days of labor in public works. George H. Moore, *Notes on the History of Slavery in Massachusetts* (New York, 1866), pp. 60–61. From the time of the enactment of the measure much of Boston's road maintenance was done by impressed Negroes. Carl Bridenbaugh, *Cities in the Wilderness* (New York, 1955), p. 163.

[24]John R. Bartlett, ed., *Records of the Colony of Rhode Island and Providence Plantations in New England*, 10 vols. (Providence, 1856–1865), 2:536. New Hamp-

with the colony's avowed determination to make all citizens "observant," either actively or passively, of military affairs; but watch service did not necessitate carrying firearms.

An armed slave was an anomaly seldom tolerated in normal times by the provincial legislatures. Hence the barring of Negroes from the militia was commonly supplemented by laws to keep weapons out of their hands. Again Virginia took the lead. In 1680 the Jamestown assembly prohibited Negroes from carrying clubs, swords, guns, or other weapons of defense or offense. The preamble of this measure explained that it was necessary because "the frequent meeting of considerable numbers of negroe slaves under pretence of feasts and burialls is judged of dangerous consequence."[25] Restated in 1705, the law substituted "slave" for "negroe or other slave,"[26] but an enactment of 1723 removed any doubt: arms were to be carried by "no negro, mulatto, or indian whatsoever," under penalty of a whipping not to exceed twenty-nine lashes.[27]

Similar precautions were taken by other provincial bodies. Negro arms-bearing was prohibited in Pennsylvania in 1700; a colored person convicted of carrying a gun, pistol, fowling piece, club, "or other weapons whatsoever" would receive twenty-one lashes on the bare back.[28] South Carolina's comprehensive slave code of 1712 required every master to have all "negro houses" searched fortnightly for guns, swords, clubs, or other "mischievous" weapons.[29] The Delaware counties prohibited blacks from bearing arms or serving in the militia "upon any pretense whatsoever." This action, taken in 1741 after the news of a Negro plot to burn New York, was considered necessary, the authorities explained, because the counties were now exposed not only to foreign enemies "but to the insults also or insurrections of our own slaves."[30]

In cases where frontier defense or game hunting might dictate arming the slave, appropriate safeguards were required. In Virginia, slaves on frontier plantations might use guns, but only if properly licensed. As a further safeguard, only the master could procure such

---

shire's comprehensive militia act of 1718, although barring Negroes from the trainings, did not list them among the groups exempt from "military watchings and wardings."

[25]Hening, *Statutes at Large*, 2:481. [26]Ibid., 3:459. [27]Ibid., 4:131.

[28]James T. Mitchell and Henry Flanders, eds., *Statutes at Large of Pennsylvania from 1682 to 1801*, 16 vols. (Harrisburg, 1896–1908), 2:79. Reaffirmed five years later (ibid., 235–36), this law was not repealed until after the colonial period (1780).

[29]Thomas Cooper and David J. McCord, eds., *Statutes at Large of South Carolina*, 10 vols. (Columbia, 1836–1841), 7:353.

[30]*Laws of the Government of New-Castle, Kent, and Sussex upon Delaware* (Philadelphia, 1741–1742), p. 178.

a permit for his servant.[31] A New Jersey ruling of 1694 allowed slaves to carry firearms if accompanied by the master or his representative.[32] Similarly, North Carolina in 1729 forbade slaves to hunt with dog or gun unless accompanied by a white man.[33] Maryland permitted its bondmen to carry offensive weapons only when on the master's premises.[34]

The general policy, therefore, in colonial America was to exclude the Negro from military participation and arms-bearing. But times of peril made for hard choices; in such a season it might be necessary to take a calculated risk. The arming of slaves was considered particularly risky in time of war; indeed, much of the legislation of Negro exclusion came when enemy danger threatened most. "The villany of the Negroes on an emergency of gov't is w't I always feared," wrote Governor Robert Dinwiddie of Virginia when informed of trouble with the Negroes near Fort Cumberland during the early months of the French and Indian War.[35]

Yet equally serious in wartime was the paucity of manpower. It was this shortage that often overcame customary caution. South Carolina, exposed to enemy attack and heavily populated with Negroes, perhaps best illustrates the provincial problem of using slaves as soldiers. Faced with an Indian threat following the outbreak of Queen Anne's War, the colony in 1703 authorized masters to arm their slaves if enemy invasion materialized.[36] Taking the big step a year later, the assembly ordered masters to furnish slaves, upon summons, for the provincial militia. Payment for their service would be made from public funds.[37] Typical of legislation authorizing Negro enlistments (and military legislation generally), this measure had a time limit; in this instance the law was to continue in force for only two years.

In 1708 the assembly passed a more comprehensive bill. Its preamble reaffirmed the necessity, in time of actual invasion, of enlisting trusted slaves, "accoutred and armed with a lance or hatchet or gun" supplied from the provincial stores. A slave who

[31]Hening, *Statutes at Large*, 4:131.

[32]Aaron Leaming and Jacob Spicer, eds., *The Grants, Concessions, and Original Constitutions of the Province of New-Jersey* (Philadelphia, 1758), p. 341.

[33]*Laws of the State of North Carolina*, 2 vols. (Raleigh, 1821), 1:125.

[34]Laws of Maryland, p. 144.

[35]Dinwiddie to Charles Carter, July 18, 1755, in Robert A. Brock, ed., *Official Records of Robert Dinwiddie*, 2 vols. (Richmond, 1883–1884), 2:101.

[36]Cooper and McCord, eds., *South Carolina Statutes*, 7:33.

[37]Ibid., 347–49.

killed or captured an enemy would be freed; a slave disabled while fighting would be liberated and thereafter maintained "at the charge of the public."[38]

When Indian troubles persisted after Queen Anne's War, the assembly again authorized the use of Negroes in the militia. In May 1715, a month after the outbreak of the Yamassee War, Governor Charles Craven informed London that he had "caused about two hundred stout negro men to be enlisted." This step was necessary, he explained, because there were so few white men ("not above fifteen hundred") in the colony.[39] Within five years the assembly again ordered that in time of danger masters were to make available to militia officers the services of trusted slaves from ages sixteen to sixty. It provided also that a slave who killed or captured an enemy was to receive ten pounds from "the Public Receiver for every killing or taking."[40]

During the following two decades South Carolina felt no need for slave recruits. But in 1739, faced by the menace of the Spanish garrison at St. Augustine, the colony again took the venturesome step. Asserting that "Negroes and slaves have behaved themselves with faithfulness and courage and demonstrated that in some instances faith and trust may be put in them," the assembly authorized the governor to empower militia captains to enlist "recommended" slaves. Only at a time of general alarm and invasion would they be armed; then each enlisted slave would be furnished with a gun, a hatchet, a powder horn, a shot pouch with ammunition and bullets for twenty rounds, and six spare flints. For killing an enemy, taking him alive, or capturing his colors, liberation was to be the reward. A slave who fought well enough "to deserve public notice" would receive yearly "a livery coat and pair of breeches made of good red Negro Cloth turned up with blue, and a black hat, and pair of black shoes, and shall that day in every year during their lives on which such action was performed be freed and exempted from all personal service or labor."[41]

A year later, when an expedition to reduce the St. Augustine garrison was proposed, General James E. Oglethorpe suggested that

[38]Ibid., 349–51.

[39]Charles Craven to Secretary of State Charles Townshend, May 23, 1715, Saunders, ed., *Colonial Records of North Carolina*, 2:178.

[40]Cooper and McCord, eds., *South Carolina Statutes*, 3:108–10.

[41]South Carolina Acts, 1733–1739 (Law Library, Library of Congress). The acts down to 1736 were printed; those for the period after 1736 are handwritten and unpaged.

1,000 Negroes be drafted, of whom 800 would be military laborers and 200 would be armed for combat.[42] The assembly voted that the pay for such slaves "shall be £10 Currency per Month, the Owners running all Hazzards" that might attend the expedition. A later provision specified, however, that the masters of any slaves between twenty and fifty years of age who were killed in action would be paid a sum "not exceeding £250 per Head."[43]

Before the South Carolina experiment of using blacks in the militia could be tested, a slave uprising took place in September 1739 at Stono, less than twenty miles from the capital. Another full-scale slave conspiracy followed nine months later in Charles Town itself.[44] To the alarmed South Carolinians two things seemed clear: the rebellious Negroes had been in possession of firearms; and they had undoubtedly been urged on, albeit not openly, by the Spaniards. The reaction was prompt. Faced with Negro revolts and plots, the lawmakers reversed their position. On December 11, 1740, the assembly ordered "that the law for encouraging armed Negroes, and for making them useful for the defense of the province be speedily revised."[45] A permanent damper fell on Negro enlistment in the militia. Twenty years later, with the colony beset by trouble with the Cherokees, a motion to arm 500 Negroes was defeated by the deciding vote of the presiding officer.[46]

The South Carolina experience was duplicated in Georgia. Three years before the Revolutionary War the Georgia assembly voted to arm slaves if such a step became necessary, and masters were required to furnish militia officers with lists of all their capable and trustworthy slaves between ages sixteen and sixty. Remarkably similar to the South Carolina law of 1739, this act promised freedom to slaves who killed or captured an enemy. A slave who fought bravely would receive annually a supply of bright-colored clothes and be excused from labor on the anniversaries of his heroism.[47] But the provisions of this act were not carried out. Subsequent

---

[42]For Oglethorpe's military labor proposal see J. Harold Easterby, ed., *The Colonial Records of South Carolina*, 7 vols. (Columbia, 1951–), 2:175–78. For the suggestion on Negro troops see John Tate Lanning, ed., *The St. Augustine Expedition of 1740* (Columbia, 1954), p. 97.

[43]Easterby, *Colonial Records of South Carolina*, 2:195, 309.

[44]Herbert Aptheker, *American Negro Slave Revolts* (New York, 1943), pp. 187–89.

[45]Easterby, *Colonial Records of South Carolina*, 2:420.

[46]John R. Alden, *John Stuart and the Southern Colonial Frontier* (Ann Arbor, 1944), pp. 113–14.

[47]Allen D. Candler, ed., *Colonial Records of the State of Georgia*, 26 vols. (Atlanta, 1904–1916), 19, part 1:324–29.

incidents, such as that of the ten slaves who ran amuck in St. Andrew's Parish after killing their overseer,[48] seemed to bring sober second thoughts concerning the arming of the Negro.

Georgia was not unique in holding misgivings and in taking precautionary steps. But in colonial America official attitudes toward arming the Negro did not always mirror actual practice. A case in point is the French and Indian War period, during which colored men were enlisted in both southern and northern colonies. A few illustrative instances may be noted. In Granville County, North Carolina, under date of October 8, 1754, a muster roll of Colonel William Eaton's company lists five Negroes and two mulattoes, a roll of Captain John Glover's company lists three Negroes, and that of Captain Osborn Jeffreys lists five Negroes.[49] And in Virginia, General Edward Braddock wrote from Williamsburg in 1755: "There are here numbers of mulattoes and free Negroes of whom I shall make bat men, whom the province are to furnish with pay and frocks."[50]

In the French and Indian War the colony of New York made extensive use of the Negro.[51] So did Connecticut; in her wartime militia colored men served in twenty-five different companies.[52] In Rhode Island, James Richardson of Stonington, advertising in May 1763 for his Negro servant, reported him as having served as a soldier earlier that year.[53] The town of Hingham, Massachusetts,

---

[48]Ulrich B. Phillips, ed., *Plantation and Frontier Documents, 1649–1863*, 2 vols. (Cleveland, 1909), 2:118–19.

[49]Walter Clark, ed., *The State Records of North Carolina*, 26 vols. (Winston and Goldsboro, 1886–1907), 22:370–72. After the war customary precautions were resumed; by an act of 1768 overseers of six slaves or more were to be fined if they appeared at musters. Luther L. Gobbel, "The Militia in North Carolina in Colonial and Revolutionary Times," *Historical Papers of the Trinity College Historical Society* 12 (1916):42.

[50]Edward Braddock to Robert Napier, March 17, 1755, Stanley Pargellis, ed., *Military Affairs in North America, 1748–1765* (New York, 1936), p. 78.

[51]For the names of Negroes serving in New York companies, with such descriptive data as date of enlistment, age, birthplace, occupation, stature, militia company, and officer who did the enlisting, see "Muster Rolls of New York Provincial Troops, 1755–1764," *Collections of the New-York Historical Society for 1891* (New York, 1892), pp. 60, 182, 284, 364, 385, 398, 402, 406, 418, 420, 426, 427, 440, 442, 498. One Negro, Salomon Jolly, is designated as free; the others, presumably, were slaves.

[52]"Rolls of Connecticut Men in the French and Indian War," 2 vols., 1:322; 2:437, *Collections of the Connecticut Historical Society*, vols. 9, 10 (Hartford, 1903–1905). The number of companies is derived from a page check of the regimental and militia affiliations of the Negroes listed (barring duplications) in the indexes of these two volumes.

[53]"Eighteenth Century Slaves as Advertised by Their Masters," *Journal of Negro History* 1 (April 1916):200.

recruiting men in 1758 for the prosecution of the war, included two Negroes, Primus Cobb and Flanders, among the thirty-six privates in Captain Edward Ward's company.[54] Jeremy Belknap expressed the belief that in Massachusetts as a whole the number of slaves declined by 1763 "because in the two preceding wars, many of them were enlisted either into the army or on board vessels of war, with a view to procure their freedom."[55]

In fine, despite the laws, Negroes were enlisted. This difference between policy and practice is but another illustration of the colonial dilemma with respect to the use of slaves as soldiers. "They are...necessary, but very dangerous domestics," commented a prominent South Carolina physician in 1763.[56] To arm the Negroes was hazardous, but the latent military strength they represented was undeniable—a manpower potential often too badly needed and too readily available to be ignored.

[54]*History of the Town of Hingham, Massachusetts*, 3 vols. (Hingham, 1893), 1:265.

[55]"Queries Respecting the Slavery and Emancipation of Negroes in Massachusetts, Proposed by the Honorable Judge Tucker of Virginia, and Answered by the Reverend Dr. Belknap," *Collections of the Massachusetts Historical Society*, 1st series, 4 (Boston, 1795):199.

[56]George Milligen-Johnston, *A Short Description of the Province of South Carolina* (London, 1770), reprinted in Chapman J. Milling, ed., *Colonial South Carolina: Two Contemporary Descriptions* (Columbia, 1951), p. 136.

2. Lord Dunmore as Liberator

I N A M E R I C A N patriotic tradition the first full-fledged villain to step from the wings as the Revolutionary War unfolded was John Murray, Earl of Dunmore. Like other royal governors in office as the crisis reached its pitch, the Crown's representative in Virginia would have been a marked man no matter how circumspect his behavior. Dunmore, lacking in diplomatic skills, was destined to furnish the colonists with a convenient hate-symbol. The one act that most thoroughly defamed his name was a deed which in Negro circles cast its author in the role of liberator. This was Dunmore's proclamation inviting slaves to leave their masters and join the royal forces.

Issued as of November 7, 1775, on board the *William* in the harbor at Norfolk, the proclamation announced that in order to defeat "treasonable purposes" the governor was establishing martial law. Colonists who refused "to resort to his Majesty's standard" were to be adjudged traitors. Then came the words which were destined to be quoted far and wide: "and I do hereby further declare all indented servants, Negroes, or others, (appertaining to Rebels,) free, that are able and willing to bear arms, they joining His Majesty's Troops, as soon as may be, for the more speedily reducing the Colony to a proper sense of their duty, to His Majesty's crown and dignity."[1]

Dunmore's proclamation had its expected effect. "The colonists," wrote a contemporary, "were struck with horror";[2] the "Poet of the American Revolution" implored the heavens to deliver the colonies from the "valiant" Dunmore and "his crew of banditti" ("who

---

[1] Original broadside, 11 by 17 inches, in University of Virginia library. For a facsimile which Patrick Henry circulated, and which differs a little in punctuation from the original, see Francis L. Berkeley, Jr., *Dunmore's Proclamation of Emancipation* (Charlottesville, 1941), frontispiece. See also *American Archives,* comp. Peter Force, 4th ser., 3 (Washington, 1837–46): 1385.

[2] David Ramsay, *History of the American Revolution* (Philadelphia, 1789), vol. 1, p. 234.

plunder Virginians at Williamsburg city").[3] Taking alarm, the Continental Congress lost no time in bestirring itself. On December 2, 1775, the delegates instructed the "Committee for fitting our armed vessels" to engage ships of war for the taking or destroying of the governor's fleet,[4] and the presiding officer urged the commander in chief of the Continental Army to take such measures against his lordship as would "effectually Repel his violences and secure the peace and safety of that Colony."[5] Two days later the Congress recommended to Virginia that she resist Dunmore "to the utmost. ..."[6]

The apprehension over Dunmore's proclamation was grounded primarily in the fear of its unsettling effect on the slaves, if not in the fear of a servile insurrection—that nightmarish dread in communities where the whites were outnumbered. A policy that would strike off their shackles would obviously have a marked appeal to the inhabitants of slave row. Moreover, there had been recent evidence that the Virginia bondmen were responsive to the offer of freedom.

Dunmore himself had furnished such evidence. For at least eight months prior to the formal proclamation, the governor had seriously considered the idea of enlisting the slaves. His reasons were plain. Rebellious planters who contemplated a resort to arms would

---

[3] *The Poems of Philip Freneau*, ed. Fred Lewis Pattee (Princeton, 1902–07), vol. 1, p. 140. "Hell itself could not have vomitted anything more black than his design of emancipating our slaves," wrote a Philadelphia correspondent to a friend abroad. *Morning Chronicle and London Advertiser*, Jan. 20, 1776, quoted in *Letters on the American Revolution, 1774–1776*, ed. Margaret W. Willard (Boston, 1925), p. 233. It was the judgment of Edward Rutledge that the proclamation tended "more effectually to work an eternal separation between Great Britain and the Colonies,— than any other expedient, which could possibly have been thought of." Rutledge to Ralph Izard, Dec. 8, 1775, in *Correspondence of Mr. Ralph Izard* (New York, 1844), vol. 1, p. 165.

[4] *Journals of the Continental Congress, 1774–1789*, ed. Worthington C. Ford et al. (Washington, 1904–37), vol. 3, p. 395.

[5] John Hancock to George Washington, Dec. 2, 1775, in *Letters of Members of the Continental Congress*, ed. Edmund C. Burnett (Washington, 1921–36), vol. 1, p. 267. The army commander shared the apprehension of Congress. "If," he wrote to a Virginia delegate, "that man is not crushed before spring, he will become the most formidable enemy America has; his strength will increase as a snow ball by rolling: and faster, if some expedient cannot be hit upon, to convince the slaves and servants of the impotency of his designs." George Washington to Richard Henry Lee, Dec. 26, 1775, in R. H. Lee, *Memoir of the Life of Richard Henry Lee* (Philadelphia, 1825), vol. 2, p. 9. Compare Washington to Joseph Reed, Dec. 15, 1775, in *The Writings of George Washington from the Original Manuscript Sources, 1745–1799*, ed. John C. Fitzpatrick (Washington, 1931–44), vol. 4, p. 167.

[6] *Journals of the Continental Congress*, vol. 3, p. 403.

be deprived of their workers and would be compelled to return to their homes to protect their families and their property. Moreover, the slaves would help fill the ranks of military laborers for His Majesty's forces, and such human *potentiel de guerre* was badly needed. And Dunmore could expect little help from British head-quarters in Boston.[7] Obviously, too, the Crown supporters and their sympathizers counted on the disaffection of the Negroes in the South.[8]

Needing supporters to hold the rebellion-bent Virginians in check, Dunmore let it be known late in April 1775 that he might be driven to set up the royal standard, adding that if he did he believed that he could count on "all the Slaves on the side of Government."[9] On May 1 the governor wrote to the Earl of Dartmouth expressing confidence that, once supplied with arms and ammu-nition, he would be able "to collect from among the *Indians,* negroes and other persons"[10] a force sufficient to hold his own.[11] Two weeks later, Gage in a letter to Dartmouth touched on Dunmore's pro-posal: "We hear," wrote the British commander, "that a Decla-

[7]General Thomas Gage wrote to Dunmore on Sept. 10, 1775: "I can neither assist you with Men, arms or ammunition, for I have them not to spare; should you draw upon me I have not the Cash to pay your Bills." Clinton Papers, William L. Clements Library, University of Michigan. For England's continuing great difficulty in getting manpower see Edward E. Curtis, *The Organization of the British Army in the American Revolution* (New Haven, 1926), pp. 51–80.

[8]"Although Virginia and Maryland are both very populous," wrote Governor Josiah Martin of North Carolina to Dartmouth on June 30, 1775, "the Whites are greatly outnumbered by the Negroes, at least in the former; a circumstance that would facilitate exceedingly the Reduction of those Colonies who are very sensible of their Weakness arising from it." Clinton Papers. This idea of Negro support was a persistent one: "The Negroes may be all deemed so many Intestine Enemies, being all slaves and desirous of Freedom." Joseph Galloway to Dartmouth, Jan. 23, 1778, *Facsimiles of Manuscripts in European Archives Relating to America, 1773–1783,* ed. Benjamin F. Stevens (London, 1889–98), vol. 24, no. 2079. For a similar expres-sion from another loyalist, see "Moses Kirkland to His Majesty's Commissioners, Oct. 21, 1778," Clinton Papers.

[9]"Deposition of Dr. William Pasteur. In Regard to the Removal of Powder from the Williamsburg Magazine," in "Virginia Legislative Papers (from Originals in Virginia State Archives)," *Virinia Magazine of History and Biography* 13 (July 1905): 49.

[10]Later that year Dunmore concocted a plan to raise the tribes, as Gage phrased it, "on the back parts of the Province of Virginia, to be Joined by such Inhabitants and Indians as may be at, and about Detroit." Gage to Guy Carleton, Sept. 11, 1775, Gage MSS. (American Series), Clements Library. This so-called Connolly Plot is briefly described in Isaac S. Harrell, *Loyalism in Virginia* (Philadelphia, 1926), pp. 35–37.

[11]Dartmouth to Dunmore, Aug. 2, 1775, *Amer. Arch.,* 4th Ser., 3:6. In this passage Dartmouth repeats the contents of a letter from Dunmore dated May 1.

ration his Lordship has made, of proclaiming all the Negroes free, who should join him, has Startled the Insurgents."[12]

In late April a group of slaves, scenting freedom in the air, went to the governor's house and volunteered their services, but Dunmore had them dismissed.[13] He was then not quite ready for the open break, but it could not be long delayed. On June 8, 1775, the governor took the decisive step of quitting Williamsburg and taking asylum aboard the man-of-war *Fowey* at Yorktown, a move he had been turning over in his mind since May 15.[14] "I have thought it best for his Majesty's Service," he wrote, "to retire from amidst such hostile appearances around me."[15] The House of Burgesses, taking note of the governor's flight, assured him that his personal safety was in no danger, but pointedly noted its displeasure that "a Scheme, the most diabolical, had been meditated, and generally recommended, by a Person of great Influence, to offer Freedom to our Slaves, and turn them against their Masters."[16]

Realizing that there was no turning back, Dunmore initiated a policy of unofficial slave solicitation to augment his tiny force of 300 white soldiers, seamen, and loyalist recruits. In early August the "Officers of the Volunteer Companies" in Williamsburg informed the Convention that the "Governor's Cutter had carried off a number of Slaves belonging to private gentlemen...."[17] Small sloops, which were employed primarily to intercept intracolonial shipments of powder, invited slaves aboard. "Lord Dunmore sails up and down the river," wrote a Norfolk correspondent on October 28, 1775, to a friend in England, "and where he finds a defenceless place, he lands, plunders the plantation and carries off the negroes."[18]

Now ready to come out into the open, Dunmore was concerned only with his timing. An apparently auspicious moment came in

[12]Gage to Dartmouth, May 15, 1775, Gage MSS. (English Series), Clements Library.

[13]"Deposition of John Randolph in Regard to the Removal of the Powder," in "Virginia Legislative Papers," *Va. Mag. of His. and Biog.* 15 (Oct. 1907):150.

[14]Dunmore to Gage, May 15, 1775, Gage MSS. (American Series).

[15]Ibid., June 17, 1775.

[16]*Journals of the House of Burgesses of Virginia, 1773–1776*, ed. John Pendleton Kennedy (Richmond, 1905), p. 256.

[17]"Proceedings of the Virginia Convention, August 3, 1775," *Amer. Arch.*, 4th Ser., 3:373.

[18]*Morning Chronicle and London Advertiser*, Dec. 22, 1775, in Willard, *Letters on the American Revolution*, pp. 271–72. The number of slaves reaching Dunmore during the preproclamation stage is indeterminate; "some accounts make them about 100; others less." Edmund Pendleton and others to Virginia Delegates in Congress, Nov. 11, 1775, Lee Family MSS., U. Va. library.

mid-November 1775 when a skirmish took place at Kemp's Landing on the Elizabeth River. In this action the colonial militia was routed and its two commanding colonels were captured. Entering the village in triumph, Dunmore, on November 14, ordered the publication of the proclamation he had drafted a week earlier on board the *William*. The final break had come—the governor had set up his standard and had officially called upon the slaves to join him.

Tidewater Virginia took alarm as rumors spread that the slaves were stampeding to the British.[19] But there were strong deterring factors. Foremost among these was the military alertness of the Virginians themselves. Before any substantial slave migration to Dunmore could get under way, the governor suffered a decisive defeat at arms. This occurred on December 9 at Great Bridge, a fortified span across the Elizabeth River some ten miles below Norfolk which dominated the land approach thereto. Dunmore had believed that an attack was impending and had rashly decided to take the offensive. His force of 600 was severely repulsed, suffering sixty-one casualties, including three dead officers. Forced to retreat after twenty-five minutes of combat, Dunmore's troops hurried back to Norfolk. Feeling that he could no longer hold the city and fearing a retaliatory attack, the governor spiked his twenty pieces of cannon and ordered his followers aboard the vessels in the harbor. He was never to regain a foothold on the Virginia mainland.

The military preparation of the colonists was matched by their promptness in adopting "home front" measures to prevent slaves from joining the governor. Newspapers lost no time in publishing the proclamation in full, as information and as a warning. To deter runaways local patrol groups were doubled, highways were carefully watched, and owners of small craft were required to exercise vigilance. Since Dunmore's action had come as no surprise, the Virginians had had time to put the colony in a "tolerable state of defense."[20] Adjacent Maryland, through its Council of Safety, ordered the military to station itself in St. Mary's County "and guard the shores from thence to the river Powtowmack, to prevent any servants, negroes, or others from going on board the Fowey ship of war."[21]

[19]"Letters mention that slaves flock to him in abundance, but I hope it is magnified." Edmund Pendleton to Richard Henry Lee, Nov. 27, 1775, *Amer. Arch.*, 4th Ser., 4:202.

[20]Ramsay, *American Revolution*, vol.1, p. 234.

[21]*Journal and Correspondence of the Maryland Council of Safety, Aug. 29, 1775–July 6, 1776*, ed. William H. Browne et. al., *Archives of Maryland* (Baltimore, 1883—in progress), 11:511–12.

To vigilance the colonists added psychological warfare. In Alexander Purdie's *Virginia Gazette* was published a letter from a subscriber urging that Negroes be cautioned against joining Dunmore. Slaves should be told that the English ministry, in refusing to stop the slave trade, had proved a far greater enemy to Negroes than their American masters, and that if the colonists were defeated, their slaves would be sold to the West Indies. They should be told, too, continued Mr. Purdie's correspondent, that Dunmore was cruel to his own black servitors. And, finally, they should be urged to place their expectation on "a better condition in the next world." If this information had been spread widely, "not one slave would have joined our enemies."[22]

A week later the *Gazette* carried another letter in a similar vein. Colonists were advised to inform slaves that Dunmore proposed to free only those who would bear arms for him, leaving the aged and infirm, the women and children, to bear the brunt of the shorn master's anger. Moreover, under the English flag the slaves would be much worse off than under Virginia masters, "who pity their condition, who wish in general to make it as easy and comfortable as possible, and who would willingly, were it in their power, or were they permitted, not only prevent any more negroes from losing their freedom, but restore it to such as have already unhappily lost it." Contrast this with the British, ran the *Gazette's* warning, who would sell the runaways to the sugar islands. "Be not then, ye negroes, tempted by this proclamation to ruin your selves."[23]

Official action was not long in coming. The Virginia Convention on December 8 appointed a committee to prepare an answer to Dunmore's proclamation. Five days later, when the committee made its report, it was directed to draw up a declaration stating that runaways to the British would be pardoned if they returned in ten days; otherwise they would "be liable to such punishment as shall be directed by the Convention." The following day, with the committee's report at hand, the delegates issued a declaration of policy. Beginning with a reminder that the time-honored penalty for a slave insurrection was death without benefit of clergy, the document stated that Negroes who had been "seduced" to take up arms were liable to punishment. But in order that they might return in safety to their duties, they would be pardoned if they laid down their arms forthwith. The proclamation concluded with a request to "all hu-

[22]Purdie's *Virginia Gazette,* Williamsburg, Nov. 17, 1775. Hereafter cited as *Va. Gaz.*
[23]Ibid., Nov. 24, 1775.

mane and benevolent persons in the colony" to convey to the slaves this "offer of mercy."[24] To insure a wide circulation, the proclamation was published as a broadside.[25]

The Virginians supplemented techniques of persuasion and sweet reasonableness with alternatives more forthright and punitive. In early December the Convention decreed that slaves taken in arms were to be sold to the foreign West Indies, with the sale money, minus expenses, to go to their masters.[26] Somewhat less severe was the fate of captured runaways who had failed in their attempts to reach the king's forces. Such slaves, if their masters were patriots, were returned to their home plantations, often after first serving a term of imprisonment. An owner of a captured runaway might be ordered to "convey him to some interior part of the Country as soon as may be. . . . "[27] Slaves of British sympathizers were put to work in the lead mines,[28] a practice which became customary in Virginia for the duration of the war. Distrusting all Negroes who had joined the governor, the Convention recommended that military officers "seize and secure" even those who came bearing flags of truce.[29]

The death penalty was used sparingly. In Northampton County the court passed such a sentence on a group of thirteen slaves who had seized a schooner at Hungers Creek and sailed into the bay, their destination the James. Overtaken by a whale boat,[30] their execution was set for April 2, 1776. But the Northampton Committee of Safety sent word to Williamsburg inquiring whether the punishment should not be mitigated since the seizing of the boat was more "intended to effect an escape to Dunmore than any other Design of committing a felony."[31] Whenever the death sentence was

[24]*Proceedings of the Convention of the Delegates in the Colony of Virginia* (Richmond, 1816), p. 62.
[25]Virginia Broadsides (V. 54), U. Va. library.
[26]William Waller Hening, *The Statutes at Large; Being a Collection of All the Laws of Virginia* . . . (Richmond, 1809–23), vol. 9, p. 106.
[27]Such was the language used by the Virginia Council to William Kirby (July 12, 1776) concerning his slave Frank. *Journals of the Council of State of Virginia*, ed. H. R. McIlwaine and Wilmer L. Hall (Richmond, 1931–32, 1952), vol. 1, p. 67.
[28]On Dec. 14, 1775, the convention ordered the Committee of Safety to employ captive slaves "in working the Lead Mine in the County of *Fincastle*, for the use of this Colony." *Amer. Arch.*, 4th Ser., 4:85. Shortly afterward four would-be followers of Dunmore who were captured at Accomac were ordered "sent up the country and employed in some publick works." Ibid., 6:1553.
[29]Ibid., 6:1524.
[30]James Kent and William Henry to Maryland Council of Safety, Feb. 28, 1776, *Arch. of Md.*, 11:191.
[31]Northampton Committee of Safety to General Committee of Safety, Apr. 23, 1776, "Va. Leg. Papers," *Va. Mag. of Hist. and Biog.* 15 (April 1908):407.

passed, as in the case of two runaways who mistook an armed vessel of the Virginia navy for a British man-of-war, it was used mainly "as an example to others."[32]

Despite preventive efforts, whether an appeal to common sense or a resort to legal reprisals, many slaves made their way to the British, spurred in part by loyalist propaganda of the governor's good treatment.[33] Some 200 "immediately joined him,"[34] and within a week after the proclamation the number had reached 300.[35] "Numbers of Negros and Cowardly Scoundrels flock to his Standard," wrote a member of the provincial Committee of Safety.[36]

Since Dunmore had no base on the mainland after mid-December 1775, the Negroes who sought his sanctuary were water-borne. Two weeks after the proclamation a group of slaves came down the James in a thirty-foot vessel, bound for the fleet off Norfolk, but they were captured near Surry.[37] Shortly afterward seven Negroes broke out of a Northampton jail and "went off in a pettinger," bound for the British ships.[38] Colonel Landon Carter of the Sabine Hall plantation made a diary notation of the break for the open water executed by ten of his retainers:

26 Wednesday, June, 1776. Last night after going to bed, Moses, my son's man, Joe, Billy, Postillion, John, Mullatto Peter, Tom, Panticove, Manuel & Lancaster Sam, ran away, to be sure, to Ld. Dunmore, for they got privately into Beale's room before dark & took out my son's gun & one I had there, took out of his drawer in my passage all his ammunition furniture, Landon's bag of bullets and all the Powder, and went off in my Petty Anger [pettiauger] new trimmed, and it is supposed that Mr. Robinson's People are gone with them, for a skow they came down in is, it seems,

---

[32]*Va. Gaz.*, Apr. 13, 1776.

[33]Northampton Committee of Safety to General Committee of Safety. Dunmore would have every reason to welcome runaways, but perhaps his reception of them fell short of the report, circulated in the *Virginia Gazette*, that on the evening the governor's forces landed on Gwynn's Island, they amused themselves "with a promiscuous ball, which was opened, we hear by a certain spruce little gentleman, with one of the black ladies." *Va. Gaz.*, May 31, 1776.

[34]Northampton Committee of Safety to Continental Congress, Nov. 25, 1775, "Va. Leg. Papers," *Va. Mag. of Hist. and Biog.* 14 (January 1907):251.

[35]Andrew Sprowel to Peter Paterson, Nov. 19, 1775, ibid., 14 (April 1907):387.

[36]John Page to Thomas Jefferson, Nov. 24, 1775, *The Papers of Thomas Jefferson*, ed. Julian P. Boyd (Princeton, 1950—in progress), vol. 1, p. 265.

[37]*Va. Gaz.*, Jan. 10, 1776.

[38]*Maryland Gazette*, Annapolis, Feb. 22, 1776. "Pettinger" and "pettiauger" (below) are corruptions of the Spanish *piragua*, "a dugout," "a two-masted, flat-bottomed boat."

at my Landing. These accursed villians have stolen Landon's silver buckles, George's shirts, Tom Parker's new waistcoat & breeches.[39]

The Negroes who reached the British were generally able-bodied men who could be put to many uses.[40] It was as soldiers, however, that Dunmore envisioned them, and he enlisted them from the beginning. By early December he was arming them "as fast as they came in."[41] He made use of Negro privates at the rout of the colonials at Kemp's Landing; indeed, slaves had captured one of the two commanding colonels.[42] In the skirmishes preceding the action at Great Bridge, two runaways who were taken prisoner testified that the garrison was manned by thirty whites and ninety Negroes, and that "all the blacks who are sent to the fort at the great Bridge, are supplied with muskets, Cartridges & strictly ordered to use them defensively & offensively."[43] By the first of December the British had nearly 300 slaves outfitted in military garb, with the inscription, "Liberty to Slaves," emblazoned across the breast of each.[44] The governor officially designated them "Lord Dunmore's Ethiopian Regiment."[45]

The first and only major military action in which Dunmore's forces were engaged was the battle of Great Bridge.[46] Of the gov-

---

[39]"Diary of Col. Landon Carter," *William and Mary Quarterly*, 1st ser., 20 (January 1912):178–79.

[40]Two women, however, were among a party of nine slaves who were seized in mid-December after putting out to sea in an open boat in an attempt to reach Norfolk. *Pennsylvania Gazette*, Philadelphia, Dec. 20, 1775.

[41]Dunmore to Sec. of State for the Colonies, Dec. 6, 1775, Peter Force-George Bancroft Transcripts, "Virginia: Official Correspondence," Library of Congress.

[42]Edmund Pendleton to R. H. Lee, Nov. 27, 1775, *Amer. Arch.*, 4th Ser., 4:202.

[43]William Woodford to Edmund Pendleton, Dec. 5, 1775, "The Woodford, Howe, and Lee Letters," *Richmond College Historical Papers* 1 (June 1915):113. Added Woodford, "The bearer brings you one of the Balls taken out of the cartirages found upon the negro Prisoners, as they were extremely well made." Ibid., p. 112.

[44]*Md. Gaz.*, Dec. 14, 1775.

[45]Dunmore to Sec. of State for Colonies, Dec. 6, 1775, Force-Bancroft Transcripts.

[46]Eyewitness accounts of the action at Great Bridge include: "...a Midshipman on board his Majesty's ship *Otter*, commanded by Captain Squires, Dec. 9," in Willard, *Letters on the American Revolution*, pp. 234–35; "...a Gentleman, dated ship *William*, off Norfolk, Virginia, Dec. 25, 1775," ibid., pp. 244–45; "Thomas McKnight to Rev. Dr. McKnight, on board the King's Fisher, Dec. 26, 1775," Miscellaneous Collection, Clements Library; "Contemporary English Accounts of the Destruction of Norfolk in 1776," comp. H. S. Parsons, *Wm. & Mary Quart.*, 2d ser., 13 (October 1933):219–24; Richard Kidder Meade to Theodorick Bland, Jr., Norfolk Town Camp, Dec. 18, 1775, in *The Bland Papers*, ed. Charles Campbell (Petersburg, 1840–43), vol. 1, p. 38; "The Woodford, Howe, and Lee Letters," *Richmond College Hist. Papers* 1:96–163, passim; William Woodford to Edmund Pendleton, Dec. 10, 1775, in *Md. Gaz.*, Dec. 21, 1775, and Jan. 4, 1776. For

ernor's troops of some 600 men, nearly half were Negroes. Of the eighteen wounded prisoners taken by the Virginians in this rout, two were former slaves. James Anderson was wounded "in the Forearm—Bones shattered and flesh much torn," and Casar was hit "in the Thigh, by a Ball, and 5 shot—one lodged."[47] After the fiasco at Great Bridge, the governor was forced to operate from his ships. Taking aboard the hardiest of his Negro followers and placing them under officers who excercised them at small arms, he sanguinely awaited recruits.

Dunmore's use of Negroes also embraced sailoring services. On the six tenders sent by the governor to cannonade Hampton in late October 1775, there were colored crewmen. Two of them were captured when the Virginians seized the pilot boat *Hawk Tender*.[48] To man the small craft that scurried in and out of the river settlements, harassing the plantations, the British depended largely on ex-slaves. Particularly were they needed as pilots. Joseph Harris, a runaway, served as pilot of the *Otter*, having come to Captain Matthew Squire with the highest recommendation from a fellow naval officer. "I think him too useful to His Majesty's service to take away," wrote the latter, because of "his being well acquainted with many creeks in the *Eastern Shore*, at *York*, *James* River, and *Nansemond*, and many others, . . ." and "accustomed to pilot. . . ."[49] Two citizens on the Isle of Wight advised the chairman of the Virginia Committee of Safety to go slow on discharging "a Negro fello, named Caesar," who was not only "a very great Scoundrel" but was also "a fello' they can't do well without being an Excellent pilot."[50]

Another service performed by Dunmore's black followers was foraging. The governor's supply of provisions, particularly fresh foods, needed constant replenishing, and the Virginia leaders understandably would not permit the British to send men ashore to

---

Dunmore's account see Dunmore to Secretary of State for the Colonies, Dec. 13, 1775, Force-Bancroft Transcripts. For the story, relished by Virginians, that a well-coached slave had been sent into Dunmore's lines with instructions to misrepresent the strength of the colonial militia, see John Burk, *The History of Virginia* (Petersburg, 1805–16), vol. 4, p. 85.

[47]Woodford to Pendleton, Dec. 10, 1775, "The Woodford, Howe, and Lee Letters," *Richmond College Hist. Papers* 1:118.

[48]John Page to Thomas Jefferson, Nov. 11, 1775, *Papers of Thomas Jefferson*, ed. Boyd, vol. 1, p. 257.

[49]George Montague to Matthew Squire, July 20, 1775, *Amer. Arch.*, 4th ser., 2:1692.

[50]Thomas Pierce and Thomas Smith to Edmund Pendleton, Dec. 17, 1775, "Miscellaneous Colonial Documents," *Va. Mag. of Hist. and Biog.* 19 (July 1911):267.

make purchases. "Back settlers" who might have been willing to supply his lordship with provisions had "no means of conveying them,"[51] and Dunmore was driven to a dependence upon the foraging abilities of his Negro recruits. Marauding parties of predominantly ex-slave composition preyed on the countryside, making a night descent upon a plantation and making off with the choice livestock. One foraging party, captured while on its way to the Eastern Shore, was made up of "one white and sixteen blacks."[52]

Allegedly one of the services of Negroes to Dunmore was germ spreading. That the charge of germ warfare was propaganda-laden did not make it less potent in arousing indignation. The accusation was that Dunmore had inoculated two Negroes and sent them ashore at Norfolk to spread the smallpox.[53] The charge was ironic in view of the fate of the Negroes who fled to the British. The majority of them were disease fatalities. Late in March the governor informed his superior in England that the recruiting of the black regiment "would have been in great forwardness had not a fever crept in amongst them, which carried off a great many very fine fellows." He added that on advice of "medical people here," he had concluded that the trouble came from the overcrowded condition on the ships and the lack of clothing, both of which "we have now provided against."[54]

But the plague persisted, killing off the Negroes and the hope of the governor alike. Writing to Germain in June, Dunmore confessed defeat. The fever, he explained, was malignant, and had "carried off an incredible number of our people, especially blacks." Had this not happened he would have enlisted 2,000 Negro followers. He was, ran his letter, separating the sick from the well and would try to keep the two groups from intermingling.[55] The governor's efforts

---

[51]"Extract of a letter to a gentleman in Scotland, dated Norfolk, Virginia, February 17, 1776," *Amer. Arch.*, 4th ser., 4:1166.

[52]Archibald Cary to R.H. Lee, Dec. 24, 1775, in Robert K. Brock, *Archibald Cary of Ampthill* (Richmond, 1937), p. 161.

[53]*Va. Gaz.*, June 15, 1776.

[54]Dunmore to George Germain, Mar. 30, 1776, *Amer. Arch.*, 5th ser. (Washington, 1848–53), 2:159–60.

[55]Dunmore to Germain, Mar. 30, 1776, *Amer. Arch.*, 5th ser., 2:162. Dunmore's policy of isolation appears to have prevented the smallpox from decimating the white troops. The monthly return of the 14th Regiment of Infantry, signed by Capt. Sam Leslie, lists a total of 128 men (with breakdowns as to rank) for Mar. 1, 1776, a total of 126 men for Apr. 1, 1776, and a total of 122 for May 1, 1776. "Monthly Return of a Detachment of His Majesty's 14th Regiment of Infantry, off Norfolk, Virginia, 1 March 1776," Clinton Papers; ibid., for Apr. 1, 1776, and for May 1, 1776. In addition to the factor of isolation, the mortality of the Negro soldiers may have been due to their performing most of the garrison and fatigue duties; at Gwynn's

were unavailing; by early June 1776 there were not more than "150 effective Negro men," although each day the black corps was augmented by from six to eight arrivals.[56]

The failure to arrest the smallpox, and the harassment by the Virginia and Maryland militia, finally brought an end to his lordship's stay in Chesapeake waters. In May 1776, faced with the likelihood "of a great reduction of our force" due to disease,[57] the fleet moved from their exposed quarters at Tucker's Mills near Portsmouth and took shelter on Gwynn's Island near the mouth of the Rappahannock. Nowhere were Dunmore and his "floating Town"[58] allowed peace; "we no sooner appear off the land, than signals are made from it," wrote Dunmore to Whitehall, "and if we come to anchor within cannonshot of either shore, guns are immediately brought to bear upon us...."[59]

Early in July the British, after suffering an attack on their shipping, took refuge on St. George's Island in the Potomac. By the end of the month the disease-ridden corps, lacking suitable drinking water, and despairing of reenforcements, prepared to make their exit. Dismantling, burning, or running aground sixty-three out of their 103 vessels, they sailed out of the Potomac on August 6, seven of the ships bound for Sandy Hook and the others setting a southward course for St. Augustine and the Bermudas.[60] With the departing fleet went some 300 Negroes, the healthiest going northward, destined for further military service, and Dunmore's schemes came to an inglorious end.[61]

Perhaps not more than a total of 800 slaves had succeeded in reaching the British,[62] and perhaps one eighth of these had been

Island the entrenchments were guarded "chiefly by the black regiment." *Va. Gaz.*, June 1, 1776.

[56]Entry of June 10, 1776, A. S. Hamond Diaries, 1775–77, U. Va. library. Andrew Snape Hamond, captain of the *Roebuck,* was the commanding officer in Virginia waters.

[57]Ibid., May 19, 1776.

[58]The descriptive phrase is Hamond's. Letter to Hans Stanley, Aug. 5, 1776, ibid.

[59]Dunmore to George Germain, July 31, 1776, *Amer. Arch.*, 5th ser., 2:166.

[60]Hamond Diaries, Aug. 6, 1776. Dunmore himself went to New York, arriving on Aug. 14. *Journals of Lieut.-Col. Stephen Kemble,* New-York Historical Society, *Collections (1883–84),* vol. 1, p. 84.

[61]Dunmore remained convinced of the soundness of his plan to arm Negroes in large numbers, reviving it even after Yorktown. See Percy Burdelle Caley, "Dunmore: Colonial Governor of New York and Virginia, 1770–1782," unpubl. diss., University of Pittsburgh, 1939, pp. 887–93.

[62]Dunmore's Negro followers were computed in general terms; e.g., "...came in a great number of Black men from the Rebels." Logs of *Roebuck* and *Fowey,* in Greenwich Museum, England, entry of June 27, 1776. Photostat in A. S. Hamond MSS., U. Va. library.

brought by loyalist masters. But Dunmore's proclamation undoubtedly had an indirect effect on thousands of additional slaves, quickening their hopes for freedom. Perhaps the imagination of colonial editors was behind such stories as that of a colored mother in New York naming her child after his lordship,[63] and that of a Negro in Philadelphia jostling whites on the streets and telling them to wait until "lord Dunmore and his black regiment come, and then we will see who is to take the wall."[64] But whether fact or fabrication, such reports reflect the attitude of expectation that Dunmore engendered among persons of color along the Chesapeake. It made no difference that he had offered freedom to the bondmen of his enemies only,[65] and that as governor he had withheld his signature from a bill against the slave trade; to those who whispered his name in slave quarters he was in truth the "African Hero" he was derisively dubbed by a Virginia patriot.[66]

If Dunmore was viewed by one group as a tyrant and by another as a liberator, this was but another paradox in a war that abounded in paradox, and another illustration of the war as a social revolution. The Negro who fled to the governor was actuated by the same love of freedom for which the colonists avowedly broke with the mother country. Dunmore's invitation to the slaves was to prefigure the thousands of runaways below the Mason-Dixon line who served as military laborers to His Majesty's forces during the Revolution and who, when peace came, sailed with them from Savannah, Charleston, and New York.

[63]Taking due note, the *New York Journal* carried an occasional poem, copied in the *Va. Gaz.*, May 25, 1776:

> Hail! doughty Ethiopian Chief!
> Though ignominious Negro Thief!
> This BLACK shall prop thy sinking name,
> And damn thee to perpetual fame.

[64]*Va. Gaz.*, Supplement, Dec. 29, 1775.
[65]John King, runaway slave of a loyalist, was ordered discharged from the *King's Fisher*. Logs of *Roebuck* and *Fowey*, Feb. 23, 1776.
[66]R. H. Lee to Thomas Jefferson, July 21, 1776, in *The Letters of Richard Henry Lee*, ed. James C. Ballagh (New York, 1912–14), vol. 1, p. 210.

3. The Revolutionary War as a Black Declaration of Independence

URING THE SUMMER of 1777 Capt. William Whipple, a soldier from Portsmouth, New Hampshire, noted that his slave, Prince, was quite dejected. Asked by Whipple to account for his moodiness, Prince explained, "Master, *you* are going to fight for your *liberty*, but I have none to fight for." Struck by the essential truth of Prince's complaint, Whipple lost no time in freeing him.[1]

Before his emancipation Prince had been one of the oarsmen who rowed George Washington and his party across the ice-choked Delaware River in a blinding snow and sleet storm Christmas night 1776. But even had Prince Whipple not taken part in one of the most significant battles of the Revolutionary War, there was nothing unusual about his longing to be free. This yearning for freedom was common among those in bondage and its roots ran deep. The contagion of liberty had long infected blacks, reaching epidemic proportions with the outbreak of the war against England. As was the case for other Americans, regional differences characterized Afro-American culture, and within each regional group status determinants such as occupation and skin color further divided both slave and free blacks. Moreover, in ever-changing early America the patterns of black life were not static from one generation to another.[2] But regardless of these distinctions, all blacks during the Revolutionary era shared a common goal—the pursuit of freedom and equality.

---

[1]Charles W. Brewster, *Rambles about Portsmouth: Sketches of Persons, Localities, and Incidents of Two Centuries: Principally from Tradition and Unpublished Sources* (Portsmouth, N.H., 1859), p. 153.

[2]On this point see Ira Berlin, "Time, Space, and the Evolution of Afro-American Society in British Mainland North America," *American Historical Review* 85 (1980):44–78; and idem, "The Revolution in Black Life," in Alfred F. Young, ed., *The American Revolution: Explorations in the History of American Radicalism* (DeKalb, Ill., 1976), pp. 351–82.

The exchange between Captain Whipple and his slave illustrated another major characteristic of Revolutionary War blacks, their tendency to differ with whites in interpreting the rhetoric and the meaning of the war itself. When whites, for example, accused England of trying to enslave them, they had in mind such measures as stamp acts and trade restrictions, royal decrees and parliamentary legislation. To white Americans the war meant freedom and liberty in a politicoeconomic sense rather than in the sense of personal bondage. Admittedly, the Revolutionary War did have its social overtones, as J. Franklin Jameson reminded us half a century ago.[3] And, as Jesse Lemisch, Alfred F. Young, and others have pointed out more recently, various underprivileged white groups, including women, had distinctive reactions to the war, each of them viewing it as an opportunity for advancement.[4]

With all due credit for its pivotal role in the history of human freedom, the American Revolution fell considerably short of the egalitarian goals it proclaimed. Like many subsequent armed outbreaks, it was essentially a colonial war of liberation; it was waged, however, against a country not unlike America itself. White Americans claimed that they were fighting for the rights of Englishmen—rights that they had long enjoyed but that the crown had tried to abrogate; they struggled to retain freedom rather than to acquire it.

Although white patriots might not have cared to acknowledge it, the American Revolution bore the overtones of a civil war; indeed, it was more a war of independence than one of revolution. Moreover, unlike other colonial wars of liberation, as Moses Coit Tyler pointed out, it was "directed not against tyranny inflicted, but only against tyranny anticipated."[5] Its inherent conservatism limited the revolutionary potential of the American War for Independence.

Slaves saw the matter differently. In its impact on them the war was truly revolutionary. Seizing the opportunity, they gave a personal interpretation to the theory of natural rights and to the slogans

---

[3] J. Franklin Jameson, *The American Revolution Considered as a Social Movement* (Princeton, 1926).

[4] Jesse Lemisch, "The American Revolution Seen from the Bottom Up," in Barton J. Bernstein, ed., *Towards a New Past: Dissenting Essays in American History* (New York, 1968), pp. 3–29; Young, *American Revolution*.

[5] Moses Coit Tyler, *The Literary History of the American Revolution, 1763–1783*, 2 vols. (1897; reprint ed., New York, 1957), vol. 1, p. 8.

of liberty and independence. Such a patriotic exhortation as "Give me liberty or give me death" carried special meaning to people in bondage.

The desire of blacks for freedom did not, of course, originate with the American Revolution. In one of his midweek lectures to Boston slaves, delivered on May 21, 1721, Cotton Mather denounced the *"Fondness* for *Freedom* in many of you, who lived Comfortably in a very easy Servitude." Obviously not alluding to religious freedom, Mather had in mind a freedom of the person which, in his opinion, was not the state God had ordained for the assembled bondspeople.[6] Half a century later, on the eve of the Revolutionary War, this fondness for freedom had become even more prevalent. The number of blacks had multiplied, and they had become more at home in provincial America and more responsive to its ways of life, particularly those tinged with egalitarianism of substance, tone, or spirit.

The special circumstances of Afro-American life sharpened the desire to be free. In sheer numbers blacks composed in 1774 a larger proportion of the total population than they ever would again: 500,000 out of 2,600,000, or nearly 20 percent. These half million blacks had become Afro-Americans in the true sense of the hyphenated word. Reinforced by more recent arrivals from overseas, they retained strong spiritual and aesthetic ties with their ancestral homelands, their rich cultural heritage already working its way into American music, dance, folk literature, and art. Indeed, in reference to Americans from Africa the term *acculturation* lacks precision; it would be better to use *transculturation,* a process of exchange and not a one-way street. Despite the persistence of their African heritage, however, most blacks by 1774 had undergone a transition from Africans to Afro-Americans and were no longer the "outlandish" blacks slave traders had deposited in the New World.

Their Americanization had resulted from a complex of influences, economic, socioreligious, and genetic. They certainly had been integrated economically, as a vital source of labor. Slaves in the southern colonies, numbering 90 percent of the total slave population, produced the agricultural staples of the late colonial period, to-

---

[6]Cotton Mather, *Tremenda: The Dreadful Sound with Which the Wicked Are to Be Thunderstruck* . . . (Boston, 1721), quoted in Lawrence W. Towner. " 'A Fondness for Freedom': Servant Protest in Puritan Society," *William and Mary Quarterly,* 3d ser. 19 (1962):201. For a penetrating analysis of Mather's views on slavery, see Daniel K. Richter, " 'It Is God Who Has Caused Them To Be Servants': Cotton Mather and Afro-American Slavery in New England," *Bulletin of the Congregational Library* 15 (1979):3–13.

bacco, rice, and sugar. A plantation required skilled laborers as well as field hands, and these too were black. As Marcus W. Jernegan pointed out, "It is hard to see how the eighteenth-century plantation could have survived if the Negro slave had not made his important contribution as an artisan."[7] In South Carolina, Peter H. Wood has noted, slaves not only engaged in the full range of plantation activities "but were also thoroughly involved wherever experiments were made with new products," such as the development of silk culture.[8] North Carolina's blacks likewise performed complex and essential tasks. "If their status often forced them into menial labor," observed Jeffrey J. Crow, "they still contributed skills and know-how to the colony's agriculture and crafts."[9]

The northern provinces also had their component of slaves with industrial skills. Slave workers in New York, as described by Edgar J. McManus, "showed proficiency in every field of human endeavor."[10] Lorenzo J. Greene, another authority on blacks in the colonial North, painted a similar picture of the slave in New England who might be called upon "not only to care for stock, to act as a servant, repair a fence, serve on board ship, shoe a horse, print a newspaper, but even to manage his master's business."[11] And in New England, as elsewhere, slave women were proficient spinners, knitters, and weavers.

Daily contacts between black worker and white owner inevitably led to a sociocultural interaction between the parties, with the slaves becoming familiar with and sometimes adopting the beliefs and behavior patterns of their owners. Such personal contacts were most frequent when a master owned only one or two slaves. The pattern of person-to-person association between the races was less pervasive on the larger plantations, but even there one would find a corps of domestic slaves, whose children, it may be added, tended to play with the children of the master.

In the absence of a slave row with its separate quarters, the slaves in New England and the middle colonies were in close and constant contact with their owners. In the cities above the Potomac, Ira Berlin

[7]Marcus W. Jernegan, *Laboring and Dependent Classes in Colonial America, 1607–1783* (Chicago, 1931), p. 23.

[8]Peter H. Wood, *Black Majority: Negroes in Colonial South Carolina from 1670 through the Stono Rebellion* (New York, 1974), p. 199.

[9]Jeffrey J. Crow, *The Black Experience in Revolutionary North Carolina* (Raleigh, N.C., 1977), p. 12.

[10]Edgar J. McManus, *A History of Negro Slavery in New York* (Syracuse, N.Y., 1966), p. 47.

[11]Lorenzo J. Greene, *The Negro in Colonial New England* (New York, 1942), p. 101.

has argued, the acculturation of blacks "was a matter of years, not generations."[12] If somewhat slower, the process also went on in the northern countryside. Traveling in rural Connecticut in 1704, Sarah Kemble Knight took note of white masters who permitted what she termed a "too great familiarity" vis-à-vis their slaves, dining at the same table with them. A terse entry in Madame Knight's diary bespoke her displeasure: "Into the dish goes the black hoof as freely as the white hand."[13]

Out of such white-black proximity, North and South emerged another force in the Americanization of blacks—their conversion to Christianity. Although many masters considered it imprudent, the idea of bringing slaves to Christ gained momentum throughout the eighteenth century. The movement was led by the London-based Society for the Propagation of the Gospel in Foreign Parts (S.P.G.), an Episcopal organization that operated mainly in the southern colonies. A handful of Puritans and Quakers, more often laboring individually than in organized groups, also took up evangelical work across the color line. In 1740 the conversion of blacks assumed major proportions with the religious revival known as the Great Awakening, with its central theme of equality before God. Negroes entered the churches in unprecedented numbers, imbibing the "New Light" ideas that characterized the crusade. Writing in 1743, Charles Chauncy, a cleric critical of the Great Awakening, complained that it permitted "women and girls; yea Negroes . . . to do the business of preachers."[14]

A significant by-product of this eighteenth-century evangelistic impulse was the emergence of a small but steadily increasing contingent of blacks who could read and write, a case of religion with letters. The S.P.G. established several schools for blacks, one of which, in Goose Creek Parish, South Carolina, employed two black teachers, the first of their race in colonial America.[15] The Quakers were especially notable for their efforts to provide education for blacks, their zeal spurred by Anthony Benezet, the leading abolitionist of his day. In 1750 Benezet established in Philadelphia a

[12]Berlin, "Time, Space, and the Evolution of Afro-American Society," p. 49.

[13]*The Private Journal of Sarah Kemble Knight: Being the Record of a Journey from Boston to New York in the Year 1704* (1825; reprint ed., Norwich, Conn., 1901), p. 52.

[14]Charles Chauncy, *Seasonable Thoughts on the State of Religion in New England* (Boston, 1743), quoted in Eldon J. Eisenbach, "Cultural Politics and Political Thought: The American Revolution Made and Remembered," *American Studies* 20 (1979):74.

[15]Frank J. Klingberg, *An Appraisal of the Negro in Colonial South Carolina* (Washington, D.C., 1941), pp. 111 and 114–15.

night school for blacks that was still in operation, and with an enrollment of forty-six, when the Revolutionary War broke out.[16] In New England many slaves received training in the "three Rs," not only so they could read the Bible but also because literate slaves brought a higher price on the market.

The close relationship between religion and literacy among blacks was reflected in the two best-known poetic publications of the period, one by Jupiter Hammon and the other by Phillis Wheatley. Hammon's work, a broadside of eighty-eight lines, bore the revealing title "An Evening Thought. Salvation by Christ, with Penetential Cries: Composed by Jupiter Hammon, a Negro belonging to Mr. Lloyd, of Queen's Village, on Long Island, the 25th of December, 1760." Far more celebrated than her predecessor, Phillis Wheatley at the age of twenty-three became in 1773 only the second woman in colonial America to publish a volume of poetry. The title of her path-breaking work, *Poems on Various Subjects, Religious and Moral,* conveys the basic outlook and orientation of a writer who had in 1771 been baptized in Boston's Old South Meeting House.

If Hammon and Wheatley personified the religious acculturation of Afro-Americans, the scientist Benjamin Banneker personified another characteristic of white-black proximity, the mixing of bloodlines. Banneker's white English grandmother had freed and married one of her slaves, Bannaky, a former African chief. As Banneker's ancestry illustrates, blacks in the thirteen colonies were by no means of exclusively African stock. Early Virginia permitted white-black marriages, but even after all the southern colonies, as well as Pennsylvania and Massachusetts, outlawed racial intermixing, miscegenation remained extensive, as evidenced by the large numbers of mulattoes, some of them blue-eyed and red-haired. "It is impossible," Winthrop D. Jordan has argued, "to ascertain how much intermixture there actually was, though it seems likely that there was more during the eighteenth century than at any time since."[17] It is hardly necessary to add that blacks, like whites, also mingled their blood with that of Indians.

As a result of the white-black contacts previously mentioned— economic, socioreligious, and sexual—the half million Afro-Americans of 1774 had begun to experience a sense of distinct identity, a race-conscious identity if you will, but one that reflected the

[16]George S. Brookes, *Friend Anthony Benezet* (Philadelphia, 1937), p. 45.
[17]Winthrop D. Jordan, *White over Black: American Attitudes toward the Negro, 1550–1812* (Chapel Hill, N.C., 1968), p. 137.

essential values of the Revolutionary era. Watered by the Revolutionary War, this sense of self-identity would flower into a collective sense of community, the latter too an affirmation of the most cherished values of the early republic.

The Revolution, with its slogans of liberty and equality, inevitably appealed to a group such as the blacks. If this were the credo of the new America, they would joyfully make the most of it. As a class black Americans were not strong on theory and would hardly have been prepared to discuss the ideological origins of the war. But they could readily understand propositions to the effect that all men were created equal and that everyone was entitled to personal freedom. Themselves short on worldly goods, most blacks did not consider private property, particularly the ownership of slaves, a basic natural right.

Like other Americans, blacks viewed the war in terms of their own interests and concerns. Perceiving what they regarded as an inescapable inconsistency between the ideals of the Revolution and the institution of slavery, they redoubled their efforts for emancipation, their methods including freedom suits, petitions to state legislatures, and military service. In states like Massachusetts that considered them not only property but also persons before the law, slaves instituted suits for freedom. Such actions cast the master in the role of defendant, obliged either to defend the validity of his title or to answer the charge that slavery itself was illegal or unconstitutional.

The effect of a judicial decree extended only to the litigants immediately involved in the case. Hence blacks seeking freedom collectively rather than individually drafted petitions to their state legislatures. Typical of such pleas was that sent in November 1779 to the New Hampshire assembly by nineteen slaves from Portsmouth. Contending that "the God of nature gave them life and freedom," the petitioners asserted that freedom "is an inherent right of the human species, not to be surrendered but by consent."[18]

Slaves in the Revolutionary War South, denied recourse to the courts or the legislatures, expressed their protests more directly. Exhibiting an insubordinate disposition, they became harder to handle. Ronald Hoffman concluded in his study of revolutionary Maryland that the Eastern Shore centers of black population "were severe

---

[18]Petition reproduced in Isaac W. Hammond, "Slavery in New Hampshire in Olden Time," *Granite Monthly* 4 (1880):108–10.

sources of strain and worry during the Anglo-American conflict."[19] By way of example, Hoffman cited a late 1775 dispatch from the Dorchester County Committee of Inspection reporting that "the insolence of the Negroes in this country is come to such a height that we are under a necessity of disarming them. We took about eighty guns, some bayonets, swords, etc."[20]

Slave discontent was further evidenced in the marked increase of runaways. To escape-minded blacks the war was a godsend; the number of fugitive slaves reached flood proportions during the conflict. Thomas Jefferson estimated that during the war more than 30,000 Virginia slaves took to their heels.[21] Attesting to their numerical strength, runaway slaves in revolutionary Georgia established communities of their own.

Blacks' desire for freedom found its greatest fulfillment in wartime service as arms-bearers. British overtures and American military necessity enabled slaves to join the armed forces and thereby win freedom with their muskets. The invitation to blacks to join the British ranks was first offered in the early months of the war by Lord Dunmore, Virginia's last royal governor. In June 1779 commander in chief Sir Henry Clinton issued the most sweeping of the slave-freeing proclamations by the British command. It promised blacks their freedom and stipulated that they would be given their choice of any occupation within the British lines. Blacks welcomed such overtures, their motivation being more profreedom than pro-British.

By 1779 the Americans too were welcoming blacks to their armies. In the early stages of the war American military and civilian authorities had adopted a policy of excluding Negroes, a policy based on the mistaken supposition that the war would be over quickly. By the summer of 1777, with the war dragging into its third year, a policy reversal began when the northern colonies and Maryland decided to enlist blacks whatever the risks.

Slaves needed no second invitation. Recruiting agents had only to mention or hint at that magic word *freedom* to bring them into the fighting forces. It is striking, for example, that of the 289 identifiable blacks in the Connecticut army, five reported "Liberty" as

---

[19]Ronald Hoffman, "The 'Disaffected' in the Revolutionary South," in Young, *American Revolution,* p. 281.

[20]Ronald Hoffman, *A Spirit of Dissension: Economics, Politics, and the Revolution in Maryland* (Baltimore, 1973), p. 148.

[21]John Chester Miller, *The Wolf by the Ears: Thomas Jefferson and Slavery* (New York, 1977), p. 26.

their surname when they signed on, and eighteen reported "Freedom" or "Freeman."[22]

Free blacks also welcomed the coming of the Revolutionary War. Just as their lot was akin to that of the slaves, so was their response. Like the slaves, the free blacks drafted petitions and joined the army. Prince Hall, for example, did both. Led by the Cuffe brothers, blacks in Massachusetts lodged an official protest against the denial of their right to vote even though they paid taxes. In a 1780 petition to the state legislature they invoked the patriotic slogan "No taxation without representation."[23]

Free blacks who joined the army were variously motivated. They shared the common hope, however, that the high-sounding affirmations of the Revolution were more than hollow rhetoric. With a touch of the wishful thinking not uncommon to those who are reform-minded, black Americans tended to take seriously the proclaimed goals of the patriots.

Hence in assessing the temper and spirit of the Revolutionary War blacks, one finds that, slave and free alike, their loyalty was not to a locality in which they were propertyless, not to an assembly in which they could not sit, and not to a social order that denied their worth. They reserved allegiance for whoever made them the best and most concrete offer in terms of man's inalienable rights, which is only to say that the loyalty of black Americans centered on the fundamental credos upon which the new nation was founded.

The hope of black Americans for a new day of equality was not realized; it was a dream deferred. True, the Revolutionary War had its positive side. It was imbued with a strong moral overtone, leading some whites to question an institution such as slavery, no matter how time-honored. To whites of a reformist turn of mind the war had exposed the inconsistencies and contradictions in American thought about the rights of man, particularly those of the black man. But if heightened sensitivity to the presence of an underprivileged black group characterized some whites, they were far outnumbered by those who detected no ideological inconsistency. These white Americans, not considering themselves counterrevolutionary, would never have dreamed of repudiating the theory of natural rights. Instead they skirted the dilemma by maintaining that

[22]David O. White, *Connecticut's Black Soldiers, 1775–1783* (Chester, Conn., 1973), pp. 57–64.
[23]Petition reproduced in Roger Bruns, ed., *Am I Not a Man and a Brother: The Antislavery Crusade of Revolutionary America, 1688–1788* (New York, 1977), pp. 454–56.

blacks were an outgroup rather than members of the body politic. They subscribed to an equation of equality that excluded nonwhites, regarding them as outside the sociopolitical community encompassed by the Revolutionary War tenets of freedom and equality.

Black Americans, not unexpectedly, gave an entirely different reading to these war-spawned concepts. To them freedom was everyone's birthright; everyone had certain inalienable rights. In black circles the feeling of independence that these beliefs had fostered outlasted the roar of the guns. Still unspent, the spirit of '76 found new outlets among blacks. The Revolutionary War as a black declaration of independence took on a power of its own, fueled by residual revolutionary rhetoric and sustained by the memory of fallen heroes and the cloud of living black witnesses. To black Americans the theory of natural rights did not lose its relevance with the departure of the British troops. Blacks were left no choice other than to oppose all efforts to derevolutionize the Revolution.

However complacent and self-congratulatory their white countrymen may have been after expelling the British, the less euphoric black Americans turned their thoughts to the unfinished business of democracy. Their sense of self-identity, forged in the colonial period and honed by the Revolutionary War, now gave way to a sense of community, of cooperative effort in a cause that was no less true-blue Americanism simply because its advocates were dark-skinned. Their problems pressing, their resources meager, black Americans took heed of the Revolutionary War slogan "Unite or die." They were brought together not so much by a blood knot or a common Old World heritage as by a shared experience, particularly during the war, and by a shared pursuit of the goals articulated by Jefferson in 1776.

Free blacks assumed the leadership roles as keepers of the flame; in 1790 they numbered nearly 60,000. The 700,000 slaves were hardly in a position to become spokesmen for the new freedom, although a growing number of skilled and literate slaves were more likely to resort to extreme measures as they recalled wartime slogans of liberty. As Gerald W. Mullin pointed out, it was just such a freedom-inspired, literate, skilled slave, the blacksmith Gabriel Prosser of Richmond, who planned one of the most ambitious slave conspiracies in United States history.[24] St. George Tucker, a Virginian and a contemporary of Prosser's, observed that there was a difference between the slaves who responded to Lord Dunmore's

[24]Gerald W. Mullin, *Flight and Rebellion: Slave Resistance in Eighteenth-Century Virginia* (New York, 1972), pp. 140–63.

proclamation in 1775 and those who took part in Gabriel's plot in 1800. The slaves of 1775 fought for freedom as a good, said Tucker, whereas those of 1800 claimed freedom as a right.[25]

The dwindling component of slaves in the post–Revolutionary War North, however, found it unnecessary to resort to overt rebellion; time was on their side and gradual emancipation the vogue, especially with the increased availability of white workers. But, like those to the south, northern slaves were not the same after the war. Even the pacifist-minded bondsman Jupiter Hammon was affected. In February 1787 he published "An Address to the Negroes in the State of New York," a poignantly worded leaflet. "That liberty is a great thing," wrote Hammon, "we may know from our own feelings, and we may likewise judge from the conduct of the white people in the late war. How much money has been spent, and how many lives have been lost to defend their liberty. I must say that I have hoped that God would open their eyes, when they were so much engaged for liberty, to think of the state of the poor blacks, and to pity us."[26]

With northern slaves quiescent in their expectation of emancipation and southern slaves under surveillance, free blacks led the movement for racial unification and solidarity. As might be expected, such leadership fell largely to those living above the Mason-Dixon line. Their counterparts in the South were not entirely stripped of citizenship rights, but their limited opportunity for independent reformist action is suggested by the title of Ira Berlin's perceptive study of their marginal status, *Slaves without Masters.*[27]

Out of this impulse toward organized independence in the North came the mighty fortress of the independent black church, a church that preached the equality of all human beings before God and had its own interpretation of the Christian theme of the apocalypse. It was a church whose mission of reconciliation was not only between God and man but also between man and his own noblest ideals, a church that envisioned a new earth as logically ancillary to a new heaven. By the end of the century the pattern of racially separate churches had been firmly fixed.

In the South small independent black Baptist churches first appeared during the Revolutionary War years. Many of these churches

[25]Ibid., p. 157.

[26]Oscar Wegelin, *Jupiter Hammon, A Negro Poet: Selections from His Writings and a Bibliography* (Miami, Fla., 1969), p. 27.

[27]Ira Berlin, *Slaves without Masters: The Free Negro in the Antebellum South* (New York, 1974).

were offshoots of white congregations which, for a time, exercised a nominal "watch-care" over them. As in the religious services held by slaves, a characteristic feature of these black churches was the singing of spirituals. If these Negro spirituals had their escapist, otherworldly overtones, they also abounded in code words and double meanings, many of them striking a note of social protest and carrying a barely concealed freedom ring. It was during the late eighteenth century that blacks began to sing one of the greatest of these spirituals with a hidden or double meaning:

> Go down, Moses,
> Way down in Egypt land.
> Tell ole Pharoh
> Let my people go.[28]

In the North, Richard Allen, a former slave who had purchased his freedom, led the movement for the independent black church. In 1786 Allen attempted to establish a separate congregation of Negro Methodists in Philadelphia. Rebuffed in this effort by an official of St. George's Methodist Episcopal Church, Allen withdrew his membership a year later when, at a Sunday morning worship service, a white trustee ordered him and two other black communicants to hie themselves to the gallery. They would never return to St. George's.[29]

By then Allen, who, in the words of biographer Carol V. R. George, had "imbibed the philosophical preferences of Revolutionary America," had come to the conclusion that an independent black church and a gospel of social deliverance would be mutually supportive.[30] Deeply religious, he would never lose sight of "that city called Heaven." But to him, to his co-workers who founded Bethel Church in 1794, and to succeeding generations of black churchgoers, the theology to which they subscribed was a theology of liberation in which God spoke out in thunder tones against chattel slavery and sharply condemned other forms of injustice inflicted upon any of His children. Thus the black church was not only a spiritual fellowship; it was also a social unit, and for this reason represented a fusion of redemptions, religious and racial.

In whatever sphere it operated, however, a given church tended

[28]Miles Mark Fisher, *Negro Slave Songs in the United States* (Ithaca, N.Y., 1953), p. 40.

[29]Charles H. Wesley, *Richard Allen: Apostle of Freedom* (Washington, D.C., 1935), pp. 52–53.

[30]Carol V. R. George, *Segregated Sabbaths: Richard Allen and the Rise of Independent Black Churches, 1760–1840* (New York, 1973), p. 9.

to confine its immediate services to members of its own congregation, its own denomination. Hence the movement toward black independence also led to the establishment of organizations that cut across denominational ties, even while retaining a broadly Christian orientation. During the early years of the republic a number of societies and organizations emerged to promote black solidarity, self-help, and self-improvement. Blacks certainly played their part in making post–Revolutionary War America a nation of joiners.

The earliest of these black secular organizations was the African Union Society of Newport, Rhode Island, founded in November 1780; it was followed seven years later by the Free African Society of Philadelphia. The 1790s witnessed the birth of the Brown Fellowship Society, located in Charleston (1790),[31] the African Society of Providence, Rhode Island (1793), the African Society of Boston (1796), and the Friendly Society of St. Thomas, in Philadelphia (1797).[32] A sense of racial identity and pride accounts for the frequent use of the word *African* in the naming of these groups.

As might be expected, the major emphases of these organizations were mutual aid programs, such as supporting one another in sickness and in want, and requirements that their members lead upright lives, minding their morals and their manners. If these goals appeared to be limited exclusively to the welfare of their own participants, however, such was not their overall design. The societies were bent on demonstrating that blacks as a class were, if given the opportunity, prepared to assume the full responsibilities of freedom and citizenship, thus disputing the argument that blacks had never amounted to anything except as slaves, and never would. In a 1794 public letter Richard Allen, founder (with slave-born Absalom Jones) of the Free African Society, urged his fellow blacks to fulfill "the obligations we lie under to help forward the cause of freedom." A special obligation, Allen insisted, fell upon those who themselves had tasted the cup "of which the slave has to drink."[33]

The wider concerns of these early societies are revealed by their interest in Africa, particularly in establishing a black Christian presence among their brethren abroad. This missionary impulse to uplift the Africans and at the same time strike an indirect blow against slavery was particularly strong in the Rhode Island societies. In

[31]E. Horace Fitchett, "The Traditions of the Free Negro in Charleston, South Carolina," *Journal of Negro History* 25 (1940):144.
[32]Floyd J. Miller, *The Search for a Black Nationality: Black Emigration and Colonization, 1787–1863* (Urbana, Ill., 1975), pp. 8, 16, and 34.
[33]Dorothy Porter, ed., *Negro Protest Pamphlets* (New York, 1969), p. 23.

Newport the movement was led by Newport Gardner, in Providence by Bristol Yamma, both literate former slaves born in Africa.[34] The efforts of these eighteenth-century black emigrationists were unsuccessful, but later blacks would echo their call, although with additional reasons, including disillusionment with the American dream.

In company with church and secular groups, the roster of late eighteenth-century Afro-American organizations included the first black secret fraternal order in this country, the Masons. If black Masonry can be said to have had a single founder, it was Prince Hall of Boston, a Revolutionary War veteran and, to use a present-day term, a civil rights activist. Determined to establish a black Masonic lodge and rebuffed by white Masonic authorities in America, he succeeded after a ten-year struggle in obtaining a charter from the British Grand Lodge. On May 6, 1787, African Lodge No. 459 (its charter number) was formally organized with Prince Hall as Master. Ten years later Hall, now bearing the title of Grand Master, established lodges in Providence and Philadelphia, in the latter instance installing Absalom Jones as Worshipful Master.[35]

In common with other black self-help and self-improvement organizations, the Masons placed great emphasis on formal education, especially reading and writing. If blacks of the colonial period deemed such education a privilege, blacks of the Revolutionary War era thought of it as an American entitlement, if not an inherent right of man. "Let us lay by our recreations, and all superfluities, so that we may ... educate our rising generation," Prince Hall urged in an address to the African Lodge on June 25, 1792. And in the same breath Hall berated the selectmen of Boston for taxing blacks while not permitting them to attend the public schools.[36]

In Philadelphia, Absalom Jones established a school for blacks in 1799. "It is with pleasure that I now inform you that the school was opened on the 4th day of March," Jones wrote to the Pennsylvania Abolition Society, expressing "unfeigned thanks for the encouragement you were pleas[ed] to give me."[37] As a result of the

[34]Miller, Search for a Black Nationality, pp. 7–9 and 15–20.
[35]Charles H. Wesley, Prince Hall: Life and Legacy (Washington, D.C., 1977), pp. 124 and 142. For a facsimile of the charter from the British Grand Lodge, see p. 49.
[36]"A Charge Delivered to the Brethren of the African Lodge...," in Dorothy Porter, ed., Early Negro Writing, 1760–1837 (Boston, 1971), p. 67.
[37]Jones to Pennsylvania Abolition Society, Mar. 11, 1799, Papers of the Pennsylvania Society for Promoting the Abolition of Slavery, and for the Relief of Free Negroes Unlawfully Held in Bondage, and for Improving the Condition of the African Race. Pennsylvania Historical Society, Philadelphia.

sacrificial efforts of such black leaders as Hall and Jones and the extensive educational operations of white-membered abolitionist societies, the pursuit of formal education became a mainspring in black life during the formative years of the new nation.

Blacks of the Revolutionary War era could work independently, as in their churches, or cooperatively with whites, as in providing schools. But neither by independent nor cooperative action could they make any headway in winning suffrage, a right so vital to the "created equal" concept in the Declaration of Independence. In the New England colonies during the colonial period, slaves had been permitted to establish mock Negro governments, electing their own "governors." Primarily a form of diversion, these slave "elections" were occasions for feasting and merriment, but as Lorenzo Greene has argued, the "governments" they set up "acted as a sort of political school wherein slaves received the rudiments of political education which could be drawn upon once they were enfranchised."[38]

Five of the thirteen states forming the new nation—New York, Pennsylvania, Delaware, Maryland, and North Carolina—did not exclude blacks from voting. Indeed, in one of these states, Maryland, a black candidate ran for public office in 1792, very likely the first of his color ever to take this bold step. Thomas Brown, a horse doctor, sought one of the two seats allotted to Baltimore in the House of Delegates. In a September 24, 1792, public letter addressed "To the virtuous, free and independent electors of Baltimore-Town," Brown asserted that he had "been a zealous patriot in the cause of liberty during the late struggle for freedom and independence, not fearing prison or death for my country's cause." Brown closed his somewhat lengthy letter with a pledge that "the corpulency of my body shall be no clog to the exercise of my genius, and agility of my limbs, which shall be kept in perpetual motion for the good of the state."[39] His vote so minuscule as not to have been recorded, Brown was defeated in his bid for office, a circumstance reflecting the times. In but a few scattered instances were blacks a political factor during the eighteenth century, and black enfranchisement in postrevolutionary America was generally short-lived. In fact after 1810 Thomas Brown himself could not even have voted, Maryland having barred blacks from the polls as of that year.

[38]Greene, *Negro in Colonial New England*, p. 255.
[39]*Baltimore Daily Repository*, Sept. 26, 1792.

Politically minded blacks could hope for little when propertyless whites were subject to disfranchisement.[40]

Postwar blacks resorted to another form of political participation, the right to petition for redress of grievances. On December 30, 1799, as the Revolutionary War era was drawing to a close, a group of seventy-four blacks from the Philadelphia area addressed a petition "To the President, Senate, and House of Representatives," requesting abolition of the overseas slave trade and modification of the fugitive slave law so as to prevent the kidnapping of free blacks. The document concluded with a plea that blacks might "be admitted to partake of the liberties and unalienable rights" to which they were entitled.[41] Although invoking the language and the spirit of the Declaration of Independence and the Constitution, the appeal was couched in the most respectful and conciliatory of tones, and it issued from a city in which the Liberty Bell once had rung, heralding the birth of the new nation. But the House of Representatives did not prove to be liberation-minded; the congressmen rejected the petition by a chilling vote of eighty-five to one.[42]

This rejection of revolutionary principles, like others, did not deter blacks from pressing for the Revolution's goals of freedom and equality. Determined and patient, they would hardly have heeded J. R. Pole's observations that "revolutions by the nature of the historical process are always incomplete" and that a revolution tends to raise hopes that it cannot satisfy.[43] Blacks of the Revolutionary War era would have been more receptive to the contention of jurist Benjamin N. Cardozo that a principle has a tendency "to expand itself to the limit of its logic."[44] For them the war and the freedom concepts it sprouted bore their own seeds of regeneration.

In fine, the Revolutionary War can be termed a black declaration of independence in the sense it spurred black Americans to seek

[40]Indeed, down to the Civil War era blacks wielded little power as voters except for a twenty-year span, 1800–1820, when the Federalist party wooed their vote. See Dixon Ryan Fox, "The Negro Vote in Old New York," *Political Science Quarterly* 32 (1917):252–75. No black would hold elective office until 1854, when the voters of Oberlin, Ohio, chose John Mercer Langston as township clerk.

[41]Petition in Porter, *Early Negro Writing*, pp. 330–32.

[42]U.S., Congress, House, *Congressional Record*, 6th Cong., Jan. 3, 1800, pp. 244–45.

[43]J. R. Pole, *The Pursuit of Equality in American History* (Berkeley, Cal., 1978), p. 325.

[44]Benjamin N. Cardozo, *The Nature of the Judicial Process* (New Haven, 1932), p. 51, quoted in A. Leon Higginbotham, Jr., *In the Matter of Color: Race and the American Legal Process* (New York, 1978), pp. 383–84.

freedom and equality. The Afro-Americans of that era stood whole-heartedly among those who viewed the war as an ongoing revolution in freedom's cause. To a degree approaching unanimity, they clothed the War for Independence with a meaning and a significance transcending their own day and time and not confined to the shores of the new republic. To them the full worth of the American Revolution lay ahead.

Blacks in Abolition and Civil War

4. Sources of Abolitionist Income

I N ENLISTING financial support the abolitionist groups employed all of the refined techniques of solicitation. With a distinct talent for organized activity the zealous antislavery workers tapped a variety of sources in the bitter struggle to lessen the breach between ends and means. Firm in the belief that giving was a moral exercise, the abolitionists neglected no one who might have an urge to contribute; the cause was receptive whether the donor was a rich merchant with an unbusinesslike taste for antislavery (" 'Beware of a Yankee when he is feeding'," wrote a leading abolitionist)[1] or a widow sending in her mite. Abolitionists were proud that "extremes meet at our treasury," and that in a random year (1837) the cause appealed to such diverse personalities as "General Sewall, of Maine, a revolutionary officer, 85 years old— William Philbrick, a little boy near Boston, not four years old— and a colored woman who made her subsistence by selling apples in the streets of New York."[2] The abolitionists had a personalized appeal to each member of their clientele.[3] Their methods of fundraising were copied by other contemporary reformist groups—the Bible, tract, and Sunday school societies and the advocates of temperance, peace, woman's rights and no capital punishment.

No abolitionist society had a permanent fund or endowment;[4] its revenues were always anticipated. The largest source of income was furnished by voluntary contributions. The cause had a handful of wealthy donors. The most generous of these was Gerrit Smith, a Peterboro, New York, landowner with diversified reform interests.

[1] Frederick Douglass, *My Bondage and My Freedom* (New York, 1855), p. xxvi.
[2] "Correspondence Between the Hon. F. H. Elmore and James G. Birney," *Anti-Slavery Examiner*, No. 8 (New York, 1838): 17.
[3] See for example the specialized appeals made to young men, to ladies, and to children, in *Second Annual Report of the American Anti-Slavery Society* (New York, 1835), pp. 49–53. The American and Foreign Anti-Slavery Society proposed to issue a series of addresses to nine different classes or interest groups. *Thirteenth Annual Report of the American and Foreign Anti-Slavery Society* (New York, 1853), p. 196.
[4] With the partial exception of the Hovey Fund, noted below.

Smith's "tide of benefaction was perpetually flowing,"[5] and as he stated himself, people concluded that he had "a sort of pecuniary plethora that requires constant bleeding to assure health and vigor."[6] For thirty years antislavery societies cashed checks in Smith's barely legible scrawl. He commonly gave $1,000 at a time.[7] His closest friend stated that Smith gave a total of $50,000 to the American Anti-Slavery Society and the New York Anti-Slavery Society.[8] Other abolitionist groups profited from his unstinting generosity.

Another large contributor was the New York merchant-philanthropist, Arthur Tappan, first president of the national society and for thirteen years president of the American and Foreign society. His brother and co-worker estimates that Arthur Tappan's yearly contribution to the national society was $3,000. This did not include "considerable sums" otherwise spent for the cause.[9] Occasionally a large donor would prefer to remain anonymous.[10]

Generous contributors, however, were few. Many wealthy men doubtless sensed the caution expressed by a friend of Tappan's who pointed out that " 'if a man of business is also a philanthropist, he is in danger, while he is laying up treasure in heaven, of losing it on earth'."[11] Aware of this precaution, the abolitionists invited rich men to include antislavery societies as beneficiaries when they were preparing their wills. One of the national societies published a form of bequests for those who wished to remember the cause.[12]

There was some response to this type of appeal. Charles Hovey, a Boston merchant, left $8,000 annually, until the trust of about $40,000 would be exhausted, for "the promotion of the Anti-Slavery Cause and other reforms."[13] The funds were to be administered

---

[5] Octavius B. Frothingham, *Gerrit Smith: A Biography* (New York, 1878), p. 98.

[6] John W. Chadwick, ed., *Sallie Holley: A Life for Liberty* (New York, 1899), p. 83.

[7] *Anti-Slavery Record* (New York), June 1836, p. 12; Nov. 1836, p. 12.

[8] Samuel J. May, *Some Recollections of our Antislavery Conflict* (Boston, 1869), p. 325.

[9] Lewis Tappan, *The Life of Arthur Tappan* (New York, 1870), p. 176. The number of years for which Tappan made this contribution is not stated. Tappan's interest in antislavery extended over a period of thirty-two years. For typical Tappan donations, see *Anti-Slavery Record*, Feb. 1836, p. 12; March 1836, p. 12; May 1836, p. 12; June 1836, p. 12; July 1836, p. 12; Aug. 1836, p. 12.

[10] Such an individual gave $1,100 to the Western Anti-Slavery Society in 1852. *Anti-Slavery Bugle* (Salem, Ohio), Aug. 28, 1852. (Hereafter cited as *Bugle*.)

[11] Tappan, *Life*, p. 64.

[12] *Ninth Ann. Rept. of Amer. and For. A.S. Soc.* (1849), p. 3.

[13] For the phraseology of this stipulation in Hovey's will, see *Ann. Rept. of Amer. A. S. Soc. for 1859*, p. 141.

by a group of Massachusetts abolitionists headed by Phillips and Garrison. This group received another windfall in the same year (1859) when Francis Jackson's will provided $10,000 in order "to create a sentiment to put an end to slavery."[14] A third Bostonian, Frances Clapp, bequeathed $1,500 in 1843 "for the benefit of the Anti-Slavery Cause."[15] Ann Greene Chapman in 1837 left a legacy of $100 to the Boston Female Anti-Slavery Society[16] and $1,000 to the American Anti-Slavery Society.[17] To the latter society in the same year, Caroline Wheelock of New York left $ 800.[18] An English reformer, J. B. Estlin, bequeathed $500 to the same organization.[19] In the 1850s the Pennsylvania society was the recipient of two legacies of $500 each.[20]

Despite such individual exceptions men of wealth as a class could scarcely be expected to support such a disruptive force as abolitionism.[21] Large donations were so rare that forty years after Appomattox one of the long-time workers distinctly remembered how her uncle had startled an antislavery convention by putting $1,000 in the contribution box.[22]

Unable to tap many large sources, and realizing that their few men of means would not continue to give liberally unless others bore some share of the financial burden, the leaders of the movement adopted certain obvious expedients. They accepted pledges,[23] appealed for annual and life memberships in the societies, devised a plan of small monthly contributions, and made provision for organizing auxiliaries and taking up collections. These money-raising plans were carried out by field agents, appointed and assigned locations either by the executive committee or (as in the larger societies) an agency committee. The smaller societies used local agents

[14] Samuel May MSS. (Boston Public Library), vol. 8 (1860–1861).
[15] *Eleventh Annual Report of the Boston Female Anti-Slavery Society* (Boston, 1844), p. 41.
[16] *Ann. Rept. Bost. Fem. A. S. Soc. in 1837*, p. 112. [17] Ibid., p. 111.
[18] *The Quarterly Anti-Slavery Magazine* 2, no. 4 (July 1837): 347.
[19] *Ann. Rept. of Amer. A. S. Soc. for 1856*, p. 50.
[20] *Thirteenth Annual Report of the Pennsylvania State Anti-Slavery Society* (Philadelphia, 1850), p. 44; *Twenty-First Ann. Rept. of Penn. State A. S. Soc., 1858*, p. 42.
[21] On the eve of the war, after twenty-five years of organized activity, abolitionism, according to Garrison, "includes not many rich, nor many powerful." *Ann. Rept. of Amer. A. S. Soc. for 1856*, p. 57.
[22] Sarah Southwick, *Reminiscences of Early Anti-Slavery Days* (privately printed, 1893), p. 8.
[23] Very little cash was collected at antislavery meetings. Pledges, however, were freely made. For the manner in which a skillful chairman like Alvan Stewart could induce an emotionally stirred audience to make liberal pledges, see L. R. Marsh, ed., *Writings and Speeches of Alvan Stewart* (New York, 1860), p. 31.

exclusively. These were professional men in the community—lawyers, physicians or clergymen—who made short trips as their other engagements permitted. For their part-time services they received traveling expenses only.[24] General agents were employed by the national society[25] and such state organizations as the Massachusetts, Pennsylvania, New York, and Western (Ohio) societies. Closely associated with the agents in function (and often combining the same duties in one person) were the colporteurs whose primary duty was to sell or otherwise dispose of the publications of the societies.[26] Like the agents they solicited subscriptions for the antislavery press. Colporteurs and agents alike tackled a Herculean job in the effort to make abolitionist publications self-supporting.

There were numerous obstacles. Much of the antislavery printed propaganda was distributed gratuitously. Particularly was this true of tracts—ten- to twenty-page publications of sermons, speeches, essays, and proceedings of meetings. In 1854 the American society began to issue tracts gratis in large quantities. By 1856 it was issuing seventeen tracts;[27] two years later the number totaled twenty.[28] The society stated that in four years it had distributed 303,000 tracts comprising five million pages of abolitionist literature at a cost of $3,281.76.[29] Frequently antislavery periodicals were sent in the hope that receivers would pay for them.[30] Zealous workers were furnished free copies of publications. In some societies, membership entitled one to receive all official publications. Officers of the organizations frequently sent documents to their friends "as a sort of missive to say 'howdy'."[31]

In order to obtain the widest possible circulation such publica-

---

[24]A. S. Examiner, No. 8, p. 17. If an absent clergyman had to pay to supply his pulpit the society assumed the expense. E. Wright, Jr. to Birney, July 16, 1836, in Dwight L. Dumond, ed., Letters of James Gillespie Birney, 1831–1857, 2 vols. (New York, 1938), vol. 1, p. 344.

[25]In the peak year of 1836 the American society reported seventy agents. Quarterly A. S. Magazine 2, no. 4 (July 1837): 348.

[26]For a distinction between the duties of the two, see Thirteenth Ann. Rept. of Amer. and For. A. S. Soc. for 1853, p. 195.

[27]Proceedings of the Massachusetts Anti-Slavery Society for 1854, 1855, 1856 (Boston, 1856), p. 68.

[28]Ann. Rept. of Amer. A. S. Soc., 1857 and 1858, p. 189.   [29]Ibid., p. 191.

[30]Having no society's agent to collect for his paper, Elihu Embree requested of recipients who did not propose to become subscribers that they wrap up The Emancipator and return it to the editor. The Emancipator (Jonesborough, Tenn.), April 30, 1820; reprinted in Nashville, Tenn., 1932.

[31]Weld to S. and A. Grimké, Oct. 1, 1837, in Gilbert H. Barnes and Dwight L. Dumond, eds., Letters of Theodore Dwight Weld, Angelina Grimké Weld, and Sarah Grimké, 1822–1844, 2 vols. (New York, 1934), vol. 1, p. 443.

tions as bound volumes, magazines and pamphlets[32] were designed to sell at cost.[33] Letter paper at 2 cents a sheet, antislavery cards at 2 cents each, music books at 4 cents each, print views of slavery at 12 1/2 cents each, a "likeness" of Lovejoy at 12 1/4 cents[34]—all were priced with the profit motive a secondary consideration. Orders in bulk brought a reduction. One portrait of Garrison sold for $1; a hundred could be purchased for $75.[35] *The Anti-Slavery Almanac,* a forty-eight page pamphlet, sold for 6 1/4 cents a single copy; 62 cents a dozen; $4 a hundred, and $25 a thousand.[36]

More difficult for the agent and colporteur than obtaining orders for pamphlets and bound volumes was the task of securing subscriptions and collecting payment for the antislavery weeklies. Selling at an average of $2 a year,[37] every one of these papers operated at a loss. As a rule abolitionist weeklies were short-lived; those which survived placed a severe strain upon their supporting agencies. *The Emancipator,* organ of the national society, showed an aggregate excess of expenditure over receipts of $10,000 for the five-year period 1835–40.[38] *The National Era,* sponsored by the American and Foreign society, was "conducted at large expense."[39] The Western society was continually going into its pocket for *The Bugle.* That paper reported in 1853 that it was losing from $600 to $1,000 annually.[40] The deficit ran to the latter figure in 1858.[41] Frederick Douglass sank $12,000 of his own money in his newspapers over an eight-year period.[42] *The Anti-Slavery Standard* "was

[32]In 1836 the national society issued 718,267 pieces of printed material. Of these, 7,877 were bound volumes and 47,250 were pamphlets. For a further enumeration see *Quarterly A. S. Magazine* 2, no. 4 (July 1837): 348. In 1838 the number of pieces issued was 724,862. *Sixth Ann. Rept. of Amer. A. S. Soc.* (1839), p. 52.

[33]In 1838 the national society published forty-three bound volumes averaging 241 pages each at an average sale price of 63 cents. It issued sixty-six pamphlets averaging sixty-seven pages at an average sale price of 12 cents. Eight tracts were published with an average of twenty pages and an average price of 1 cent. *Anti-Slavery Almanac* (New York, 1839), rear cover. In 1850 the American and Foreign society issued twenty-seven bound volumes at an average price of 58 cents; twenty-nine pamphlets averaging 15 cents; and twelve tracts averaging $1.93 per hundred. *The Liberty Almanac for 1851* (New York, 1851), p. 36.

[34]*A. S. Almanac,* back cover. [35]Ibid.

[36]*Anti-Slavery Standard* (New York), Oct. 20, 1842. (Hereafter cited as *Standard.)*

[37]Of the twenty-six abolitionist weeklies in 1843, twenty sold at $2 a year; three sold at $2.50; two at $1; two at 50 cents; and one at $1.50. *The Legion of Liberty* (New York, 1844), rear of title page.

[38]*Ninth Annual Report of the Massachusetts Anti-Slavery Society* (Boston, 1841), xvi. This paper is not to be confused with Embree's earlier sheet of the same name.

[39]Tappan to Scoble, Nov. 14, 1847, in A. H. Abel and Frank Klingberg, *A Side-Light on Anglo-American Relations, 1839–1858* (Lancaster, Pa., 1927), p. 228.

[40]*Bugle,* Oct. 8, 1853. [41]Ibid., Nov. 6, 1858.

[42]Douglass, *Bondage and Freedom,* xxiv.

never supported by its subscribers."[43] Its existence had become so precarious in 1861 that the executive committee of the American society sent out a confidential circular and Samuel May wrote, sub rosa, that he feared it would be discontinued.[44]

The abolitionists knew the reasons for their failure to make their weeklies pay. They owned no press—their work was done by commercial printers.[45] Adding to the overhead were the postage rates, which were relatively high prior to 1850.[46] However ably conducted, a paper designed to change public opinion was doomed to a limited appeal.

Agents could do nothing about these obstacles. But they were expected to reduce the chief financial liability of abolitionist periodicals, namely, the failure of their subscribers to pay up. Executive committees and editors were constantly lamenting the large number of abolitionists who ignored their newspaper bills. Of the 1,700 subscribers to *The Emancipator* in 1835, 500 were in arrears.[47] The American and Foreign society appealed to the pride of the readers of *The National Era;* antislavery men were "supposed to be more exact than men in general" in redeeming their obligations.[48] The hard-pressed *Bugle* reported in 1850 that $1,800 was due from subscribers.[49] In 1857 the Western society reported that $3,800 was due on subscriptions for the preceding six-year period.[50] Of the 845 *Bugle* subscribers in 1858, only 334 had paid in advance; 244 were in debt for one year; 131 were in debt for one to two years, and 136 were being dropped for a delinquency exceeding two years.[51] *The Bugle's* editor expressed wonder and shame that professing abolitionists should "subscribe, read and neglect to pay."[52] An editor of another antislavery sheet reported a "very long list of nonpaying and a very short list of paying subscribers." He discovered "an amazing disparity between the disposition to read and the disposition to pay."[53]

---

[43] *Standard,* Sept. 2, 1852.

[44] May MSS., May to C. C. Burleigh, June 27, 1861.

[45] Real estate owners were reluctant to imperil their property by permitting its use for the housing of an antislavery press.

[46] The abolitionists were constant petitioners for cheap postage. They were overjoyed at the reduction of rates in 1850. *Bugle,* March 15, 1851, contrasted the old schedule with the new.

[47] Wright to Weld, Jan. 9, 1835, *Weld-Grimké Letters,* vol. 1, p. 195.

[48] *Liberty Almanac for 1849,* p. 3.   [49] *Bugle,* Sept. 28, 1850.

[50] Minute Book of Western Anti-Slavery Society (Western Reserve Historical Society, Cleveland), Sept. 4, 1857.

[51] Ibid., April 4, 1858.   [52] *Bugle,* March 29, 1851.

[53] *Frederick Douglass' Paper* (Rochester, N. Y.), June 16, 1854.

Agents were urged to be persistent in pushing subscriptions. In some instances, commissions were given for building up a paying circulation. To any agent procuring five subscriptions and forwarding the money, Benjamin Lundy gave one subscription gratis to *The National Enquirer*.[54] Agents for *The National Era* were given 50 cents for each new subscriber, and 25 cents for each renewal.[55] In the interests of *The Bugle*, the Western society paid an agent 25 percent of her collections from delinquent, present, or new subscribers.[56]

In order that the bulk of the funds raised by subscriptions and pledges might be applied directly to the promotion of the cause, the societies paid agents a very modest stipend. Field workers were familiar with the principle behind the expenditure of funds for salaries. The services of agents were due to the slave as a freewill offering. It followed that all who were in a position to do so would work in the vineyard without material recompense. Others—those "who had no extrinsic means of livelihood"—were allowed "what they consider absolutely indispensable to a bare subsistence."[57]

In an extremely rare instance an agent might receive $1,000 a year.[58] As a rule the top salary for an agent with a family was $600 a year and traveling expenses.[59] The Massachusetts society in 1860 paid $500 to George Thompson,[60] a prominent English abolitionist. For the services of an outstanding advocate like Theodore D. Weld the national society offered a yearly salary of $416.[61] The society offered $300 a year to the Negro clergyman Daniel Payne.[62]

General agents employed for a period less than a year were paid accordingly. Susan B. Anthony in 1857 received $10 a week and expenses.[63] In the same year the Western society paid A. Brooke $1.50 a day plus expenses—"he to furnish a horse and buggy."[64] An inexperienced agent might be required to raise enough money to pay his own salary.[65] An impoverished society might make an

---

[54]*National Enquirer* (Philadelphia), Aug. 3, 1836.
[55]*Liberty Almanac for 1848*, p. 2.   [56]Min. Bk. West. A. S. Soc., Sept. 4, 1857.
[57]*Fourteenth Ann. Rept. of Mass. A. S. Soc.* (1846), p. 48.
[58]Amos A. Phelps received this sum from the Massachusetts society in 1836. *Ann. Rept. Bost. Fem. A. S. Soc. in 1837*, p. 25.
[59]Wright to Birney, July 16, 1836, *Letters of James Gillespie Birney*, vol. 1, p. 334.
[60]May MSS., May to Webb, May 12, 1861.
[61]Wright to Weld, Dec. 31, 1833, *Weld-Grimké Letters*, vol. 1, p. 122.
[62]Daniel Payne, *Recollections of Seventy Years* (Nashville, 1888), p. 67.
[63]Ida H. Harper, *The Life and Work of Susan B. Anthony*, 3 vols. (Indianapolis, 1898–1908), vol. 1, p. 151.
[64]Min. Bk. West. A. S. Soc., Oct. 18, 1857.
[65]Lucy N. Colman, *Reminiscences* (Buffalo, 1891), p. 25.

arrangement by which an agent, after deducting his expenses, might take as his salary half of the monies he collected.[66] Having, in most instances, contracted to pay expenses, the societies urged agents "to use a faithful economy in regard to the expenses of traveling."[67] As a rule this was not difficult because abolitionist agents and colporteurs were gratuitously entertained. They always accepted such private hospitality; indeed their hosts, reformers themselves, would have refused payment for accommodations.

In fine, of the many duties of a general agent, the collecting of money came first. The national society required that agents mail all monies to the treasurer without delay; other societies required agents to render accounts bimonthly, monthly, and quarterly.

As zealous as the agents in securing finances for the cause were the female antislavery societies. Money-raising was practically the sole reason for the existence of these auxiliaries.[68] They employed an identical method—the conducting of fairs or bazaars. Begun in 1834, by far the most successful of these organizations was the Boston group, which worked in the interests of the American society. While overshadowing the others in its scope of activities, the Boston bazaar was typical in modus operandi.

This bazaar (variously called the National Bazaar, the National Festival and the Massachusetts Fair) obtained its merchandise from a variety of sources. The most reliable of these were the sewing circle societies. Most of these met weekly. One of the group would read from the Bible or some other book on religion, while the others sewed.[69] Throughout Massachusetts, female societies worked for the Boston fair. Such groups numbered thirty-two in 1837.[70] In Worcester county in 1844 there were thirteen sewing circles working for the fair.[71] Juvenile antislavery societies made their contributions. The Boston fair reported in 1858 (for the bazaar of the preceding year) a box of knitted hosiery from a group of local

[66]*Proceedings of the First Annual Meeting of the Ohio State Anti-Slavery Society, 1860* (n. p., n. d.; undoubtedly Xenia, 1860), p. 6. This society was made up of Negroes under the leadership of John Mercer Langston.

[67]Printed commission to Weld from American society, Feb. 20, 1834, *Weld-Grimké Letters*, vol. 1, p. 128.

[68]Officially the Boston Female Society existed for the purpose of "raising money to educate and direct the public mind, and to stimulate and strengthen the public heart." *Report of the Twenty-Fourth Annual National Anti-Slavery Festival* (Boston, 1858), p. 12.

[69]*A. S. Examiner*, No. 8, p. 7.

[70]*Ann. Rept. of Bost. Fem. A. S. Soc. in 1837*, p. 90.

[71]*Eleventh Ann. Rept. of Boston Fem. A. S. Soc.*, p. 39.

children.[72] In 1838 the Hingham Juvenile Anti-Slavery Society sent "$15 worth of things," to one of the fairs.[73] The six- to fifteen-year-old misses who comprised the juvenile antislavery group of Elyria, Ohio, met weekly to sew for the slave.[74] The Providence society, a group of some thirty girls averaging twelve years of age, pledged $100 in 1836 to the state society. It planned to raise this sum by sewing for a fair.[75]

The managers of the fair solicited contributions in kind from manufacturers and merchants.[76] The policy was to buy nothing; the managers insisted on wholesale prices for their few purchases. In asking for goods the Boston women were more reticent than their Philadelphia sisters who sent out a form request,[77] or than the Salem, Ohio, committee which took pains to inform each of the common occupational groups—saddlers, tailors, shoe dealers, coopers, cutlers, brushmakers, tinners, hatters, milliners, foundrymen, etc.—as to the precise articles each could furnish.[78]

British abolitionists gave considerable support. Richard D. Webb, a reformer in Dublin, acted as foreign agent for the Boston fair. In a typical week preceding the bazaar a packet ship (used because of cheaper freight charges than a steamship) would bring a case of goods each from Edinburgh, Dublin, Belfast, Perth, Manchester, Coventry, and Rochdale.[79] In a typical year, 1853, a total of fifteen boxes was sent. Edinburgh, London, and Dublin sent two each; supporters from Glasgow, Newcastle, Leeds, Manchester, Cork, Perth, Liverpool, and Paris shipped the remainder.[80] In the peak year of 1857 the bazaar received twenty-four cases from across the Atlantic; twenty of these came from the British Isles, two from Paris, one from Rome, and one from Florence.[81]

With the wares collected, the volunteer workers would proceed to decorate the hall. On six occasions the Boston fair was held at

[72] *Rept. of Twenty-Fourth Nat. A. S. Festival*, p. 24.
[73] Minute Book of Hingham Juvenile Anti-Slavery Society (Western Reserve Historical Society, Cleveland), p. 3.
[74] E. C. Reilly, "The Early Slavery Controversy in the Western Reserve" (Unpublished Ph.D. thesis, Western Reserve University, 1939), p. 179.
[75] *Proceedings of the Rhode Island Anti-Slavery Convention for 1836* (Providence, 1836), p. 15.
[76] For an acknowledgment of gifts from merchants, see *Standard*, Jan. 27, 1853.
[77] For its phraseology, see L. B. C. Wyman and A. C. Wyman, *Elizabeth Buffum Chace*, 2 vols. (Boston, 1914), vol. 1, p. 164.
[78] *Bugle*, July 20, 1850.
[79] May MSS., May to Estlin, Dec. 14, 1847.
[80] Ibid., Dec. 20, 1853.   [81] *Rept. of Twenty-Fourth Nat. A. S. Festival*, p. 27.

Faneuil Hall.[82] Although three days' work was required to disguise its shabby, barnlike appearance, the hall had historic associations with liberty; furthermore as a municipally owned property its use was free when properly requested by taxpayers. As the bazaar was held during Christmas week, the hall was festooned with spruce, pine, rhododendron, and other evergreens. The hampers, barrels, tubs, and boxes were unloaded and their contents displayed on decorated sales tables. There the prospective buyer could pick over toys, needlebooks, bedquilts, card baskets, aprons, workboxes, bookmarks, socks, and shirts.[83] For those with long purses there were Honiton laces, Paisley shawls, Afghan blankets, and Bohemian glassware.

The most distinctive sales piece on display at the Boston bazaar was *The Liberty Bell,* a gift book. *The Bell* was a series of literary miscellanies—essays, stories, poems, dialogues—brought together in a single volume. Its originators, Maria Weston Chapman and her sister, Anne Warren Weston, solicited articles from prominent abolitionists[84] and other reformers. No article was welcomed that did not have a direct bearing on antislavery.[85] None of the contributors—among them Longfellow, Emerson, Elizabeth Barrett Browning, Harriet Martineau, and Bayard Taylor—was paid, unless receipt of a copy of *The Bell* could be so considered. Donations were solicited to cover the costs of publication.[86] Mrs. Chapman intended to bring out an issue annually; fifteen were published over the eighteen-year-period 1839–57. Generous donors to the fair received a free copy of *The Bell;* otherwise it was placed on sale. Its appearance was designed to commend it as an appropriate Christmas gift but in order to suit different purses its material makeup varied as to quality of paper and of cover.

The pattern set by the Boston women was followed closely by other groups.[87] They, too, issued gift books[88] and solicited dona-

[82]For an enumeration of the halls where each of the Boston fairs was held, 1834–1856, see *Standard,* Jan. 26, 1856.

[83]For an extensive list of the varied articles on sale, see *Standard,* Dec. 18, 1851; Jan. 27, 1853.

[84]Joshua R. Giddings MSS. (Ohio State Archaeological and Historical Society, Columbus), M. W. Chapman to Giddings, Sept. 5, 1847. See also Smith MSS. (University of Syracuse, Syracuse, N. Y.), A. W. Weston to Smith, Sept. 10, 1852.

[85]Caroline H. Dall MSS. (Massachusetts Historical Society, Boston), Edmund Quincy to Caroline H. Dall, Dec. 28, 1851.

[86]Through the pages of the *Standard* the managers of the fair made acknowledgment of such sums. See issues of Jan. 29, 1852; Jan. 27, 1853.

[87]Following are the most important of these other bazaars and the dates of their

tions from varied sources. There were a few minor differences; the Worcester bazaar was generally held during "Cattle Show" week; the Philadelphia ladies charged a small admission fee,[89] and the Salem fair requested vegetables, turkeys, chickens and deer.[90]

There were differences in the amounts raised. The receipts of the Boston fair ranged from $360 in 1834 to $5,250 in 1856. From twenty-three of the twenty-four fairs the total amount received was $65,826.23, an average of $2,860 a fair.[91] Expenses, generally amounting to 20 percent, were deducted from these gross receipts. The Pennsylvania fair showed a net profit of $9,807.27 over the six-year period 1850–56.[92] The Cincinnati women generally raised $800; the periodic bazaars in Salem and Rochester averaged a $300 profit.

The bazaar managers might have become quickly discouraged were it not for rewards other than financial. The fairs served as a channel for female energies,[93] and they provided a congenial setting for an informal coming-together of kindred spirits. But measured against the effort expended, so meager was the return in dollars and cents that after 1857 the Boston ladies abandoned the bazaar. They asked their supporters to send money, not merchandise, to the "National Anti-Slavery Subscription Anniversary."[94] The lead-

---

origin: Pennsylvania fair, 1836; Salem (Western) fair, 1849; Cincinnati fair, 1849; Rochester fair, 1853.

[88]Most novel of these was the *Anti-Slavery Alphabet* (Philadelphia, 1847), published for the Pennsylvania fair. Its opening stanzas read thus:

A is an Abolitionist—   B is a Brother with a skin
   A man who wants to free   Of somewhat darker hue,
The wretched slave—and give to all   But in our Heavenly Father's sight
   An equal liberty.   He is as dear as you.

For an analysis of the literary quality of these publications, see Ralph Thompson, "The *Liberty Bell* and Other Anti-Slavery Gift-Books," *The New England Quarterly* 7 (March 1934): 154–68.

[89]Ladies, 12 1/2 cents; children, 6 cents. *National Enquirer*, Dec. 24, 1836.

[90]Frequently the receipt of such perishables necessitated raffling. The eastern women, frowning on this practice, handled only those wares which, if not disposed of at the first offering, might be held for a subsequent bazaar.

[91]Each of the yearly figures comprising this compilation was taken from one of the following sources: reports of the antislavery festival, annual reports of the Massachusetts society, annual report of the New England society, May MSS., and the *Standard*.

[92]Figures from annual reports of Pennsylvania society or the *Standard*.

[93]This was an important outlet, especially since non-Garrisonian abolitionists were reluctant to admit women to membership in the societies.

[94]In 1859 the Pennsylvania fair assumed the title, "National Bazaar." *Standard*, Feb. 12, 1859.

ing figure in the movement had come to the conclusion that "fairs are like an Excise; good only if no other mode is practicable."[95]

A conjecture as to the total funds collected by abolitionist societies would be extremely random. The number of societies fluctuated widely. Prior to 1830 there were perhaps fewer than fifty such organizations. With the formation of the national society in 1833 there was a marked increase. In May 1835, there were 200 societies; five months later there were 300.[96] The number climbed to 527 in May, 1836;[97] by July 1837 it had jumped to 1,006.[98] This was the peak. Further expansion was arrested by the panic of 1837, the split in the national society in 1840, and the growing belief of thousands of non-Garrisonians (led by Birney) that the desired end could be better reached through political action than by abolitionist agitation.

One year after the formation of the national society it was impossible (as the society informed an inquirer) to ascertain the total annual income of the numerous organizations.[99] However, the records of the largest societies are revealing indices. During the first six years of its existence the American society collected a total of $158,849.43.[100] Its largest income for a single year was $47,111.74.[101] In three typical years during the mid-1850s the American society collected $34,466.69, $33,646.53, and $38,162.66.[102] Of the state organizations, the Massachusetts society collected approximately $6,000 annually; the Pennsylvania society during the five-year period 1850–54 averaged $5,935, and the yearly income of the Western society fell between $2,000 and $3,000. Other societies ranged from $3,000 downward to the sum of $221.62 reported in 1859 by a society in Ohio.[103]

All in all, the antislavery crusade was financed very modestly. When times were good, the societies had difficulty making ends meet; when times were out of joint, secretaries, editors, and agents

---

[95]Anne Warren Weston MSS. (Boston Public Library), M. W. Chapman to E. P. Nichols, Jan. 25, 1860.

[96]*Quarterly A. S. Magazine*, 1, no. 1 (October 1835): 104.

[97]Ibid., 1, no. 3 (April 1836): 310.   [98]Ibid., 2, no. 4 (July 1837): 340.

[99]*A. S. Examiner*, No. 8, p. 16.

[100]Compiled inclusively from the first to the sixth annual reports of the American society.

[101]The bulk of these sums was raised by the society's auxiliaries.

[102]*Ann. Rept. of Amer. A. S. Soc. for 1855*, p. 60; Ibid. (1856), p. 59; Ibid. (1857 and 1858), p. 173. The American and Foreign society did not publish its annual receipts. Inasmuch as it sent out no agents, its income was perhaps not more than $5,000 yearly.

[103] *Proc. of First Ann. Meet. Ohio State A. S. Soc.*, p. 8.

went unpaid,[104] and operations were skeletonized.[105] But the work went on. The conclusion is inescapable that in proportion to the scope of their program, the funds of the abolitionists were smaller than those of any other reform enterprise in the history of our country.

[104]In 1840 the salary of agent Henry B. Stanton was two years in arrears. Weld to Tappan, April 10, 1840, *Weld-Grimké Letters,* vol. 2, p. 828. Stanton's approaching marriage to Elizabeth Cady gave the matter a certain urgency.

[105]"I shall read your speech.... The fact is, our Society [the American Anti-Slavery] is so poor this year that we don't subscribe for the *Globe.*" Giddings MSS., Oliver Johnson to Giddings, March 6, 1858.

5. Ministers without Portfolio

DURING the two years preceding the outbreak of the Civil War a most eloquent friend of the slave, Sarah Parker Remond of Salem, Massachusetts, lectured in many of the large cities and towns of England, Scotland, and Ireland. Her avowed mission was "to extend the active sympathy of the whole British nation toward the cause of abolitionism in America." In pleading the cause of her black brothers, Miss Remond generally avoided the sensational and the sentimental. She might mention that female slaves were "liable to the brutality of the vilest wretches," but the purposeful young miss from Salem was not a four-handkerchief speaker; she did not specialize in heartrending tales of Tom and Topsy. She made her points, wrote one of her admirers, by a "clear elucidation of just principles—no claptrap."

Despite her failure to fire her audience with tales of slave derring-do, or to dissolve them in tears, Miss Remond was a most persuasive advocate. An educated young woman, she had a beguiling air of refinement—a genteel pattern of manners so highly esteemed as an ideal of womanhood in Victoria's England. Her speech was dulcet-toned and quiet, and her fluent vocabulary was pure of unladylike turns of phrase. She had an air of high seriousness, and she conveyed to others her own belief that tomorrow's sun would set upon a better world. For these reasons the Leeds Young Men's Anti-Slavery Society, at its December 1859 meeting, hired her as its agent.

The society gave her a crowded schedule. On December 23 she spoke at Leeds, followed four days later by an appearance at Wortley, where she addressed an audience composed of "working men and factory operatives." Just before the old year was snuffed out, she went to Bramley, where she won all hearts at the "large and commodious" Wesley Chapel. At Hunslet on the fourth day of the new year, her audience "was enthusiastic and encouraging in the extreme." When she appeared at Warrenton in March, her address was signed by the mayor, by the rector of the parish, by the member of parliament for the borough, and by 3522 inhabitants; no address in Warrenton, wrote a native of the town, had "ever been more numerously signed."[1] At Dublin, where she also filled a March engagement, her packed audience included clergymen and university professors. Summing up the worth of her services, the Leeds society reported that thousands who heard her would never forget the experience, and that the principles which she advocated would find an abiding place in many hearts and "materially aid in building up the Anti-Slavery sentiments of Great Britain."[2]

The services of Sarah Remond and other Negro abolitionists in keeping alive the antislavery spirit in Leeds and elsewhere throughout the British Isles was a notable contribution to the winning of the Civil War. For in this conflict the South had counted heavily on winning English support; specifically, the Confederacy expected England to recognize her as an independent nation. In turn, so the South hoped, the continental countries would follow the lead of the British Foreign Office, and the Confederacy would have the moral backing and perhaps the financial assistance of the European concert of nations.

Jefferson Davis and his colleagues had reason to expect British recognition. More than one Englishman in five gained his daily bread from the cotton industry and almost half of England's export trade was in manufactured cotton goods. From Dixie's land came more than 80 percent of the baled cotton used in English factories on the eve of the war. For years the cry, "Cotton is King," had been echoed throughout the southern regions, and the South's leaders were confident that her fleecy fields of white would enlist transatlantic support for the Confederacy.[3]

There were other reasons for the South's expectation of diplomatic recognition. She was against high tariffs and so was England. Once John Bull extended the hand of diplomatic fellowship, his cotton mills would find a waiting outlet for their manufactured drygoods in the low-tariff or free-trade markets of the South. Obviously, too, the English ruling class would prefer to deal with two American nations rather than one. The English government was made up of men drawn largely from the aristocracy and, as John Bright informed his American friend, John Bigelow, "it must be

[1] *Anti-Slavery Advocate* (London), April 1859. For a sketch of Miss Remond see Dorothy Porter, "Sarah Parker Remond, Abolitionist and Physician," *Journal of Negro History* 20 (1935): 287–93.

[2] *Annual Report of the Leeds Young Men's Anti-Slavery Society for Year Ending December 1860* (Leeds, 1861), p. 6.

[3] See Frank L. Owsley, *King Cotton Diplomacy* (Chicago, 1931), notably chapter 1, "The Foundation of Confederate Diplomacy."

hostile to your greatness and the permanence of your institutions."[4]
Englishmen whose genealogies were listed in *Burke's Peerage* were
congenitally inclined toward the Southern gentlemen-planters as
over against the bargain-driving, nouveau-riche Yankees, making
their money in trade. "London club life was Southern in its sym-
pathies." Moneyed men in England took their cue from the landed
aristocracy; so did the military services and the majority of the
newspapers.

All this the South's leaders knew. A month before the first shot
was fired, Confederate Secretary of State Robert Toombs appointed
three commissioners to go abroad and seek diplomatic recognition
from the European nations, and then to make treaties of commerce
and amity. One of the commissioners, William L. Yancey, described
his mission in a bland letter to the *London Daily News*. He sought,
wrote he, "simply to obtain a recognition of those states as a government whose people are producers of cotton, tobacco, corn, and
naval stores, and who desire to offer manufacturing Europe the
benefits of free trade in the peaceful interchange of those valuable
products for the woolen, cotton, silk and hardware fabrics of the
Old World, unrestricted and unvexed by prohibitory tariffs."[5]

Despite their sweetness-and-light approach, the Confederate
commissioners soon found that they had an uphill fight to secure
recognition. As Yancey and his colleagues quickly discovered, there
was a deeply rooted hostility to slavery among the day laborers,
the middle-class element, and "the quiet and religious people." In
their first dispatch to the Confederate secretary of war, dated May
21, 1861, the commissioners sent word that "the public mind here
is entirely opposed to the Government of the Confederate States of
America on the question of slavery and that the sincerity and uni-
versality of this feeling" embarrassed the British Foreign Office "in
dealing with the question of our recognition."[6]

This British antislavery sentiment was in no small measure the
product of American Negroes. In the twenty years preceding the
Civil War, a procession of colored agitators paraded throughout
the British Isles, pleading the cause of the chain-burdened slave.
The full extent of their antislavery activities in shaping British opin-

---

[4] Letter dated Jan. 3, 1863, in R. Barry O'Brien, *John Bright* (London, 1910),
p. 144.
[5] *London Daily News* in *London Morning Post*, Jan. 27, 1862.
[6] James M. Callahan, *The Diplomatic History of the Southern Confederacy* (Baltimore, 1901), p. 112.

ions was to become evident when the North and the South vied to enlist English support.

This impressive roster of visiting blacks began in 1840 with Charles Lenox Remond. Older brother of Sarah, he sailed for England as a delegate to the World's Anti-Slavery Convention, held in London. He remained abroad for two years, lecturing throughout the British Isles. Everywhere he was favorably received; he inspired one of his English admirers to express his praise in poetic strain, "On Hearing Mr. C. L. Remond, a Young Man of Talent but Slight Education, Lecture on Prejudice Against Color in the United States."

Remond's influence, as marked as it was, paled before that of the next of the visiting Negroes, the celebrated Frederick Douglass. For nineteen months, beginning in August 1845, the youthful Douglass, not yet turned thirty, created something of a sensation wherever he went. Britishers found their attention rivetted when they caught their first glimpse of this well-built Negro with his white stand-up collar and gleaming white shirt, relieved by a close-fitting stock and a black broadcloth coat. When he opened his mouth, his listeners heard a deep and melodious voice that hinted of its readiness to shade into wit, irony, invective or pathos.

During Douglass's sojourn in the British Isles, mayors presided over assemblies gathered to hear him, and the large audiences invariably remained attentive during the two and a half hours he spoke. Usually after his address, people crowded forward, eager to shake hands. The demand to hear him was great—in March 1847 he gave an address every night of the month, including Sundays.

Douglass's influence in England was not limited to the spoken word. For he set a widely-copied example by selling his autobiography. His *Narrative of the Life of Frederick Douglass* was a slim volume of 125 pages, published in May 1845, and prefaced by letters from William Lloyd Garrison and Wendell Phillips. During his tour of the British Isles, Douglass sold the book on the spot, suitably autographed, or took orders for it. The *Narrative* sold well; in Bristol alone nearly 200 copies were purchased. Sympathizers who could spare a few shillings bought the book, read it, and then circulated it among prospective converts.

This fugitive slave literature, in which dramatic incidents were mingled with abolitionist argument, was destined to be a powerful lever in the British Isles. "America had the mournful honour of adding a new department to the literature of civilization—the autobiography of escaped slaves," observed the English clergyman,

Ephraim Peabody. These slave narratives, however crude from the standpoint of belles lettres, went right to the hearts of their readers. Often ghost-written, or told by an anonymous collaborator, and always heavy on sermonizing, these stories nonetheless made a lasting impression on British do-gooders.

In his travels abroad William Wells Brown, like Douglass, made effective use of both speechmaking and autobiographical writings. Leaving America in July 1849, Wells went to Paris to attend the International Peace Conference. Here he made it a point, as was customary by Negro speakers at international gatherings, to call attention to America's weakness in its aspiration to give moral leadership to the world. The escaped fugitive condemned American slaveholders for prating about peace "while they practiced a form of tyranny which was inevitably driving their country into internecine war." There could be no peace, Brown added, until chattel slavery became a relic of the past.

After the Paris meeting, Brown remained in Europe for five years and two months. Most of his time was spent in the British Isles, where he delivered more than 1,000 addresses, and traveled some 12,000 miles, riding coaches "over nearly every railroad."[7]

During Brown's sojourn abroad, a number of other prominent American Negroes embarked for British shores to bear witness against the sin of slavery. One of these was the scholarly clergyman J. W. C. Pennington, who spent several months in Great Britain in 1849 and 1851. Hired as a lecturer by the Glasgow Female New Association for the Abolition of Slavery, Pennington traveled the length and breadth of Scotland. As a result of his eloquence, particularly of his effective use of tearful tales which excited sympathy and sorrow, "the friends of the Slave were much stirred up in many places." Pennington's labors elsewhere in the British Isles were also telling: "The work which he has done in England on behalf of his enslaved brethren," wrote a provincial reporter, "and the interest he aroused on their behalf has been very great."[8]

In May 1851 Pennington was one of a quartet of American Negroes who were guests at a soiree given by the British and Foreign Anti-Slavery Society at Freemason's Hall, London. Sharing honors with Pennington were Alexander Crummell, Henry Highland Garnet, and Josiah Henson. The last named, soon to win lasting note as the "original Uncle Tom," had come to England to raise funds for a manual labor institute for fugitives at Dawn, Ontario. At the

---

[7] *Leeds Anti-Slavery Series*, no. 34 (London, n.d.), p. 12.   [8] Ibid., p. 16.

World's Fair, held in London, Henson placed on exhibition four boards of black walnut, seven feet in length and four inches in width, in the hope that the planed and polished lumber, gleaming like a shimmery sea, would induce fair-goers to place sales orders. On one occasion no less a personage than Queen Victoria came to the Crystal Palace Exhibition and moved toward the Henson display. The Negro clergyman bowed to the waist, and as Her Majesty passed, he heard her murmur, "Is he indeed a fugitive slave?"[9]

In England at the same time as Henson, Pennington, and Brown, and sometimes speaking from the same platform, was Henry Highland Garnet. Invited to England in 1850 by the Friends of Free Labor, Garnet first went to Frankfort to attend the World Peace Conference. Teaming up with Pennington, he addressed two large audiences at the Evangelical church, urging that free-labor stores be established throughout Germany. The two Negroes spoke through an interpreter, but their addresses were reported to have increased "considerably" the number of friends of the slave.

Garnet remained in Great Britain for three years, speaking and lecturing. His was a potent influence over an audience. Grandson of a Mandingo chieftain and warrior, he was a princely man in appearance, showing little indication that his right leg had been amputated. His head was well-proportioned—a broad nose and a large, firm mouth, flanked by low sideburns. A Presbyterian clergyman, Garnet had a voice of vast compass; once heard, said John Cromwell, it "echoed and re-echoed throughout the chambers of memory."

In 1853, as Garnet returned to America, two other Negro leaders sailed for England. One of these was Samuel Ringold Ward, formerly a pastor of the Congregational church of South Butler, New York, whose all-white membership stood in sharp color contrast to their pastor, whose semicircle of black chin-whiskers could be observed only at close quarters. Ward had subsequently edited two reform weeklies, and had lectured for the Liberty Party. As agent of the Anti-Slavery Society of Canada, Ward came to England "to plead in behalf of my crushed countrymen in America, and the freed men of Canada."

Like other Negro visitors, Ward had no dearth of speaking engagements. His public appearances were not confined to the many abolitionist societies that flourished throughout the British Isles; before Ward had been in England a single month he had been, so

---

[9] Josiah Henson, *Autobiography* (Boston, 1879), p. 191.

he related, "on the platforms of the Bible, Tract, Sunday School, missionary, and Peace, as well as Anti-Slavery, societies."

The other Negro notable who came to England in 1853 was the youthful, light-skinned William G. Allen, a graduate of Beriah Green's Oneida Institute, and formerly editor of the *National Watchman,* published at Troy, New York. Allen had left America somewhat in a hurry. He had been teaching languages and literature at Central College, McGrawville, New York, which had two other Negroes on the faculty, George B. Vashon and Charles L. Reason. At Central College, Allen had formed an acquaintanceship, extending over a year and a half, with one of the white students, Mary E. King.

When it became evident that the two were planning to marry, the townspeople thought it advisable to caution the Negro professor. On a Sabbath evening in January 1853, they paid Allen a visit "armed with tar, feathers, poles, and an empty barrel spiked with shingle nails." Miss King's parents removed her to a neighboring county, but she gave her guardians the slip, joined her fiancé in New York, married him, and sailed with him, nine days later, for Liverpool.

Once in England, Allen sketched in a few additional details to the picture of American injustice. He published in 1853 an account of his experiences, *The American Prejudice Against Color: an Authentic Narrative, Showing How Easily the Nation Got into an Uproar.* Priced at one shilling, the book moved quickly from the stalls. At the 1853 meeting of the British and Foreign Anti-Slavery Society, held at Exeter Hall, Allen indicated that he would embark upon a lecture tour "as soon as the season comes around." His reception among British reformers was cordial: "We welcome all refugees from foreign tyrannies," editorialized the *Anti-Slavery Advocate,* "when, like Professor Allen, they are industrious and self-reliant, asking only for a clear stage, and begging no special favor."

Allen never returned to America. In England "he gained the confidence of all he met." His British friends subsequently raised enough money to purchase control of the Caledonia Training School at Islington, and thereupon they installed him as master, "the first instance in this country of an educational establishment being under the direction of a man of colour."[10]

Like Allen, William and Ellen Craft, who had come to England

---

[10] *Anti-Slavery Reporter* (London), July 1, 1863.

after the passage of the Fugitive Slave Law of 1850, never returned to the United States. They remained under the Union Jack, moving English audiences to sniffles with the thrilling story of their almost incredible escape from slavery. Their youth, good looks and modesty made them popular in reform circles. In 1854 they began to attend school, assisted financially by the generosity of well-wishers, particularly that of Joseph B. Estlin, a clergyman and physician of Bristol.

On the eve of the war, British anti-slavery sentiment was measurably increased by a visit by Martin R. Delany, fresh from a safari into equatorial Africa. Delany had been in London only a few weeks when he almost precipitated a diplomatic breach between Her Majesty's government and the United States. Because of his explorations he had received a royal commission to attend the sessions of the International Statistical Congress, an organization made up of distinguished scientists and other learned men. At the opening convocation, held on July 16 at Somerset House in London, His Royal Highness, Albert, prince consort of England, welcomed the assembled delegates and the invited diplomats.

After Prince Albert had eased himself into the royal crimson chair, Lord Brougham, who was seated on his left, arose to preside. Henry Peter Brougham, excitable and impulsive, was then over eighty, and for fifty years had been an outspoken foe of slavery. Only a few weeks earlier he had ordered his carriage driven to the suburban home of William and Ellen Craft, where he sat for an hour chatting with their house guest, the persuasive Miss Remond. Now, rising to preside at the opening session of the congress, Brougham caught a glimpse of Martin R. Delany, his black face made more highly visible by the surrounding sea of white skins. Thereupon Brougham made an unscheduled remark, "I call the attention of Mr. Dallas to the fact that there is a Negro present, and I hope he will have no scruples on that account."

Seated to the immediate right of the prince, George Mifflin Dallas, the United States minister to England, could scarcely believe what he heard. A dignified career diplomat of distinguished manners, he had never met a situation like this before, either at the court of the czars or that of St. James. As he combed his mind for precedents in protocol, his habitual calm was further ruffled when Delany "with all his blackness," rose up in full view of the curious gaze of the scientists of the world. With mouths agape, the delegates listened as Delany's voice rang out: "I rise, your Royal Highness, to thank his lordship, the unflinching friend of the Negro, for the remarks which he has made in reference to myself, and to assure your Royal Highness that *I am a man.*"

As Delany took his seat, a clapping of hands commenced on the stage, which was quickly echoed from the floor. In a moment, like a barrage of giant firecrackers, peals of loud applause resounded throughout the hall. Seconds later the sound of hand-clapping was completely drowned out by what the London *Times* described as "the wildest shouts ever manifested in so grave an assemblage."

Amid the commotion there was one who sat in frozen disapproval. Mr. Dallas, who had freely confessed that "my individual opinion as to the races being unequal in intellect is strong," debated the advisability of taking a walk. He had no doubt, wrote he in his diary for July 16, that the act "was a premeditated contrivance to provoke me into some unseemly altercation with the colored personage. I balked that by remaining silent and composed." The minister raised a question with himself: "Is not the government answerable for this insult? Or must it be regarded as purely the personal indecency of Lord Brougham?"

A day later Lord Brougham, realizing that his impulsive act might have international repercussions, sent an American messenger to Dallas, who assured the minister that Brougham had no intention of wounding his feelings. Dallas informed the messenger that "he would receive nothing from Brougham at second-hand." When Brougham himself called, Dallas told his doorman "to refuse him." When Brougham came back later in the day, Dallas made it a point to be at the Kensington Museum, drinking in the Turners and the Hogarths.

Although Brougham finally succeeded in making a personal apology to Dallas, Great Britain sent no word of regret. Secretary of State Lewis Cass favored making an official request for a disclaimer, and he informed Dallas that the president and the cabinet commended him for preserving silence, but that they felt he "should have taken a walk after the incident," as a rebuke.[11]

After his impromptu statement, Delany was a center of attraction at the congress throughout the remaining five days of meetings. At the closing session the delegates cheered as he made a short speech

[11] For this incident see Frank A. Rollin, *Life and Public Services of Martin R. Delany* (Boston, 1883), pp. 99–126; Susan Dallas, ed., *Diary of George Mifflin Dallas* (Philadelphia, 1892), pp. 407–9; Lewis Einstein, "Lewis Cass," in Samuel F. Bemis, ed., *The American Secretaries of State and Their Diplomacy* (New York, 1928), vol. 6, pp. 309–11.

of thanks and gratitude for the cordial manner in which he had been received. Before leaving London he received a special request from the Royal Geographical Society to read a paper on his African explorations, and his subsequent seven months in England and Scotland were filled with speaking engagements.

From Charles L. Remond's journey to England in 1840 to that of Delany twenty years later, American Negroes had been strengthening the current of antislavery sentiment in Great Britain and on the continent. Their audiences were large and sympathetic; their influence was great. Negro agitators had laid their groundwork well; after nearly a quarter of a century of listening to their unsparing condemnation of human bondage, the British public would have found it difficult to conceive of one good argument in favor of slavery.

During the first eighteen months of the war—the critical period in diplomatic relations between the United States and England— American Negroes continued their treks to the land of the sympathizing British and, once there, to stiffen English opinion against the Confederacy. Late in 1861 Henry Highland Garnet, William H. Day, and the Boston clergyman J. Sella Martin, among others, were in England informing all who would listen of the inseparable connection between slavery and the war.[12]

Martin, who had arrived in London in October 1861 and remained abroad for nearly six months, was surprised to see so many Negroes in London. "There is no end," he observed, "to the colored here." Martin traveled in company with the zealous George Thompson, then a salaried agent of the American Anti-Slavery Society, who scheduled meetings "all over the kingdom," as Martin wrote in a letter to a member of his congregation.[13] Self-assured and eloquent, Martin won converts wherever he went. He so moved his English audiences with the story of his sister Caroline and her two children, that they raised over $2,000 to purchase the freedom of these three slaves from the Columbus, Georgia, clergyman whose son was the father of Caroline's young ones.[14]

Perhaps the most influential of the Negroes who came to the British shores in 1862 was Jefferson Davis's escaped coachman, William Andrew Jackson. Arriving at Liverpool on November 5 armed with a letter of introduction from William Lloyd Garrison,

---

[12] *Anti-Slavery Reporter*, Jan. 1, 1862.
[13] J. Sella Martin to unnamed correspondent, Oct. 16, 1861. Manuscript in Moorland Collection, Howard University Library, Washington, D. C.
[14] *Liberator*, Oct. 24, 1862.

the ex-coachman was met by George Thompson, who took him to London and installed him as a house guest.[15] Thompson's wife and daughter tutored the former slave so that he might be "better qualified to serve his brethren than at present."[16]

Thompson found "constant occupation" for Jackson. He took him to Staffordshire for a series of engagements, and at every meeting Jackson delivered "an interesting and telling address." He spoke at "several Sabbath schools" and addressed upwards of 3,000 children. He accompanied Thompson to Manchester and Sheffield and on a tour to "the west of England."[17] Jackson traveled solo to fill engagements in South Wales, Derbyshire, and Lancashire. Thompson was highly pleased to send word to Garrison that everywhere that Jackson went, he produced a favorable impression: "I shall," continued Thompson, "be able to obtain for him as much work as he can do for some time."[18]

So busy did Jackson keep, in speaking and in attending meetings, that he felt duty-bound to address a letter to Jefferson Davis, informing him that he could not be with him in Richmond on December 24, 1862, the day on which Davis had to produce him or "discharge a bond of $1,500" to his former master.[19]

Thompson and Jackson did much of their touring as agents of the two antislavery societies that came into existence expressly to prevent England from extending the right hand of political friendship to the Confederacy—the London Emancipation Society and the Union and Emancipation Society of Manchester. The former, born in the closing weeks of 1862, was the lusty offspring of the London Emancipation Committee, which had come into existence in June 1859 at the Bloomsbury residence of Frederick W. Chesson, Thompson's son-in-law. Prominent at this organizational meeting were William Craft and the Baron de Pradine, the Haitian minister to the Court of St. James. Founded to "diffuse information on the slavery question," the group selected Thompson as president and Chesson as secretary.

With the birth late in 1862 of these two influential emancipation societies, there was less need for American Negroes to journey to England to bolster antislavery sentiment and thus forestall diplomatic recognition of the Confederacy. Dating from the Emancipation Proclamation, the Union trumpet no longer gave forth an

---

[15] Ibid., Nov. 28, 1862. [16] Ibid., Dec. 26, 1862.
[17] Thompson to Garrison, Dec. 12, 1862. *Anti-Slavery Letters to William Lloyd Garrison and Others*, Boston Public Library.
[18] Ibid. [19] Ibid.

uncertain sound. Thenceforth anti-Confederate sentiment in England could be left safely in the hands of native reformers such as Harriet Martineau. Moreover, with the coming of 1863 the agitation of Negro abolitionists would be less needful as Northern successes on the battlefield began to sharpen the military intelligence of Lord John Russell, the perceptive British foreign secretary. And, finally, after 1862 the British working classes, already instinctively hostile to slavery, had come to realize that they had a strong personal stake in a Northern victory since the freeing of the American Negro might well bring in its wake an improvement in their own condition in England.[20]

But before 1863, before these things had come to pass, the Negro's role in strengthening British anti-Confederate sentiment had been significant, and that these things had come to pass was in a measure a result of that significant role.

[20] This point is developed in Frank J. Klingberg, "Harriet Beecher Stowe and Social Reform in England," *American Historical Review* 43 (1938): 542–52.

6. Antebellum Free Blacks and the "Spirit of '76"

 N AN ABOLITIONIST observance of the Fourth of July in 1860 at Framingham, Massachusetts, under the auspices of the Massachusetts Anti-Slavery Society, a young black orator advanced a novel reason for the cracking of the Liberty Bell the first time it had been rung. The bell cracked, said H. Ford Douglas, the featured speaker of the occasion, because it simply did not have enough brass to tell the lie conveyed by its inscription, "Proclaim liberty throughout the land unto all the inhabitants thereof."[1]

More than a personal pique, this quip by Douglas revealed an attitude that was common among antebellum blacks. They were less likely than others to be carried away by the patriotic, spread-eagle "spirit of '76," with its glorification of the Declaration of Independence, and its annual flag-waving, band-playing, fireworks celebration of that document's natal day, July 4. White Americans might regard the Declaration of Independence as a beacon light. To a black spokesman like H. Ford Douglas, however, it was a flickering torch at best, its flame fitful.

Afro-Americans had a critical sense of their country's history, their condition permitting no easy escape into a national folklore, no matter how illustrious its origins or how alluring its accents. Their experiences had taught blacks that the great affirmations of the Declaration of Independence did not mean the same thing to whites as to blacks. Before the Revolutionary War had come to a close, it had become clear that to most whites the blacks in their midst did not fall within the abstractions of the Declaration of Independence.

White Americans, whether slaveholders or not, found it possible

[1]*Liberator* (Boston), July 13, 1860.

to proclaim a deep attachment to the Declaration of Independence as an abstract truth while simultaneously denying that it applied to blacks, slave or free. Along with the theory of man's inalienable rights went a tacit proviso that blacks were outside the pale. The central paradox of white American society was to think equality but to practice inequality—a succession of English monarchs had been replaced by an equally divine-right aristocracy of skin color. The Declaration was declared to be off-limits to blacks from the day of founding father Edmund Randolph, who wrote that slaves could "never pretend to benefit" from the Declaration inasmuch as they were not "constituent members of our society," down to the eve of the Civil War when, in the Dred Scott case, the high court ruled that "the enslaved African race were not intended to be included, and formed no part of the people who framed and adopted this declaration: for if the language, as understood in that day, would embrace them, the conduct of the distinguished men who framed the Declaration of Independence would have been utterly and flagrantly inconsistent with the principles they asserted.... "[2]

If the majority opinion in the Dred Scott decision absolved the signers of the Declaration of Independence from "universal rebuke and reprobation" for any alleged inconsistency, it found no echo in black circles. Antebellum black spokesmen found fault with the Declaration on the grounds of its inconsistency and the closely related grounds of its hypocrisy and its ineffectuality.

Inevitably this self-contradictory aspect of the Declaration drew sharp criticism from blacks. In an oration at New York's African Zion Church on July 4, 1827, in commemoration of the abolition of slavery in New York, William Hamilton took note of the "inconsistency of men holding slaves and at the same time declaring in the most solemn manner" their attachment to the self-evident truths in the Declaration.[3] David Ruggles, assister of scores of runaway slaves who had succeeded in reaching New York, pointed out that to stigmatize a man "for wearing the complexion he received from his Creator, or conceding to slavery the right to incarcerate humanity as a chattel personal" was at variance with his notion of the Declaration of Independence.[4] Climaxing a nearly two-year tour of the British Isles in March 1847, Frederick Douglass informed a London audience that the very men who drew up the Declaration

[2]Dred Scott v. John F. A. Sandford, 19 Howard 410.
[3]*Freedom's Journal* (New York), July 13, 1827.
[4]*Liberator*, February 10, 1842.

of Independence "were trafficking in the bodies and souls of their fellow-men."[5] In a speech at Chatham, Ontario, in 1854, Douglass minced no words. America was a nation of liars, "for in her Declaration of Independence, and the gateway to her Constitution, she proclaims 'all men equal,' while she holds in bondage three millions and a half of her subjects...."[6]

To some black critics the Declaration was the ultimate in hypocrisy. At a dinner of the Friendship Society of Baltimore, commemorating the abolition of slavery in New York in 1827, one of the eleven toasts was devoted to the Declaration: "We hold these truths to be self-evident, that all men are born free and equal has been resounded from one end of the Union to the other by white Americans. May they speedily learn to practice what they so loudly proclaim."[7] In a speech to the American Anti-Slavery Society in 1840, Henry Highland Garnet, still a student at Oneida Institute, said that the nation was guilty of a breach of faith in its response to the principles laid down in the Declaration.[8] In similar vein, another student, Thomas Paul of Dartmouth College, in an address to the Massachusetts House of Representatives in 1841, quoted from the Declaration, following it with the assertion that America "presented the rare spectacle of a nation brooding on equal rights while a large part of the population are the most oppressed and degraded beings that crawl on the face of the earth."[9] Writing to abolitionist Wendell Phillips in 1849, runaway slave William Wells Brown attributed a novel quality of thought to those who held slaves. "This is an age of discoveries," he noted, "but I will venture the assertion that none but an American slaveholder could have discovered that a man born in a country was not a citizen of it. Their chosen motto, that 'all men are created equal,' when compared with their treatment of the colored people of the country, sinks them lower and lower in the estimation of the good and wise of all lands."[10]

Black condemnation of the Declaration centered basically in its failure of implementation. Salem-born Charles Lenox Remond informed a London audience in 1840 that his Negro countrymen were driven headlong into perdition because the privileges guar-

[5]*Report of the Proceedings at the Soirée Given to Frederick Douglass, London Tavern, March 30, 1847* (London, 1847), p. 16.
[6]*Frederick Douglass' Paper* (Rochester, N.Y.), Aug. 18, 1854.
[7]*Freedom's Journal*, July 20, 1827.
[8]*Colored American* (New York), May 30, 1840.
[9]*Anti-Slavery Standard* (New York), April 1, 1841.
[10]*Liberator*, November 30, 1849.

anteed in the Declaration and the Constitution were denied them.[11] John Mercer Langston, Oberlin College graduate and a practicing lawyer, tersely stated the problem in an address before the American Anti-Slavery Society in 1855: "The question is with us, shall the Declaration of American Independence stand?"[12] Delivering a speech in Delaware County, Pennsylvania, H. Ford Douglas informed his attentive listeners that he was born a slave in Virginia, birthplace of the "Father of his Country," and the author of the Declaration of Independence, "which proclaimed life, liberty and the pursuit of happiness the inalienable rights of man." Yet, he continued, were he, or anybody else, to go there, or to any other slave state, and "exercise the liberty of speech," he would "find himself dangling to the nearest tree."[13]

No black made a more bitter attack on the Declaration than David Walker, a Boston-based dealer in clothes, in his "Appeal to the Coloured Citizens of the World," a seventy-six-page work first published in 1829. In a call to militant action, Walker exploded his full fury on the Declaration in his closing pages, asking "the attention of the world of mankind to the declaration of these very American people, of the United States." After quoting from it at length, Walker addressed himself to his countrymen: "See your Declaration Americans!!!" With characteristic bite he bade them to "compare your own language above, extracted from your own Declaration of Independence, with your cruelties and murders inflicted by your cruel and unmerciful fathers and yourselves on our fathers and on us. . . ."[14]

Inevitably the coolness of many blacks toward the Declaration of Independence was transferred by association to Thomas Jefferson, its chief architect, few changes having been made on his draft by his colleagues on the committee assigned to the task. To blacks Jefferson was something less than an apostle of liberty; the Jefferson image in the Afro-American mind was essentially negative. To antebellum blacks the cardinal, overriding fact about Jefferson was that he had held slaves. To them his personal life belied his political principles. Jefferson's black critics were little moved by his condemnation of slavery, by his alleged kindness to his own slaves,[15]

---

[11]*Colored American*, August 8, 1840.

[12]*Standard*, May 19, 1855.   [13]Ibid., July 25, 1857.

[14]Herbert Aptheker, *One Continual Cry: Walker's Appeal . . . to the Coloured Citizens of the World . . .* (New York, 1965), pp. 142–43.

[15]"Old master very kind to servants," remembered one of them. Rayford W. Logan, ed., *Memoirs of a Monticello Slave as Dictated to Charles Campbell by Isaac, One of Thomas Jefferson's Slaves* (Charlottesville, 1951), p. 23.

or by the story that when he returned from Paris in December 1789 his slaves met his carriage, unhitched the horses and drew the vehicle up to the lawn in front of the door at Monticello.[16] Black leaders knew of the story of Jefferson's demonstration of interracial togetherness in his alleged semiconjugal relationship with slave Sally Hemings; indeed the title page of William Wells Brown's historical novel, *Clotel: or the President's Daughter: A Narrative of Slave Life in the United States* (London, 1853), bore a passage from the Declaration of Independence and, as if to remove all doubt, Clotel was identified in the narrative as "the daughter of Thomas Jefferson, a president of the United States; a man distinguished as the author of the Declaration of American Independence, and one of the first statesmen of that country."[17]

The ever-militant Robert Purvis seized upon the Clotel theme in an address before the Pennsylvania Anti-Slavery Society in October 1860. "It is said that Jefferson sold his own daughter," said Purvis as his predominantly white audience listened with mixed emotions. If true, continued Purvis, his voice rising, his manner "highly impassioned," this proved Jefferson "to have been a scoundrel as well as a tyrant!" Purvis had been led to this outburst by the assertion, made by a preceding speaker, that Jefferson was antislavery. Purvis had been quick to dissent: "Thomas Jefferson was a slaveholder; and I hold all slaveholders to be tyrants and robbers."[18]

This was the crux of the matter as far as blacks were concerned. To them whatever Jefferson did, said or wrote as to equality and liberty was found wanting when weighed against his holding slaves.[19] Jefferson's contradictory roles as author of the Declaration and slave-owner were challenged as early as 1791 by Benjamin Banneker of Maryland, America's first black scientist of note. Along with an almanac he compiled, Banneker enclosed a lengthy letter in which he took the liberty, in the courteous formal language of the times, to remind Jefferson of his lapse from logic in penning the Declaration of Independence on one hand and in holding slaves

[16]Sarah N. Randolph, *The Domestic Life of Thomas Jefferson* (New York, 1955), p. 153.

[17]William Wells Brown, *Clotel; or the President's Daughter: A Narrative of Slave Life in the United States* (London, 1853), p. 218.

[18]*Anti-Slavery Standard,* November 3, 1860.

[19]For Jefferson's views on slavery and Negroes see Frederick M. Binder, *The Color Problem in Early National America As Viewed by John Adams, Jefferson and Jackson* (The Hague, 1968), pp. 48–81; Daniel J. Boorstin, *The Lost World of Thomas Jefferson* (Boston, 1948), pp. 88–98; Robert McColley, *Slavery and Jeffersonian Virginia* (Urbana, Ill., 1964); and Merrill D. Peterson, *The Jeffersonian Image in the American Mind* (New York, 1960), pp. 173–87.

on the other. Jefferson, then secretary of state, returned a prompt and equally gracious reply. Although he expressed the hope that the condition of the blacks would be bettered, he pointedly ignored Banneker's reference to the Declaration.[20] Banneker's letter, however, was put to good use by black reformers, Frederick Douglass, for example, reading it to a Philadelphia audience in 1859.[21]

Jefferson was treated less gently by William Hamilton, who, in an oration in 1827, referred to him as "an ambidexter philosopher, who can reason contrarywise, first tells you 'that all men are created equal, and that they are endowed with the unalienable rights of life, liberty, and the pursuit of happiness,' next proves that one class of men are not equal to another, which bye the bye, does not agree with the axioms in geometry, that deny that things can be equal, and at the same time unequal to one another." Hamilton found Jefferson remiss in moral principles and "true philosophy."[22]

If antebellum blacks found Jefferson guilty of violating his own political principles, they were likewise sharply critical of his views as to the mental and moral capacity of the Negro. In a speech to the Female Benevolent Society of Troy in 1848, clergyman Henry Highland Garnet charged Jefferson with being the chief American propagator of "the old doctrine of the natural inferiority of the colored race."[23] David Walker, not unlike Garnet in his militant spirit, was moved to bitter condemnation by Jefferson's racial views, railing against him for asserting that the inferiority of the blacks was not due "merely to their condition of life." Walker urged every black "who had the spirit of a man" to buy a copy of Jefferson's *Notes on Virginia* and put it into the hands of his son. The assignment of reputing Jefferson's charges fell inevitably upon the blacks themselves, exhorted Walker, "for we must remember that what the whites have written respecting this subject, is other men's labours, and did not emanate from the blacks."[24]

Walker's challenge was taken up by J. McCune Smith, a physician who somehow found time to become a leading abolitionist and one of the ablest of spokesmen in refuting scholarly contentions as to the shortcomings of blacks. Smith addressed himself to Jefferson's

[20]For this exchange of correspondence between Banneker and Jefferson, see Dorothy Porter, ed., *Early Negro Writing, 1760–1837* (Boston, 1971), pp. 324–28.

[21]*Douglass' Monthly* (Rochester), November, 1859.

[22]Porter, *Early Negro Writing*, p. 101.

[23]"The Past and Present Character and Destiny of the Colored Race," *Speech delivered at 15th anniversary of Female Benevolent Society of Troy, N.Y., February 14, 1848* (Troy, 1848), p. 15.

[24]Aptheker, *One Continual Cry*, p. 15.

assertion (advanced "as a suspicion only," as Jefferson put it) that blacks were inferior to whites in the endowments both of body and mind. Smith proceeded, point by point, to examine the physical differences between whites and blacks—the bones of the body, the muscles, the texture of the brain and the color of the skin. His findings, reported Smith, led him to the inescapable conclusion that Jefferson never would have doubted the equal capacity of the Negro if he had "been acquainted with the philosophy of human progress."[25]

On one Jefferson viewpoint blacks were in full agreement—his warning that in the event of a conflict between the slaves and the masters, God would side with the slaves. This dread possibility of "supernatural interference" on behalf of the exploited downtrodden had moved Jefferson to a dire reflection: "Indeed I tremble for my country when I reflect that God is just: that his justice cannot sleep forever."

This "tremble for my country" quotation was carried on the masthead of the black weekly, *African Sentinel and Journal of Liberty*;[26] it was used by Frederick Douglass in a speech at Rochester,[27] by William J. Watkins in an appearance before a legislative committee convened in Boston,[28] and by William Allen, professor of Greek and Latin, and of rhetoric and belles-lettres, in a book excoriating white Americans for their hostile reaction to his marriage to one of his white students at New York Central College in McGrawville.[29]

The coldly critical eye which antebellum blacks fastened on the author of the Declaration of Independence extended to the natal day of that historic pronouncement, the Fourth of July. To the great majority of the blacks of that era July 4 was a white American holiday. They felt that if observed at all, it should be as a day of national atonement, one on which the people would repair to their places of worship, asking God's forgiveness.

In one instance, however, the blacks wholeheartedly celebrated the Fourth of July. On that day in 1827 slavery officially ended in the state of New York. Blacks in New York City gathered at the

---

[25]Smith, "On the Fourteenth Query of Jefferson's 'Notes on Virginia,'" *Anglo-African Magazine* (New York), August 1859: 225–38.

[26]Stephen B. Oates, *The Fires of Jubilee: Nat Turner's Fierce Rebellion* (New York, 1975), p. 130.

[27]Douglass, *My Bondage and My Freedom* (New York, 1855), p. 440.

[28]William J. Watkins, *Our Rights as Men: An Address Delivered in Boston...* *February 24, 1853* (Boston, 1853), p. 11.

[29]William Allen, *The American Prejudice Toward Color* (London, 1853), p. 27.

African Zion Church to listen to an oration by William Hamilton, who opened by invoking "the ever memorable words" of the Declaration.[30] Blacks throughout the state held similar celebrations. At a Fredericksburg meeting, the Declaration was read in its entirety.[31] The meeting at Cooperstown drew some sixty whites, led by curiosity "to be auditors at so novel a scene."[32] At one New York town the blacks fired guns, although instead of firing as many as there were states in the Union, they "fired only the number of those that acknowledged the African's right to breathe the air of liberty."[33]

For a few years blacks resorted to observing July 5, in part in celebration of emancipation in New York.[34] A fuller explanation was offered by Peter Osborne, speaking at the New Haven African Church: "On account of the misfortune of our color, our Fourth of July comes on the fifth." Osborne said that he hoped and trusted that when the Declaration of Independence became operative "we may then have our Fourth of July on the Fourth." He added, however, that there were many who thought that this was as likely to come to pass as for the leopard to change his spots.[35]

By the mid-1830s the fifth of July had been superseded by August 1 as the "high feast day of freedom" by blacks, as by their white abolitionist co-workers. The act of Parliament freeing the slaves in the British West Indies took effect on August 1, 1834, a day quickly seized upon by black Americans as their freedom day.[36] But their annual glorification of August 1 did little to lessen their long-standing coolness toward the Fourth of July.

Reflecting a common sentiment among blacks, Peter Williams, in a "discourse" on July 4, 1830, at the church of which he was rector, St. Philip's in New York, pointed out that the "festivities of this day serve but to impress the minds of reflecting men of colour a deeper sense of the cruelty, the injustice, the oppression, of which they have been the victims." The meeting at St. Philip's was to raise money "for the benefit of the Coloured Community of the Wilberforce in Upper Canada," and Williams, as befit his calling, had

---

[30]*Freedom's Journal*, October 12, 1827.

[31]Ibid., July 13, 1827.   [32]Ibid.   [33]Ibid., July 20, 1827.

[34]For July 5 observances in 1828 by blacks, see *Freedom's Journal*, July 11 and 18, 1828.

[35]*Liberator*, December 1, 1832.

[36]For August 1 celebrations in 1840 by blacks in Hartford, Newark, Wilmington, Rochester, Buffalo, Albany and Pittsburgh, see *Colored American*, August 15, 1840. For August 1 celebrations in general by antebellum blacks, see Benjamin Quarles, *Black Abolitionists* (New York, 1969), pp. 123–29.

words of advice for his listeners: "Give what you would probably expend in celebrating the 4th of July, to your brethren in Canada."[37]

Other articulate blacks voiced similar anti-Fourth sentiments. Charles Lenox Remond remarked that he was tired of reading Fourth of July speeches, effusions which he branded an insult.[38] In her diary for July 4, 1857, the young and sensitive Charlotte Forten, then a teacher at the Salem (Massachusetts) Normal School, posted a bitter entry: "The celebration of this day! What a mockery it is! My soul sickens of it."[39] According to William Wells Brown, in a speech at Framingham in 1859, the soul of the slave was also sickened on the Fourth, "the great day of sale in the Southern states." To the slave, explained Brown, the firing of cannons and the ringing of bells on that morning were "the signals of separation from each other and from their families."[40]

The black condemners of the Fourth were joined by the most prominent black abolitionist, the editor-orator Frederick Douglass. In an editorial taking note of the Fourth of July celebration in Rochester in 1848, Douglass wrote that if bell-ringing, banner-waving, powder-burning and firearms-discharging were evidence of a devotion to the principles of the Declaration of Independence, then Rochesterians were lovers of liberty without peer. But, he added, these patriotic demonstrators had no desire to put such principles into operation—theirs was a "white liberty."[41] To a Poughkeepsie audience at an August 1 celebration in 1858, Douglass characterized July 4 "not as a festival of Liberty," but as a "day selected for the assassination of Liberty." Behind the bewitching rhetoric of Fourth of July orators loomed "the hideous and bell-black imp of Slavery."[42]

The incompatibility of slavery with the Fourth of July furnished the topic for the most widely publicized of any of the tens of hundreds of stirring speeches ever made by Douglass over a span of more than fifty years. Invited in 1852 by the Rochester Ladies'

---

[37]The full speech by Williams may be found in Porter, *Early Negro Writing*, pp. 294–302.

[38]Remond, in a letter to the West Newbury Anti-Slavery Society, September 16, 1842, in *Liberator*, October 7, 1842. For a similar sentiment by Remond see his speech to the Massachusetts Anti-Slavery Society, July 4, 1857, in *Liberator*, July 10, 1857.

[39]Ray Allen Billington, ed., *The Journal of Charlotte L. Forten* (New York, 1953), p. 103.

[40]*Anti-Slavery Standard*, July 16, 1859.   [41]*North Star*, July 7, 1848.

[42]*New York Times*, August 3, 1858, in Philip S. Foner, ed., *The Life and Writings of Frederick Douglass, 1844–1860*, supplementary volume 5 (New York, 1975), pp. 403, 406.

ANTEBELLUM FREE BLACKS AND THE "SPIRIT OF '76"

Anti-Slavery Society to deliver a Fourth of July oration, he ignored the traditional patriotic themes, addressing himself instead to the question, "What, to the American slave, is your Fourth of July?" It was, answered the speaker, "a day that reveals to him, more than all other days in the year, the gross injustice and cruelty to which he is the constant victim. To him, your celebration is a sham, your boasted liberty, an unholy license; your national greatness, swelling vanity . . . your prayers and hymns, your sermons and thanksgivings . . . are, to him, mere bombast, fraud, deception, impeity, and hypocrisy—a thin veil to cover up crimes which would disgrace a nation of savages." The almost exclusively white audience, sobered if not shocked, hardly needed Douglass's reminder: "This Fourth of July is *yours,* not *mine. You* may rejoice, *I* must mourn."[43]

As he ended his philippic against the Fourth, however, Douglass sounded a note of hope. Expressing his belief in the high destiny of the United States, he drew courage, he said, "from the Declaration of Independence, the great spirit it contains, and the genius of American Institutions."

This hate-love attitude as to the spirit of '76, this condemnation of the Declaration on one hand and a publicly avowed, sincere reverence for it on the other, was a common phenomenon among antebellum blacks. Optimistic and forward-looking in the main, most of them believed that their country would right itself, and that the Declaration of Independence, as the most enduring legacy of the American Revolution, would come to mean to others what it had always meant to them. For all their criticisms of the Declaration, to most black leaders it was a lodestar, a sacred pledge. To revitalize the Declaration blacks were prepared to act as something of a cross between a whip-and-spur and the keeper of the nation's conscience.

The viewpoint of these black proponents of the Declaration was not hard to fathom; they held that its sina qua non was its all-embracing outreach. To them the Constitution of the United States was to be interpreted only within the context of the philosophy of the Declaration, and that every branch and agency of the government, on every level, should operate within a similar compass.

This subsuming power of the Declaration was set forth by James Forten, who had served as a powder boy on the Pennsylvania privateer, the *Royal Lewis,* during the Revolutionary War. The principles of the Declaration, wrote Forten in 1813, along with the Constitution, "embraces the Indian and European, the savage and

[43] *Oration, Delivered in Corinthian Hall, Rochester, by Frederick Douglass, July 5, 1852* (Rochester, 1852).

the Saint, the Peruvian and the Laplander, the white man and the African...."[44] Hosea Easton of Hartford expressed a similar inclusive appraisal, if in less sweeping fashion. There was nothing, he wrote, "to show that color was a consideration in the Declaration of Independence."[45] In terms more scriptural, fellow-clergyman Samuel Ringold Ward interpreted the Declaration as saying "that no enactments, no constitutions, no consent of the man himself, no combinations of men, can alienate that which is by God's *fiat* made *unalienable*."[46] Henry Highland Garnet, addressing a Massachusetts Liberty Convention, said that the Declaration meant "not this man here, and that man there, but *all men*."[47] A group of New York state blacks, meeting in Albany, averred that the Declaration ruled against basing a man's rights on "accidental circumstances or factitious arrangements."[48]

Viewing the Declaration as a freedom document, black antebellum spokesmen put it to a variety of uses in their efforts to better the lot of their kinsfolk. From its inception in 1830 the colored convention movement, an organized expression of protest against racial discrimination by Negroes in the North, invoked the Declaration. In the opening line of its "Address" to fellow-blacks, the Convention of 1830 referred to the Declaration, characterizing it as "that inestimable and invaluable instrument."[49] At the first annual convention the following year, the delegates recommended that the Declaration and Constitution of the United States be read at all black conventions inasmuch as "the truths contained in the former are incontrovertible...."[50]

In its "Declaration of Sentiment" the Convention of 1834 asserted that their principles were "drawn from the book of divine revelation, and are incorporated in the Declaration of Independence."[51] The Convention of 1847, as if to reassure the wav-

---

[44]Carter G. Woodson, ed., *Negro Orators and Their Orations* (Washington, 1925), p. 42.

[45]Hosea Easton, *A Treatise on the Intellectual Character and Civil and Political Condition of the Colored People of the United States* (Boston, 1837), pp. 28–29.

[46]Samuel Ringold Ward, *Autobiography of a Fugitive Slave* (London, 1855), p. 76.

[47]*Emancipator and Free American* (New York), March 4, 1842.

[48]*Colored American*, January 2, 1841.

[49]*Constitution of the American Society of Free Persons of Colour...* (Philadelphia, 1831), p. 9. For a literatim reproduction of the official reports of these meetings, see Howard H. Bell, ed., *Minutes of the Proceedings of the National Negro Conventions, 1830–1861* (New York, 1969). For convenience, Bell's compilation will be used in this paper.

[50]*Convention of 1831*; Bell, p. 5.

[51]*Convention of 1834*; ibid., p. 29.

ering, passed a resolution denoting that "the Declaration of Independence is not a lie."[52] At a gathering in Rochester six years later, the delegates, in an address "to the People of the United States," assured their countrymen that they were citizens "by the principles of the Declaration of Independence," among other qualifications.[53]

In addition to giving a thrust to a broad-based program of black uplift, as embodied in the convention movement, the Declaration served any number of single reforms and concerns. Blacks who inveighed against the efforts of the American Colonization Society to ship them to Africa, for example, were quick to invoke the Declaration. Indeed one of their criticisms of Thomas Jefferson was his insistence that any freeing of the slaves must be conditioned upon their leaving America ("removal beyond the reach of mixture").

The strong black protest against deportation, begun within months after the formation of the American Colonization Society in 1816, reached a high point in the early 1830s, when blacks had become more accustomed to cooperative action. A meeting of Brooklyn blacks in June 1831 condemned colonization as a denial of the "equal rights" conferred by the Declaration of Independence.[54] Wilmington blacks, meeting a month later, were agreed that the effort to colonize blacks was "wholly incompatible" with the Declaration.[55] The first of a series of resolutions passed by a group of Pittsburgh blacks, meeting at the African Methodist Episcopal Church later that year, was a verbatim passage from the Declaration, followed by an assertion that the colored people of that city "were just as much natives here as are the members of the Colonization Society."[56]

A series of resolutions by Harrisburg, Pennsylvania, blacks likewise opened with a passage from the Declaration, characterizing it as "the language of America, of reason, and of eternal truth."[57] In the same year, 1831, Providence blacks protesting colonization cited the Declaration, pointing out in the same breath that their fathers

---

[52]*Convention of 1847;* ibid., p. 16.

[53]*Convention of 1853;* ibid., p. 11.

[54]William Lloyd Garrison, *Thoughts on African Colonization* (Boston, 1832), p. 25. Part 2 of this work is entitled, "Sentiments of the People of Color," and is a reproduction of the official minutes and proceedings of black groups condemning colonization. In 1969 the Arno Press reproduced this work with a preface by William Loren Katz.

[55]Garrison, ibid., p. 36.   [56]Ibid., pp. 34–35.

[57]Ibid., p. 41.

had done their share in the struggle for American independence and freedom.[58] An address from a "numerous meeting" of blacks in Lewiston, Pennsylvania, in January 1832, quoted from the Declaration, following it with the observation that all measures to enslave or degrade blacks were contrary to its spirit.[59] Criticizing the legislature of Ohio for passing a bill in 1829 requiring blacks to leave the state if they could not post a bond of $500, Samuel Cornish expressed a doubt that the legislators had ever read the Declaration or the Constitution.[60]

In a rare instance, the Declaration might be summoned by those favoring voluntary separation from whites. In reply to those who criticized his espousal of all-black settlements, Lewis Woodson of Pittsburgh countered by charging them with forgetting the history of the United States inasmuch as "the very act which gave it political independence was an act of separation," otherwise the Declaration of Independence was a "weak and foolish" pronouncement.[61] In a memorial to the New York legislature in 1851, William P. Powell began by stating that he was the grandson of Elizabeth Barjona, who, as cook to the Continental Congress, gave its members the necessary strength of mind and body to produce the Declaration of Independence. After thus establishing his identity, Powell asked the assembly to pass a special act providing him and his family with the means to leave "this country" which denied to them the rights guaranteed by the Declaration of Independence, "in which he had so great an hereditary interest."[62]

Blacks bent on remaining in America would naturally seek the right to vote and, equally as a matter of course, would base their claim in part on the Declaration. In a rally in support of the Liberty Party in 1840, Albany blacks contended that denying them equal franchise with whites contravened the principles of the Declaration of Independence.[63] Later that year, also in Albany, a state convention of black spokesmen issued a formal statement which in three instances referred to the Declaration, including its assertion that governments derive their just powers from the consent of the governed.[64] Twenty years later, in a tract issued for statewide distribution, "The New York City and County Suffrage Committee of

[58]Ibid., p. 45.   [59]Ibid., p. 49.
[60]*Rights of All*, August 14, 1829.   [61]*Colored American*, July 28, 1838.
[62]*Anti-Slavery Standard*, July 17, 1851. For a sketch of Powell, see Louis Ruchames, ed., *The Papers of William Lloyd Garrison*, vol. 4, *From Disunion to the Brink of War, 1850–1860* (Cambridge, Mass., 1975), p. 42.
[63]*Colored American*, May 23, 1840.
[64]Ibid., December 19, 1840.

Colored Citizens," invoked the Declaration in its plea to the electorate to eliminate the property requirement for voting imposed only on blacks.[65]

In an address to the citizens of New Jersey in 1849, a convention of blacks gathered in Trenton for the sole purpose of seeking the ballot couched its plea in the phraseology of the Declaration.[66] Blacks in Ohio in 1856 petitioned the general assembly to strike the word "white" from the suffrage requirement, "in the name of our common humanity, in the name of the Declaration of Independence, and the Bill of Rights of the State of Ohio."[67] In 1864 a group of Louisiana blacks sent a similar franchise-seeking petition to the president and the Congress, containing a similar pressing reminder of the Declaration.[68]

In a number of other ways the Declaration might be put to use by antebellum blacks, such as in justification for publishing a weekly (as in the case of the short-lived *Sentinel and Journal of Liberty*); in protest against Jim Crow in public transportation (as in the ejection of David Ruggles from a train coach en route from New Bedford to Boston);[69] in fighting against segregation in the public and state-supported education (such as in the case of the Boston public schools);[70] or in petitioning the legislature to permit blacks to serve in the state militia (as in the case of Massachusetts in 1853).[71] The final important way that might be noted here, however, is the use of the Declaration in slavery-related matters.

In their attacks on slavery, black reformers, like their white allies, read the Declaration of Independence as an abolitionist tract. When the act of Congress prohibiting the foreign slave trade went into effect on January 1, 1808, Peter Williams, pastor of the African Church in New York, hailed the occasion as a fulfillment of the principles of the Declaration by "the angel of mercy."[72] In his incendiary "Address to the Slaves" in 1843, Henry Highland Garnet

---

[65]*Principia* (New York), October 20, 1860.

[66]For a copy of this address, see Marion T. Wright, "Negro Suffrage in New Jersey, 1776–1875," *Journal of Negro History* (April 1948):188–89.

[67]"Proceedings of the State Convention of Colored Men...," in Herbert Aptheker, ed., *A Documentary History of the Negro People in the United States: From Colonial Times to 1910* (New York, 1951), p. 383.

[68]*Liberator*, April 1, 1864.   [69]*Anti-Slavery Standard*, July 29, 1841.

[70]"Appeal of the Colored People of the City of Boston. To the Honorable, the Mayor and the Aldermen of Said City," in *Liberator*, August 10, 1849.

[71]William J. Watkins, "Our Rights as Men" (Boston, 1853), p. 10. This petition is carried in Dorothy Porter, ed., *Negro Protest Pamphlets* (1837).

[72]Williams, "An Oration on the Abolition of the Slave Trade...," in Philip S. Foner, ed., *The Voice of Black America*, vol. 1, 1797–1900 (New York, 1975), p. 33.

quoted at length from the Declaration, condemning masters for acknowledging its truths while simultaneously "reducing you to slavery."[73] William Wells Brown informed his former master that his slaves, "like yourself," were entitled to the inestimable blessings of life, liberty, and the pursuit of happiness.[74]

Blacks appealed to the Declaration in condemning attempts to recapture runaway slaves, or to punish those who assisted them. At one of the many meetings protesting the seizure of George Latimer and his imprisonment in a Boston jail late in 1842, Charles Lenox Remond and Frederick Douglass "ably sustained" a resolution which asserted that it was thievery to reduce anyone to servitude in light of the sentiments embodied in the Declaration.[75] In 1844 blacks in Northampton, Massachusetts, held a sympathy meeting for Charles T. Torrey and Jonathan Walker, each of whom had been apprehended for underground railroad operations, men whose only crime, according to the Northampton protesters, was that of "acting in harmony with the sentiments expressed in the Declaration of Independence."[76] Another slave-freeing white activist who landed in jail, William L. Chapin, was eulogized by a black-conducted "Fugitive Slave Convention" at Cazenovia, New York, in August 1850, for "loving his neighbor as himself" and for "practically maintaining" the self-evident truths proclaimed in the Declaration.[77]

The thirty-eight persons, thirty-five of them black, arrested in the highly publicized slave-rescue attempt, the "Christiana Riot" of 1850, were in the unusual position, wrote the black journal *Impartial Citizen*, of being tried for treason against a government founded upon the very principles the jailed men had upheld—the principles spelled out in the Declaration, notably the "liberty" specification.[78] In the equally celebrated Oberlin-Wellington rescue case, black defendant Charles H. Langston, in an eloquent address before a packed courtroom, asserted that John Price, the man whom he had helped to escape, was really not a slave but a man and brother who had a right to his liberty under the Declaration of Independence.[79]

---

[73] *Liberator*, June 2, 1843.

[74] Brown to Capt. Enoch Price, November 23, 1849, in *Liberator*, December 14, 1849.

[75] *Emancipator and Free American*, November 17, 1842.

[76] *Liberator*, August 30, 1844.

[77] *Anti-Slavery Standard*, September 5, 1850.

[78] *Impartial Citizens*, in *Liberator*, October 3, 1851.

[79] *Should Colored Men Be Subject to the Pains and Penalties of the Fugitive Slave*

By the nature of things the bitter condemnation of the Fugitive Slave Law of 1850 by reformers, black and white, led them to the inexhaustible arsenal of the Declaration.[80] At a mass meeting of New York City blacks at Zion Chapel in late October 1850, that law was denounced as being at variance with the spirit and the letter of the Declaration. A similar Fugitive Slave Law protest meeting, held two weeks later by Philadelphia blacks at the Brick Wesley Church, fashioned a lengthy series of resolutions headed by a recital of the "created equal" paragraph of the Declaration, almost as if it were a secular version of the Lord's Prayer.[81] A statewide gathering of blacks in Albany in the summer of 1851 charged the Fugitive Slave Law with violating both the Constitution and the Declaration.[82] Convening in Cleveland in September of the following year, black leaders in Ohio debated a resolution to the effect that the "only way to mitigate the evils of the Fugitive Slave Law is for each . . . to enforce for himself . . . the right to life, liberty and the pursuit of happiness" whatever the course of action necessary.[83] A "Committee of Thirteen appointed to secure the legal defense of persons claimed as Fugitive Slaves," formed in New York as a result of the Fugitive Slave Law, drew up an address to Louis Kossuth which characterized his mission for Hungarian freedom as a "kindred effort" to the Declaration.[84]

Despite the Fugitive Slave Law and other slave-related pronouncements which blacks regarded as setbacks, such as the Dred Scott decision, they did not lose their faith in the Declaration. Three months before John Brown's bold thrust at Harpers Ferry, William Wells Brown voiced the belief that the day was nigh when men would indeed be free, as "written in the Declaration of Independence."[85] Often expressed previously by wishful thinking blacks, this strong belief in the inevitable triumph of the "spirit of '76" bordered on conviction after the stirring raid led by John Brown and his elevation to martyrhood following his hanging on December 2, 1859. "Did not Capt. Brown," wrote one of his black eulogizers, "act in accordance with the . . . pure and holy principles . . . that all men are created equal, and have the inalienable right to life and liberty?"[86]

Law? Speech of C. H. Langston, before the U.S. District Court of the Northern Dis. of Ohio, May 12, 1859 (Cleveland, 1859), p. 10.
   [80]*Anti-Slavery Standard*, October 10, 1850.   [81]*Liberator*, November 8, 1850.
   [82]Howard H. Bell, "Expressions of Negro Militancy in the North, 1840–1860," *Journal of Negro History* (January 1960):15.
   [83]Ibid., p. 16.   [84]*Anti-Slavery Standard*, December 18, 1851.
   [85]Ibid., July 16, 1859.   [86]*Cleveland Plain Dealer*, November 18, 1859.

To blacks the outbreak of the Civil War seemed to herald the longed-for new day. Frederick Douglass informed the Lincoln administration that it would win the support of liberty lovers at home and abroad if it placed itself upon the "immutable truths" of the Declaration.[87] As if not to be taught a lesson in first principles, Lincoln asserted, in a speech at Independence Hall on Washington's birthday in 1862, that he "never had a feeling politically that did not spring from the sentiments embodied in the Declaration of Independence."[88]

As the Civil War drew to its close, with slavery withering away, blacks once more but with greater ardor, invoked the Declaration. Sergeant H. J. Maxwell, addressing a state convention of Tennessee blacks, identified his "prerogatives" as life, liberty and the pursuit of happiness—life and liberty to share in the government and to pursue the rights "guaranteed by the Infinite Architect."[89] The impending death of slavery was interpreted by a state convention of Ohio blacks, meeting at Xenia in January 1865, as a "practical assertion of the fundamental truths laid down in the great Charter of Republican Liberties, the Declaration of Independence."[90] And as the war entered its final week the *New Orleans Tribune* informed its predominantly black constituency that next to life, "as set forth in the Declaration of Independence," is liberty and the pursuit of happiness. After indicating that blacks were "now striving for this boon," the editorial closed with a rhetorical question, "Is it surprising that we now bring into the debate some persistency and warmth?"[91]

Lincoln had reminded his countrymen that they could not escape history. Antebellum blacks had done their part to make sure that the Declaration of Independence would be one aspect of the American past that would remain an inescapable commitment, a mandate not forgotten.

[87]*Douglass' Monthly,* August, 1861.
[88]Roy P. Basler, ed., *The Collected Works of Abraham Lincoln,* vol. 4 (New Brunswick, N.J., 1953), p. 240.
[89]*Colored Tennessean* (Nashville), August 12, 1864.
[90]Aptheker, *Documentary History,* vol. 1, p. 529.
[91]*New Orleans Tribune,* April 1, 1865.

7. Black History's Antebellum Origins

EFORE THE Civil War those who championed freedom for the slaves and a better lot for the free Negroes were constantly beset by the charge that blacks as a race had an unworthy past, whether in Africa or the United States. The claims that blacks were entitled to freedom and equality could be legitimately refuted, ran this line of thought, because their historical record—their achievements and contributions to civilization—had been so negligible, so abysmally low. "The African race is notoriously idle and improvident," wrote James H. Hammond in 1845, and not characterized by "reason and order."[1] Believing that blacks were inferior, Hammond held that other than as slaves they had never amounted to anything and never would. A towering figure in his native South Carolina, and not without influence throughout the South, Hammond voiced a sentiment that was more than sectional. Many whites elsewhere shared the belief that blacks, past as well as present, had a genetic predisposition to low aim and lesser achievement, destined indefinitely to lag below the historical horizon.

The theory of an ignoble Afro-American past was a challenge antebellum black leaders and spokesmen could not ignore. They could hardly be expected to concede that the black past was a chamber of horrors, and that the least said about it the better. Their response took two predictable and related forms—a denial of the indictment and the bringing forth of data to refute it.

In assailing the charge that the Afro-American past was inglorious when it was not insignificant, that it was shrouded in mystery when it was not covered with shame, blacks asserted that what passed for and was accepted as the history of their group was a misrepresentation, a distortion. "The disposition to disparage everything related to Africa, or of African origin, is one of the most stereotyped instincts of American slavery," wrote William Whipper, a shaper

[1]Hammond to Thomas Clarkson, Jan. 28, 1845, in *Governor Hammond's Letters on Southern Slavery: Addressed to Thomas Clarkson* (Charleston, 1845), p. 21.

of thought in antebellum black circles for a quarter of a century.[2] In a similar vein Russell Parrot of Philadelphia asserted that "the people of colour have ever been the victims of misrepresentation," adding that they were held to be "but a remove from the brute, with all the bad propensities of man, without one of his good qualities."[3]

It was bad enough, charged black intellectuals, for white recorders to misinterpret the historical sources they had ostensibly examined. But this failure of deduction was compounded by a deficiency even more grievous—bias by omission. Blacks charged that when white researchers came across references to black achievers they were seized as if by a selective inattention, an urge to pass on to other things. An editorial in *Freedom's Journal*, the first black weekly, accused whites of confining their attention to those blacks who were slaves, "omitting through ignorance or illiberality what ancient sages have written and handed down" about dark-skinned peoples of earlier times.[4] In a similar vein, Samuel Ringgold Ward, a Presbyterian minister, asserted that to whites "our history is that of the chain, the coffle gang, the slave ship, the middle passage, the plantation-hell!" This belief might be excusable, added Ward, on the part of those who knew nothing of the Negro except as they saw him in slavery or in menial occupations. "But scholars deserve no such extenuation."[5]

Some blacks felt that their group alone had been singled out for exclusion by historians, a belief lacking in point of fact but understandable in the color-conscious context of the times. In a Fourth of July address at Framingham, Massachusetts, on the eve of the Civil War, H. Ford Douglass of Illinois, a former runaway slave from Virginia, spoke of this black code of interdiction: "All other races are permitted to travel over the wide field of history and pluck the flowers that blossom there, to glean up heroes, philosophers, sages and poets, and put them into a galaxy of brilliant genius and claim all credit to themselves; but if a black man attempts to do so, he is met at the threshold by the objection, 'You have no ancestry behind you.' "[6]

Blacks held that this lack of knowledge of their past—these missing pages in their history—hindered them in their fight for full

---

[2]Whipper to Julia Griffiths, Feb. 3, 1859. *Douglass' Monthly* (Rochester, N.Y.), March 1859.
[3]*Freedom's Journal* (New York), July 27, 1827. [4]Ibid.
[5]Ward, *Autobiography of a Fugitive Negro* (London, 1855), pp. 185–86.
[6]Douglass, *Anti-Slavery Standard* (New York), July 14, 1860.

citizenship. Meeting in Rochester, New York, in 1853, a convention of black leaders drafted "An Address of the Colored National Convention to the People of the United States," which held that "modern American historians" had forgotten to record the services and sacrifices of their black compatriots, "a knowledge of which is essential to an intelligent judgment of the merits of our people."[7] Seeking equal voting rights in 1860, the New York City and County Suffrage Committee of Colored Citizens sent out a statewide appeal: "Our countrymen do not know us. They are strangers to our characters, ignorant of our capacity, and oblivious of our history."[8]

Blacks contended with especial fervor that the role of their group in America's wars had been ignored or slighted. "History has thrown the colored man out," said William Wells Brown in an address at the American Anti-Slavery Society in May 1860 in New York. "You look in vain to Bancroft and other historians for justice to the colored." The role of blacks in America's wars was there for the telling, continued Brown, but "the historian passes it by."[9] Addressing the same society at an earlier convention, Henry Highland Garnet, another former slave and later United States minister to Liberia, asserted that "scarcely an inch on the pages of history" had been allotted to the blacks who fell in the Revolutionary War.[10]

The journalist-reformer Thomas Van Rensselaer held that in giving an account of the role of blacks in that war it was necessary to depend upon "traditional rather than written history." He proceeded to expound on the defects in the latter: "It seems to have been then, as now, the settled policy of the white man to have permitted the colored man to an equal participation with himself in the dangers to which they are exposed in securing Republican institutions, but when secured, he is content to enjoy them alone, hence the absence (almost) in American history of any mention of the noble achievements of colored men."[11] In delivering the eulogy at the death of the wealthy sailmaker James Forten, who had served as a powder-boy in the Revolutionary War, William L. Douglass, the rector of St. Thomas's Protestant Episcopal Church in Philadelphia, faced this dilemma of word-of-mouth history versus the written version. "We have heard," ran his remarks, "something relating to his connection with the trials of the American Revolution

[7]*Proceedings of the Colored National Convention held in Rochester, July 6, 7, 8, 1853* (Rochester, 1853), p. 13.
[8]*The Liberator* (Boston), Nov. 2, 1860.
[9]*Anti-Slavery Standard*, May 26, 1860.
[10]*The Emancipator* (New York), May 15, 1840.
[11]*The Colored American* (New York), Feb. 27, 1841.

but as the facts have not come to us in a regular way, we must be permitted to pass over it."[12]

The tendency by white writers to ignore the black role in American life was viewed as a dereliction of duty by James McCune Smith, a physician who had found it necessary to go to Scotland to obtain his professional training. In a long letter to Horace Greeley, editor of the *New York Tribune*, a man regarded by blacks as being not unsympathetic, Smith called attention to the long-range academic implications of neglected black history. "The loss of the Alexandrian Library and its wealth of ancient lore is a deep grief to scholars," wrote Smith, "but I am convinced that there will be a profounder grief among thinkers a century hence that there is not now placed on record a succinct account of the true relation which blacks now bear to this Republic."[13] Sounding a similar warning, a correspondent to a black weekly urged its readers to become collectors and preservationists. We should, he advised, "take measures to effect a speedy collection of those valuable evidences of the genius and integrity of our gifted brethren." Such an enterprise was due to them, to ourselves, and to posterity, he added.[14]

The neglect of their history was a challenge to blacks to bestir themselves. Writing in 1833, the black lecturer Maria W. Stewart of Boston cogently expressed this summons to action: "When I cast my eyes on the long list of illustrious names that are enrolled in the bright annals of fame among whites, I turn my eyes within, and ask my thoughts, 'Where are the names of our illustrious ones?' "[15] Two years earlier, in an address at the African Masonic Hall, Mrs. Stewart had urged black women to become history-makers: "O, ye daughters of Africa! What have ye done to immortalize your names beyond the grave? What examples have ye set before the rising generation?"[16]

Experience had taught blacks that, despite the valued assistance of white friends, there were some things they must do for themselves, however ill-prepared they might be and however imperfect the end result. They realized that in throwing light on the black

[12]*Anti-Slavery Standard*, May 5, 1842.
[13]Smith to Greeley, Sept. 1, 1851, in *Frederick Douglass' Paper* (Rochester), Sept. 25, 1851.
[14]Ibid., Sept. 23, 1853.
[15]Maria W. Stewart, *Religion and the Pure Principles of Morality* (Boston, 1831), in Dorothy Porter, ed., *Early Negro Writing, 1760–1837* (Boston, 1971), p. 482.
[16]This address appears in *Productions of Maria W. Stewart* (Boston, 1835), in Bert James Loewenberg and Ruth Bogin, eds., *Black Women in Nineteenth-Century American Life* (University Park, Pa., 1976), p. 195.

past they would have to take the lead. "If we do not vindicate ourselves, who will do it for us?"[17] asked Samuel Ringgold Ward in referring to the Afro-American past.

In the effort to disinter their history, black leaders were motivated primarily by racial considerations. Obviously they hoped to reach some whites, particularly those who were influential, whether in church or state, the courts or the counting houses. But it was even more imperative to reach their fellow-blacks, ignorance of the black past not being confined to whites. Uncounted numbers of blacks knew little or nothing about the Afro-American past. Worse still, many of them repudiated blackness as a typology, historical or otherwise. It was common knowledge, wrote William J. Wilson in a letter to a Negro weekly, "that a black girl would as soon fondle a black imp as a black doll." Once, wrote Wilson, when he "suddenly introduced" such a doll to a group of twenty colored girls they greeted it with such a scampering and screaming as could only be imagined.[18]

Racial pride was thus a central motif in antebellum black history. Like other Americans of their day, blacks were engaged in the quest for self-identity. Because blacks bore heavy burdens, however, black self-identity more readily flowed into group identity, with history a connecting link, in effect becoming history-as-identity. Sometimes, as was to be expected, this sense of racial pride became exuberant, even to the point of role reversal. Meeting in Cleveland in 1854, the National Emigration Convention of Colored People passed a resolution to the effect "that we shall ever cherish our identity of origin and race, as preferable in our estimation, to any other people."[19] Six years later, a member of that convention, abolitionist orator H. Ford Douglass, asserted at a predominantly white gathering that he was "proud of the Negro race, and I thank God today that there does not course in my veins a single drop of Saxon blood."[20]

Antebellum blacks had little interest in recovering the past for its own sake. History to them was no idle pastime—it was a means to an end. *The Rights of All,* an early weekly published in New York, urged its readers to acquire "some knowledge of the history of nations," as a preparation for the responsibilities of full citizen-

---

[17]Ward, *Autobiography*, p. 186. [18]*Frederick Douglass' Paper*, Mar. 11, 1853.
[19]*Proceedings of the National Emigration Convention of Colored People Held at Cleveland, Ohio, on 24th, 25th and 26th of August, 1854* (Pittsburgh, 1854), p. 27.
[20]*The Liberator*, July 3, 1860.

ship.[21] Amos Gerry Beman, a Congregational minister, instructed the readers of another black journal that the purpose of history was "to show what principles ought to prevail and what ones will ruin any individual, people or nation."[22]

As construed by antebellum blacks, history's main function was to furnish them with a more positive self-perception. They felt that they needed a more heroic image of themselves so that they might respond in like fashion. "What Cyprian, Augustine, Tertullian and others in the Church were, colored men may be again," editorialized *The Colored American* in its plea for role-model history.[23] It is to be noted that in proof of the Negro ancestry of such figures of the past, antebellum blacks often relied upon physical characteristics. Euclid, according to Samuel Ringgold Ward, "had a black complexion, woolly hair, thick lips and elliptical ankle-bones."[24]

In moving to counter unfavorable assessments of their role in history, blacks were not unmindful of the small company of white writers who came to their defense. Of these the most widely quoted by blacks and their friends was Henri Grégoire, a French cleric, author of *An Enquiry Concerning the Intellectual and Moral Faculties, and Literature of Negroes; Followed with an Account of the Life and Works of Fifteen Negroes and Mulattoes, Distinguished in Science, Literature and the Arts* (to give it the title of the translated version, published in 1810).[25] "I have taken upon myself," wrote the bishop, "the task of proving that negroes are capable of virtues and talents; and this I have established by reasoning, and still more by facts."[26] Grégoire's countryman and contemporary Brissot de Warville had come to a similar conclusion. In his *New Travels in the United States Performed in 1788* (London, 1792), Brissot challenged the theory that blacks were inferior to whites in mental capacity.[27]

Similarly, if at a later date, Wilson Armistead, president of the Leeds Anti-Slavery Society, produced a lengthy volume, *A Tribute for the Negro*. Published in Manchester in 1848, it was dedicated

[21]*The Rights of All* (New York), May 29, 1820.
[22]*The Colored American*, Mar. 6, 1841. [23]Ibid., May 6, 1837.
[24]*Frederick Douglass' Paper*, Jan. 27, 1854.
[25]Passages from Grégoire may, for example, be found in *Freedom's Journal*, Nov. 24, 1828, and *The Northern Star and Freeman's Advocate* (Albany, N.Y.), Mar. 3, 1842. William Whipper, in a eulogy on William Wilberforce on Dec. 6, 1833, called attention to Grégoire's treatise. For this eulogy see Philip S. Foner, ed., *The Voice of Black America, 1757–1900* (New York, 1972), pp. 72–78.
[26]Grégoire, *An Enquiry Concerning the Intellectual and Moral Faculties, and Literature of Negroes* (1810), p. 248.
[27]Brissot, *New Travels*, p. 285.

"to James W. C. Pennington, Frederick Douglass, Alexander Crummell and Many Other Notable Examples of the Elevated Humanity of the Negro." *The North Star,* edited by Douglass, felt that Armistead's work fell somewhat short "in arrangement and literary ability," but deemed it quite important "as the repository of a luminous and brilliant array of testimony, in favor of our class to be regarded as equal members of the great human family, with the rest of mankind."[28]

The tone and temper of the history propounded by blacks took it cue from its premises. To white disparagement, blacks countered with racial glorification and pride, with objectivity a lesser consideration. Holding that truth was where you found it, blacks did not hesitate to use sources that might have been considered speculative by others. The charge that their reading of the past was more hearsay history than anything else would have left them unmoved. To them, the task of combatting deep-seated errors and grievous omissions as to the black role in history would seem to justify the use of part-truths pending the arrival of the whole truth, especially since the latter was notorious for taking its own good time.

If the writers of antebellum black history sought to influence all who would lend an ear, they wrote primarily for the general reader. The title of the pioneer work in the field, *A Text Book of the Origin and History of the Colored People,* by James W. C. Pennington, published in 1841 at Hartford, Connecticut, and running to ninety-six pages, indicated its introductory bent. It would "be found useful to families, juvenile readers, and lecturers in history," said *The Colored American.*[29] Although recommending the book ("every colored family ought to have it"), the black weekly criticized Pennington for not giving more attention to the history content even if this had forced him to curtail the sections on prejudice—"the historical part being but little understood, while all are more or less familiar with the nature and character of prejudice."[30]

Pennington's volume was followed three years later by another "claim-the-world" type of history, *Light and Truth; Collected from the Bible and Ancient and Modern History, Containing the Universal History of the Colored and Indian Race, from the Creation of the World to the Present Time,* by Robert B. Lewis of Hallowell, Maine. Published in Boston in 1844 by a "Committee of Colored Gentlemen" who had paid the printing bill and to whom Lewis had

[28] *North Star* (Rochester), Apr. 9, 1849.
[29] *The Colored American,* Jan. 9, 1841. [30] Ibid., Feb. 27, 1841.

transferred the title,[31] it was a massive work, four times the length of Pennington's. It was, however, much like the latter in tone and approach. A review in an abolitionist weekly (and hence an organ inclined to be sympathetic) described *Light and Truth* as "a curious collection of historical facts, connected, in some way or other, with those portions of mankind not commonly called 'white.' Its arrangement is not very methodical, and its aim not very definite, and as there are no references, the authenticity of some of the statements is likely to be questioned."[32]

Both authors, Pennington and Lewis, viewed history as falling into two categories, sacred and profane. The latter was regarded as far the lesser and was, wrote clergyman Pennington, to be valued "in proportion as it has the coincidence of sacred history."[33] Indeed, antebellum black history was not without its messianic overtones, reflecting the church-oriented background of the group. "Beloved brethren—here let me tell you, and believe it, that the Lord our God, as true as he sits on his throne in heaven, and as true as our Saviour died to redeem the world, will give you a Hannibal," wrote David Walker in his fiery pamphlet *Appeal to the Coloured Citizens of the World.*[34]

During the last decade of the antebellum period, the viewpoint that history was illustrative and confirmative of divine revelation was not as frequently voiced in black circles. The later commentators were also likely to document their sources, and to have read more widely than their predecessors. There was less likelihood that they would require the apologetic explanation voiced by *Freedom's Journal* about a columnist who was doing a series of articles on ancient Africa: "The readers of 'African Genealogy,' doubtless, will excuse all inaccuracies when told that the writer of it is quite a youth."[35]

Whether young or old, whether their knowledge of the past was superficial or solid, the advocates of black history focussed on certain common themes. Alike they called attention to the role of blacks in the ancient world, with due mention of Africa's influence on Greece and Rome. In the Western Hemisphere they dwelt upon the history of Haiti after she had won her independence. Moving on

[31]For a copy of this transfer of title see *The Liberator*, Mar. 22, 1844.
[32]*The Emancipator and Free American* (New York), Feb. 29, 1844.
[33]Pennington, *A Text Book of the Origin and History of the Colored People* (Hartford, 1841), p. 19.
[34]*Walker's Appeal...to the Coloured Citizens of the World*, 3d ed. (Boston, 1830), p. 20.
[35]*Freedom's Journal*, Aug. 31, 1827.

to the United States these evokers of the past were especially pleased to recount the role of their forebears in the nation's wars. To these ancestral arms-bearers for America they added the company of blacks who at one time or another had come to public notice as rebels and radicals or as achievers in the arts or the professions. These basic themes in antebellum Afro-American history may be briefly noted in turn.

Those who addressed themselves to blacks of ancient times tended to couch their observations in somewhat general terms, without specific reference to time or place. The delegates to the Colored Convention of 1834, meeting in New York, formulated a "Declaration of Sentiment" proclaiming that "the coloured population of the United States" lay claim "to be the offspring of a parentage, that once, for their excellence of attainment in the arts, literature and science, stood before the world unrivalled."[36] Similarly without furnishing a bill of particulars, H. Ford Douglass assured a Fourth of July audience that "the remains of ancient grandeur which have been exhumed from the accumulated dust of forty centuries were wrought by the ingenuity and skill of the Negro race ere the Saxon was known in history."[37] At a meeting of Boston Negroes at Joy Street Church late in 1860, author-abolitionist William Wells Brown spoke in a similar broad vein, reflecting on the Negro of "three thousand years ago, when in the period of their greatness and glory, they held the foremost ranks in the march of civilization; when they constituted, in fact, the whole civilized world of their time."[38]

History-minded blacks who made no reference to any specific locales as to the theater of ancient black genius felt that such a place identification was hardly necessary. Where could it have been other than Africa? Where else could these things have come to pass except in the historic land of the blacks?

"Everything that relates to Africa shall find a ready admission into our columns," editorialized *Freedom's Journal* on the first page of the first issue.[39] As held by antebellum blacks, this interest in Africa was variously motivated. Africa offered a refuge from American oppression; it held possibilities for trade and commerce, and it was a fertile field for evangelization—"I long to preach to the poor African the way of salvation," said one of the pioneer black

---

[36]*Minutes of the Fourth Annual Convention of the Free People of Colour in the United States* (New York, 1834), p. 27.
[37]*Anti-Slavery Standard*, July 14, 1860. [38]*The Liberator*, Oct. 26, 1860.
[39]*Freedom's Journal*, Mar. 16, 1827.

colonizing missionaries, Lott Cary, in his farewell sermon in the First Baptist Church in Richmond in 1825.[40]

It is to be noted that the suspicion blacks had about the motives of the American Colonization Society in deporting blacks led to some expressions of coolness toward identifying with Africa. "We do not trace our ancestors to Africa alone," ran a resolution of an anticolonization meeting in New York. "We trace it to Englishmen, Irishmen, Scotchmen, to Frenchmen; to the German; to the Asiatic as well as the African."[41] At an anticolonization meeting, Charles Lenox Remond, the most prominent black abolitionist lecturer before Frederick Douglass, stated that "if we should note and count this audience we should be obliged to come to the conclusion that the fatherland of the coloured people was almost anywhere else than Africa (great laughter)."[42] A similar point of diverse racial origins was raised by James McCune Smith in response to Horace Greeley who had, in the columns of the *New York Tribune,* urged blacks to "consecrate their lives to the work of regenerating and civilizing the land of their forefathers." Smith asked for clarification: "Did you mean foremothers?"[43]

Deportation schemes espoused by white organizations such as the American Colonization Society would expectedly lead some blacks to reaffirm their Americanization and to raise questions about Liberia and West Coast Africa in general as suitable places to which to migrate. Such reservations, however, did not deter the majority of articulate blacks from identifying with an Africa of antiquity. For if there were some doubts about modern Africa, not so with ancient Africa. Antebellum blacks could, by identifying themselves with the latter, bestow upon themselves an ancestry of freedom, not one of slavery and stigma. As sons and daughters of early precolonial Africa they were heirs of her ancient glory, however unapostolic the succession.

The Africa heralded by antebellum blacks was not West Coast Africa, the seat of the transoceanic slave trade and hence the ancestral homelands of the vast majority of Afro-Americans. They knew little about that region, and not they alone. The discovery of historical West Africa would have to await new techniques and new sources, including archeological findings, linguistic studies, oral evidence, and the writings of North African and Arab historians and travelers. As a consequence it was natural for antebellum blacks to

---

[40]*The Genius of Universal Emancipation* (Baltimore), Nov. 12, 1825.
[41]*The Liberator,* Apr. 4, 1851.
[42]*Anti-Slavery Standard,* May 3, 1849.   [43]Ibid., Sept. 11, 1851.

focus on East Africa with its more accessible records. Hence they invoked Egypt and Ethiopia, the former especially. "Our traducers," wrote Prince Saunders in 1818, "pretend to have forgotten what the Egyptians and the Ethiopians, our ancestors, were."[44]

Saunders and many other literate blacks held that Negro Americans were genetically related to ancient Ethiopians and Egyptians, and they attacked those who would deny such a relationship, including Samuel G. Morton, a highly regarded naturalist who specialized in the comparative study of human skulls. In his influential *Crania Americana,* published in 1839, Morton asserted that beyond all question "the Caucasian and Negro races were as perfectly distinct in that country [Egypt] upwards of three thousand years ago as they are now."[45] Morton's views were challenged by Frederick Douglass in a lengthy, thoughtful address at Western Reserve College in Hudson, Ohio, in 1854, *The Claims of the Negro Ethnologically Considered.* Stating that *Crania Americana* revealed Morton's low opinion of blacks, Douglass undertook to refute each of his reasons for holding that Egyptians bore no ethnic ties to Negroes. James McCune Smith, like Morton a physician, found the address by Douglass to be "full of new and fresh thoughts on the dawning science of race-history."[46]

Those who disparaged the idea of any linkage between the Negro race and the early Egyptians were ridiculed by H. Ford Douglass. "I know that ethnological writers tell us that we do not look like the Egyptian," said the young orator. "They dig up an Egyptian mummy that has been dead and buried three thousand years, over whose grave the storms of thirty or forty centuries have swept, and because it does not look just like a Mississippi Negro of today, set it down that there is a difference of species between them."[47] Henry Highland Garnet noted that despite the historical proof to the contrary "there are those who affirm that the ancient Egyptians were not of pure African stock."[48]

Holding that the term "African" encompassed Egypt, history-minded antebellum blacks found a source of pride in their Old World ancestry. The "glorious" past of Africa became a recurrent

[44]Saunders, *Haytian Papers* (Boston, 1818), p. 153.

[45]Morton, *Crania Americana* (Philadelphia and London, 1839), p. 88.

[46]Douglass, *The Claims of the Negro Ethnologically Considered* (Rochester, 1854), pp. 17–22. Smith's appraisal is in his introduction to Frederick Douglass, *My Bondage and My Freedom* (New York, 1855), p. xxviii.

[47]*The Liberator,* July 13, 1860.

[48]Garnet, *The Past and the Present Condition and Destiny of the Colored Race* (Troy, N.Y.), p. 3.

theme in black expression, sacred and secular. When David Nickens announced that "Africa was the garden and nursery where learning budded and education sprang," his paean was hardly a revelation to the audience assembled at the Chillicothe, Ohio, AME Church on July 5, 1832. "All the now civilized world," added the clergyman, "is indebted to sable Africa for the arts of civilization."[49]

The glorifiers of ancient Africa were not likely to forget to call attention to her significant influence on the civilizations that would develop in the Mediterranean basin, from whence it would spread into northern Europe, eventually making its way across the Altantic. Afro-American speakers and writers confidently asserted that Ethiopia and Egypt were the sources of Greek thought and culture. It was to Africa, "the cradle of Art and Science," said clergyman Sampson White, that "the wise men of Greece had gone in search of wisdom."[50] In turn the Greeks would transmit this rich legacy to the Romans, who would carry it far and wide, eventually to the shores of the British Isles. "The Romans, Saxons and Normans who swallowed up the Britons and gave them a name and a language, received their civilization from Egypt and Ethiopia," explained William Wells Brown to a Boston audience.[51]

If antebellum blacks found it satisfying to dwell upon ancient Africa and its civilizing influence they had to give some thought to the question: Why had the light faded? Why did the Africa of their day compare so unfavorably with the Africa of the pharaohs? Blacks who were church-minded had a ready answer. James W. C. Pennington found that the theology of the early Africans was their downfall, asserting that "when a man has adopted the idea of more gods than one, he has unhinged his mind from anything like the truth."[52] Fellow clergyman Samuel Ringgold Ward took note of "the wickedness of the ancient Negroes," who committed the same sins as other people and hence were treated accordingly by an impartial Jehovah.[53] The Almighty, observed Maria W. Stewart, "gave our glory unto others" because of "our gross sins and abominations." Not to close on a note of despair, Mrs. Stewart reminded her readers of the prophecy in the Book of Psalms so often quoted in black circles, clerical and lay, "Ethiopia shall again stretch forth her hands unto God."[54]

Africa's own shortcomings were not, however, the only reasons

[49]*The Liberator*, Aug. 11, 1832. [50]*Weekly Anglo-African*, Mar. 31, 1860.
[51]*The Liberator*, Oct. 26, 1860. [52]Pennington, *Text Book*, p. 33.
[53]Ward, *Autobiography*, p. 188.
[54]Maria W. Stewart in Porter, ed., *Early Negro Writing*, pp. 130–31.

for her decline. Austin Stewart, a runaway slave turned grocer, placed the blame on "Christian Englishmen." They had brought to ruin a once "powerful nation" by invading her coasts with rum, inciting her chiefs to intertribal warfare, and "by purchasing with gaudy, but worthless trinkets, her conquered captives."[55] Thomas L. Jennings of New York viewed Columbus as the chief culprit in the chain of events that had transformed Africa from "a land flowing with riches" into an "unhappy country" whose sons and daughters had been dispersed throughout the globe. "I would that Columbus had never been born," wrote Jennings, "or that he had been buried at the bottom of the sea, ere he contemplated or discovered this Western Hemisphere, the theatre of all our misfortunes."[56]

There was one spot in the Western Hemisphere, however, that history-minded blacks could hail, the island of Haiti, which had freed itself from French rule in 1804. To prove the mettle of the Negro people, said David Walker, there was no need to "refer to antiquity" since one had only to turn to Haiti, "the glory of blacks and the terror of tyrants."[57]

Ignoring differences in language and religion, Negro Americans saw Haiti as a proving ground for black abilities. The history of the bloody struggles for Haitian independence "in which the blacks whipped the French and English," said lawyer-physician John S. Rock, in a Crispus Attucks Day celebration at Faneuil Hall in Boston, "will be a lasting refutation of the malicious aspersions of our enemies."[58] At a celebration of Haitian independence held by Baltimore blacks in 1825 the orator of the day, William Watkins, Jr., showered praises on the island republic as "an irrefutable argument that the descendants of Africa were never designed by their Creator to sustain an inferiority, or even a mediocrity in the chain of beings."[59] Similarly glowing was the appraisal of *The Rights of All*, whose editor viewed Haiti's progress "in commercial relations, in respectability, and in every interest, as being not only equal to, but unparalleled by, that of any other modern nation."[60]

Taking a bachelor's degree from Bowdoin College on September 26, 1825, John B. Russwurm devoted his short commencement address to Haiti, crediting her with having "effected wonders" since

[55] Austin Stewart, *Twenty-Two Years a Slave, and Forty Years a Freeman* (Rochester, 1857), p. 197.
[56] *Freedom's Journal*, Apr. 1, 1828.   [57] *Walker's Appeal*, p. 21.
[58] *The Liberator*, Mar. 12, 1858.
[59] *The Genius of Universal Emancipation*, Aug. 15, 1825.
[60] *The Rights of All*, Oct. 9, 1829.

becoming independent and predicting for her "a career of glory and happiness."[61] J. Dennis Harris, whose emigrationist activities left him little time to practice his trade of shoemaking, characterized Haiti as "a land of historical facts, and the field of unparalleled glory," her past unsullied by anything "low or cowardly."[62] Maria W. Stewart was unhappy over the reluctance of the United States to extend diplomatic recognition to the black republic. "You have," ran her accusation, "acknowledged all the nations of the earth, except Haiti."[63]

In praise of Haiti no voice was as insistent as that of James Theodore Holly, rector of St. Luke's Church in New Haven, Connecticut. Staunchly supporting the emigrationist efforts that took shape in the 1850s, coincident with the growing sectional crisis over slavery, Holly proclaimed Haiti as a refuge from oppression and, with even greater fervor, a land of promise in its own right. Following a visit to the island in 1855, Holly prepared a lecture which he delivered upon occasion in 1856 and which was published in 1857 as a forty-six-page pamphlet, *A Vindication of the Capacity of the Negro Race for Self-Government, and Civilized Progress, as Demonstrated by Historical Events of the Haytian Revolution; and the Subsequent Acts of That People Since Their National Independence.* Holly began his long discourse by announcing that he would challenge the assumption that the Negro was lacking in those qualities upon which "the great mass of Caucasians" based their claims of superiority. Holly then proceeded with his defense, basing it on "the undoubted facts of history." He concluded by ruling on the merits of his case. He had "summoned the sable heroes and statesmen of that independent island of the Caribbean," tried them by the high standard of modern civilization, fearlessly compared them "with the most illustrious men of the most enlightened nations," and in this examination they had not fallen "one whit behind their contemporaries."[64]

To antebellum blacks no name in Haitian history could rank with that of slave-born Toussaint L'Ouverture, the dominant figure in freeing the island from foreign rule. Black periodicals dwelt upon his character and exploits: *Freedom's Journal,* for example, pub-

[61]Foner, ed., *The Voice of Black America,* p. 43.
[62]Harris, *A Summer on the Borders of the Caribbean Sea* (1860), in Howard H. Bell, ed., *Black Separatism and the Caribbean, 1860* (Ann Arbor, 1970), p. 117.
[63]Maria W. Stewart in Loewenberg and Bogin, eds., *Black Women in Nineteenth-Century American Life,* p. 191.
[64]James Theodore Holly, *A Vindication of the Capacity of the Negro Race* (New Haven, 1857), pp. 4, 5, 44.

lishing a three-part article on his career in its issues of May 4, 11, and 18, 1827, and the *Anglo-African Magazine* carrying a eulogistic sketch in its March 1859 number. Speakers at black gatherings extolled his virtues. At a meeting in Clinton Hall, New York, in 1841 for the benefit of the Colored Orphan Asylum, James McCune Smith lectured on Toussaint's life and character.[65] At a fund-raising affair on behalf of the New York Literary Association, a group of young blacks bent on self-improvement, the white speaker, C. W. Elliott, eulogized the Haitian liberator, to the demonstrated approval of the "tolerably numerous audience."[66]

When the young schoolteacher Charlotte Forten heard Wendell Phillips deliver his famed oration on Toussaint, she was transported. "My enthusiastic enjoyment knew no bounds," she wrote in her diary, appending quotations from the speech.[67] Black newspapers carried William Wordsworth's moving sonnet "To Toussaint L'Ouverture," and a few black parents gave his name to their offspring. One of the children of the Martin R. Delanys was named after the Haitian hero,[68] and at the first concert of the Juvenile Afric-American Philharmonic of Detroit in September 1859, the youngster who "presided at the melodeon" was billed as Toussaint L'Ouverture Lambert.[69]

As satisfying as it was to reflect upon Haiti's history and her heroes, black Americans experienced a much deeper sense of identification with the black history-makers within their own shores. However much they might hail the achievements of blacks of other countries and of earlier times, they found their most acceptable historic role models in the United States, the land of their more recent forefathers. This sense of having roots in America was expressed in a resolution that a convention of blacks in Albany addressed to the people of New York: "We can trace our ancestry back to those who first pierced the almost impenetrable forest. When the vast and trackless wilderness spread itself before the earliest settlers, our fathers were among those who, with sinewy frame and muscular arm, went forth to humble the wilderness in its native pride."[70]

[65]*The Emancipator*, Feb. 18, 1841. [66]*Frederick Douglass' Paper*, Mar. 2, 1855.
[67]Entry dated Dec. 16, 1857, in Ray Allen Billington, ed., *Journal of Charlotte Forten* (New York, 1953), p. 112.
[68]For the racially historic Christian names of Delany's other children see Dorothy Sterling, *The Making of an Afro-American: Martin Robinson Delany, 1812–1885* (New York, 1971), p. 86.
[69]*Weekly Anglo-African*, Oct. 7, 1859.
[70]*The Emancipator*, Dec. 10, 1840.

Black Americans let it be known that their progenitors had played an important part in levelling the forests, tilling the land, and cultivating the great agricultural staples—tobacco, sugar, rice, and cotton.[71] But it was not on these more orderly phases of the past that blacks placed their major emphasis. They took their greatest pride in the role of their ancestors in the nation's wars. The Peace and Benevolent Society of Afric-Americans, meeting in August 1831 in New Haven, would have the record reveal that their fathers had "fought, bled and died" in defense of the nation.[72] The blood of blacks "has been freely poured out on every battlefield, from the earliest to the latest conflict, in behalf of American liberty and independence," ran a memorial sent by Boston blacks to the state legislature denouncing the Dred Scott decision.[73]

Especially inviting to blacks was a contemplation of the Revolutionary War. This conflict not only had its complement of blacks who had made the supreme sacrifice, but it also had been fought in the name of freedom and equality. Evoking this war and its black arms-bearers was an effective way, thought many black leaders, of reminding their white countrymen of the nation's unkept commitments. Believing that whites were betraying their history by their incomplete and partial reading of it, blacks were prepared to offer instruction.

The tutors included groups and individuals. A meeting of the "Colored Citizens of Cleveland" sent word that during the storms of the Revolutionary War black men, in proportion to their numbers, contributed as much as white men in redeeming the country from despotism.[74] In a memorial drafted in 1855 blacks in Philadelphia informed the state legislature that "the bones of our fathers have whitened every field of the revolution—the blood trickling from their feet crimsoned the snows of Jersey."[75]

Lamenting the fact that "scarcely an inch of the page of history has been appropriated" to the memory of the black arms-bearers of the Revolutionary War, Henry Highland Garnet sought to redress the balance in an address before the American Anti-Slavery Society in 1840. Truth, he predicted, would eventually give these forgotten men "a fair share of the fame that was reaped upon the field of

---

[71]William P. Powell to editor of *Anti-Slavery Standard*, in *Standard*, Aug. 22, 1851.

[72]*The Liberator*, Aug. 13, 1831. [73]Ibid., Feb. 26, 1858.

[74]*The Anti-Slavery Bugle* (Salem, Ohio), July 14, 1849.

[75]*A Memorial to the Honorable Senate and House of Representatives of the Commonwealth of Pennsylvania. By the Colored Citizens of Philadelphia* (Philadelphia, 1854), p. 18.

Lexington and Concord." Truth would affirm that blacks "participated in the immortal hour that adorned the brow of the illustrious Washington."[76] Twenty years later William Wells Brown deemed it necessary to go over the same ground. The Negro's blood, he orated, had mingled with the soil "of every battlefield made glorious by revolutionary reminiscence, and their bones have enriched the most productive lands of the country."[77]

Evocations of the black role in the Revolution were often couched in a tone of accusation, of contrasting the sacrifices of the black patriots with the discriminations visited upon their descendants. "Our fathers fought, bled and died for the Liberties of this country, that we might enjoy equal rights with other Americans," ran a resolution adopted at a meeting of blacks in Buffalo in 1841.[78] Runaway slave Lewis Clarke said that his father, a Revolutionary War soldier, fought under the illusion "that *he* was to have a share in the freedom as well as the white folks."[79] In a Fourth of July speech in 1830 Peter Williams, rector of St. Phillip's Church in New York, permitted himself a rare burst of bitterness in referring to blacks in the Revolution: "We are natives of this country; we ask only to be treated as well as foreigners. Not a few of our fathers suffered and bled to purchase its independence; we ask only to be treated as well as those who fought against it."[80]

To their recall of the Revolution some blacks inserted a family touch. On trial in 1859 for having assisted a runaway slave, Charles H. Langston, in an impassioned address before a crowded Cleveland courtroom, alluded to his father's services as a revolutionary soldier in Lafayette's command, adding "that he fought for my freedom as much as his own."[81] On the grounds that his grandmother, Elizabeth Barjona, was "a heroine of the Revolution," having served as "a cook to the Continental Congress," William P. Powell petitioned the New York legislature to appropriate funds to help him and his wife and seven children to migrate to England.[82]

If an individual black honored a family forebear of the Revolution, the single figure most revered by blacks collectively was mulatto Crispus Attucks, a runaway slave. Attucks had not been a participant in the war. He was, however, one of the five who fell at the Boston Massacre on March 5, 1770, and hence became a

---

[76]*Anti-Slavery Standard*, June 11, 1840.   [77]*The Liberator*, Oct. 26, 1860.
[78]*The Colored American*, Jan. 9, 1841.
[79]*Anti-Slavery Standard*, Oct. 20, 1842.
[80]Williams in Porter, ed., *Early Negro Writing*, p. 297.
[81]*Weekly Anglo-African*, July 23, 1859.
[82]*Anti-Slavery Standard*, July 17, 1851.

martyr figure. Of the score or more of revolutionary blacks whose exploits would be recited by succeeding generations of blacks, his was the foremost by far.

"Who was the first martyr in your revolutionary war?" asked Robert Purvis at a meeting of the American Anti-Slavery Society. Purvis answered his own rhetorical question: "Crispus Attucks a Negro. It was a black man's blood that was the first to flow in behalf of American Independence."[83] In a petition seeking the ballot for blacks in Ohio, John Mercer Langston informed the state legislature that the first revolutionary martyr, one who "died on the plains of Boston," was a Negro.[84] In somewhat sweeping terms Martin R. Delany described Attucks as "the first who headed, the first who commanded, the first who charged, who struck the first blow, and the first whose blood was spilt on the altar of American Liberty."[85]

At a convention of New England blacks meeting at Boston's Tremont Temple, "a stone's throw from the spot where fell the colored man, Crispus Attucks," the delegates vowed to do their part "in obtaining for ourself and our posterity the full measure of blessings and rights which his love of liberty and martyr death should long since have secured."[86] In jail at Charlestown, Virginia, awaiting execution for complicity in the John Brown raid at Harpers Ferry in October 1859, John A. Copeland took comfort in Attucks. During America's fight for freedom "the blood of black men flowed as freely as that of white men," wrote young Copeland. "Yes, the *very first* blood that was spilt was that of a Negro... the blood of that heroic man (though black he was), Cyrus Attuck [*sic*]." Copeland added that some of the last blood shed in the Revolution was also that of blacks, a fact that history, "although prejudiced, is compelled to attest."[87]

The task of forcing history to do right by Revolutionary War blacks was undertaken by William C. Nell of Boston, a copyist and accountant with some experience in journalism. Nell's efforts to bridge the gap in historical knowledge had been spurred by an article written by the poet John Greenleaf Whittier, a friend and co-worker in the abolitionist crusade. "Of the services and suffer-

[83]*The Liberator*, May 18, 1860.
[84]*Frederick Douglass' Paper*, June 16, 1854.
[85]Martin Delany, *The Condition... of the Colored People* (New York, 1968), p. 69.
[86]*Weekly Anglo-African*, Aug. 6, 1859.
[87]Copeland to his brother, Dec. 10, 1859, in Robert S. Fletcher, 'John Brown and Oberlin,' *The Oberlin Alumni Magazine* (Feb. 1932), p. 137.

ings of the colored soldiers of the Revolution, no attempt has, to our knowledge, been made to preserve a record," wrote Whittier in 1847. "They have had no historian."[88]

Aspiring to fill this role, Nell in 1851 brought out a twenty-three-page pamphlet, *Services of Colored Americans in the Wars of 1776 and 1812*. In subsequent reprintings Nell expanded this work, culminating in 1855 with a 396-page volume, *The Colored Patriots of the American Revolution, with Sketches of Several Distinguished Colored Persons: To Which Is Added a Brief Survey of the Condition and Prospects of Colored Americans*. This latter work was the high-water mark in antebellum black historical literature.

Although anecdotal in tone and thin and sketchy in content, Nell's data were generally reliable (although he did make the mistake, repeated later by others, of attributing a Negro identity to Deborah Gannett, who had served as a soldier in the Revolutionary War by passing herself off as a man). The bulk of Nell's information was documented, some of it derived from personal interviews and visits to cemeteries. At abolitionist meetings he placed on exhibit some of the objects and materials he had collected, including honorable discharge papers to black soldiers, and army flags and banners of companies in which blacks had served.

Although Nell was disappointed in the number of blacks who bought his book, he could find no fault with the expressions of praise by those who did. "A copy ought to be in the hands of every colored man," editorialized Frederick Douglass.[89] Meeting in Columbus in January 1853 the Ohio State Convention of Colored Freemen recommended the work to the people of the state, white and black.[90] Echoing cries of commendation came from Nell's white co-workers in the abolitionist crusade. Wendell Phillips applauded the book, adding that as good as it was it had not told half the story.[91] John Greenleaf Whittier, in a letter to Nell, said that *Colored Patriots* had strengthened his conviction that blacks would eventually obtain the honor they deserved "in spite of all the falsehoods and omissions of historians writing with the fear of 'Massa' before their eyes."[92]

Theodore Parker appraised *Colored Patriots* as "quite a valuable book" in a letter to George Bancroft, the historian. Parker's lengthy

[88]Whittier, 'The Black Men of the Revolution and the War of 1812,' *National Era* (Washington), July 22, 1847.
[89]*Frederick Douglass' Paper*, Dec. 3, 1852.
[90]*Aliened American* (Cleveland, Ohio), Apr. 5, 1853.
[91]*The Liberator*, Mar. 12, 1858.
[92]Whittier to Nell, Jan. 29, 1858, in *Liberator*, Mar. 12, 1858.

letter touched upon several of the blacks who served in the Battle of Bunker Hill, informing Bancroft that his data came not only from Nell's book but also from a personal request for additional detail. Parker's letter ended with a request: "When you publish your volume I wish you would send Nell a copy. Negroes get few honors."[93]

To Nell, too, went the credit for enhancing the fame of Crispus Attucks. Nell headed the committee of seven Boston blacks who in 1851 urged the Massachusetts legislature to appropriate $1,500 for a monument in memory of Attucks. When the request was turned down, an embittered Nell pointed out that the same legislature had approved a similar request for a memorial to Isaac Davis. "Both promoters of the American Revolution," wrote Nell, "but one was white, the other was *black.*"[94]

The events of the crisis-laden 1850s enabled Nell to keep alive the memory of Attucks. In response to the Dred Scott decision of 1857, Nell initiated Crispus Attucks Day. Appropriately enough the first of these annual observances, held on March 5, 1858, was held in Faneuil Hall, the building from which Attucks had been buried. On display for the occasion were a number of Revolutionary War relics, including a small cup allegedly owned by Attucks and a picture of Washington crossing the Delaware in which black Prince Whipple was seen pulling the stroke oar.

With Nell in the chair, the speakers included such abolitionist stalwarts as Garrison, Phillips, Theodore Parker, Charles Lenox Remond, and John S. Rock. The audience was treated to original songs, one of them by Charlotte Forten and another by Frances Ellen Watkins, whose literary gifts were already in bloom. Numbered among the singing groups was the Attucks Glee Club, a youthful quintet.[95] In similar fashion Fifth of March commemorations would be held at the same site in 1859 and 1860, the latter taking due note of a martyr more recent, John Brown.

To antebellum blacks bent on rescuing their past the War of 1812 offered no single figure comparable to Attucks. This did not mean, however, that the black role in that war was unworthy of mention.

[93]Parker to Bancroft, Mar. 16, 1858, in John Weiss, ed., *Life and Correspondence of Theodore Parker*, 2 vols. in 1 (New York, 1869), vol. 2, p. 234. The forthcoming volume to which Parker referred was volume 7 of Bancroft's *History of the United States from the Discovery of the American Continent*. Published in Boston in 1858, this volume did mention the presence of blacks at the Battle of Bunker Hill, June 17, 1775 (p. 421).
[94]Nell, *Colored Patriots of the American Revolution* (Boston, 1855), p. 18.
[95]*The Liberator*, Mar. 12, 1858.

Indeed, according to their chroniclers, the blacks had played a role, however passive, in causing the United States to declare war against England. The war, wrote Nell, "was undertaken because of the impressment of three seamen, two of whom were colored."[96]

As reported by these latter-day remembrancers, blacks acquitted themselves well, whether on the home front or in battle. "In the War of 1812 what class of inhabitants showed themselves more loyal and patriotic than the free people of color? None, sir," lectured Robert Purvis at a Cooper Union gathering.[97] Not to be forgotten was the gallantry of the blacks in Capt. Oliver Hazard Perry's notable victory at the Battle of Lake Erie, a major naval engagement. "The splendid naval achievements on Lakes Erie and Champlain were owing mostly to the skill and prowess of colored men," ran an address issued by New York blacks. Perry's fame was gained at the expense of their "mangled bodies and bleeding veins."[98]

Out of the War of 1812 came the two most widely quoted documents in antebellum black historiography—the proclamations issued by Gen. Andrew Jackson to the blacks in Louisiana prior to the Battle of New Orleans. On September 21, 1814, nearly four months before the battle, Jackson issued a proclamation addressed "To the Free Colored Population of Louisiana," although he had in mind two black regiments that had a long and distinguished military record, including service in the Revolutionary War. Calling them "sons of freedom," Jackson summoned them "to rally round the standard of the Eagle, to defend all which is dear in existence." Jackson assured them that in "pursuing the path of glory" they would be acclaimed by their countrymen.[99]

Nearly three months later, on December 18, following a review of the black troops, Jackson issued a second proclamation. He told them that although he had expected much of them they had exceeded his expectations. The president, James Madison, would be told of their praiseworthy conduct. Jackson's proclamation concluded with a word of assurance. Our brave citizens are united, it said. "Their only dispute is, who shall win the prize of valor, or who the most glory, the noblest reward."[100] On January 21, 1815, nearly two weeks after the crucial Battle of New Orleans, Jackson issued an order thanking and complimenting the two corps of col-

[96]*Anglo-African Magazine* (New York), Jan. 1859, p. 30.
[97]*The Liberator*, May 18, 1860.
[98]"Address of the Convention of the Citizens of Color at Albany, August, 1840, to the People of the State of New York," in *The Emancipator*, Dec. 10, 1840.
[99]*Niles' Weekly Register* (Baltimore), Dec. 3, 1814, p. 205.
[100]Ibid., Jan. 28, 1815, p. 346.

ored volunteers for their courage and perseverance and praising their commanding officers. It was, however, the first two prebattle pronouncements, with their more stirring and exhortatory phrases, that antebellum black spokesmen would keep in circulation.

Portions of Jackson's proclamations were often forthcoming at national Negro conventions, whether in gracing a speech, adorning a resolution, or in lending weight to an address directed to fellow blacks or to the public at large.[101] A reference to the Jackson proclamations, or an excerpt from them, was part of the repertoire of black orators like Hosea Easton and William J. Watkins, part of the schooling of black journalists like Nell and Douglass, and part of the literary background of authors such as Samuel Ringgold Ward and Martin R. Delany. In his reference to the proclamations, which his book carried in full, Delany appended a note commonly struck by its other publicists. It was, he wrote, "a moral homicide— an assassination" to deny equal rights to men, and to their descendants, who were capable of such deeds as were acknowledged in the edicts of General Jackson.[102]

Not confining their attention exclusively to those who took part in America's wars, history-minded antebellum blacks added the names of some half-dozen individual rebels and radicals along with a like quota of achievers in the more peaceful arts. Among blacks the most revered name in the Valhalla of the rebels was that of Nat Turner, leader of the bloody slave revolt in Southampton County, Virginia, in 1831. At the time of the Turner outbreak black spokesmen did not believe that revolutionary violence was a prerogative open to them. But with the mounting dissension between the North and the South in the 1840s and 1850s black leaders began to reassess the possibilities of militant direct action against slavery, and hence to look afresh at Nat Turner.

Foremost among the black leaders invoking the memory of Turner was the clergyman Henry Highland Garnet. At a political party convention in Boston in 1842 he referred to the Southampton outbreak as an occasion "when the colored man rose and asserted his rights to liberty and humanity."[103] A year later, at the Negro national convention held in Buffalo, Garnet characterized "the patriotic Nathaniel Turner" as one whom future generations would

[101]The national conventions of 1833 and 1853 carried both proclamations in full. *Minutes and Proceedings of the Third Annual Convention of the Free People of Colour... 1833* (Philadelphia, 1833), pp. 21–23. *Proceedings of the Colored National Convention, Held in Rochester... 1853* (Rochester, 1853), pp. 15–16.

[102]Delany, *The Condition... of the Colored People*, p. 78.

[103]*Emancipator and Free American* (Boston), Mar. 4, 1842.

remember for his nobility and bravery. At the conclusion of this ninety-minute "Address to the Slaves of the United States," the convention, according to the official report, "was literally infused with tears."[104] Turner loved liberty more than he feared death, explained William Wells Brown, and he knew that his cause was just. He did not wish to kill; he only sought freedom.[105]

After the hanging of John Brown on December 2, 1859, blacks inevitably linked his name with that of Turner. At the Attucks Day observance in 1860 John S. Rock expressed the opinion that the only events in American history that should be commemorated were "the organization of the Anti-Slavery Society and the insurrections of Nat Turner and John Brown."[106] *The Anglo-African Magazine* for December 1859 carried a detailed comparison of the two insurrectionists, its analysis preceded by a reprint of "The Confessions of Nat Turner," an interview given by the jailed leader as he awaited his sentence. In black circles the remembering of Nat Turner was sometimes accompanied by a reference to Denmark Vesey, who was hanged in Charleston, South Carolina, in 1822 for conspiring to overthrow slavery by armed revolt.

Not likely to be forgotten were those who struck for freedom while on the high seas. These included Madison Washington, who in 1841 led a revolt of 130 slaves aboard the *Creole*, en route from Richmond to New Orleans. The brig was steered to Nassau, where the British authorities let the slaves go free. People in bondage should follow "the glorious example of Madison Washington," ran a resolution adopted on October 1, 1850, at a mass meeting of New York blacks ("with a slight and visible sprinkling of white abolitionists") protesting the Fugitive Slave Law of 1850.[107] In a four-installment article in his weekly, Frederick Douglass ran an account of the exploit, entitling it "The Heroic Slave."[108]

Washington's seizure of a slave ship was outmatched, in drama as in public attention, by the revolt of fifty-four Africans aboard the *Amistad* in 1839. Led by Joseph Cinque, son of an African king, the slaves took control of the vessel off the coast of Cuba and attempted to navigate it back to their African homelands. The *Amistad*, however, wound up in a Connecticut port, and for two years

---

[104] *Minutes of the National Convention of Colored Citizens Held at Buffalo...* *1843* (New York, 1843), p. 13.
[105] *The Narrative of William Wells Brown, a Fugitive Slave*, 2d ed. (Boston, 1848), p. 55.
[106] *The Liberator*, Mar. 5, 1860.
[107] *Anti-Slavery Standard*, Oct. 10, 1850.
[108] *Frederick Douglass' Paper*, Mar. 4, 11, 18, 25, 1853.

the case of the imprisoned Africans was before the courts. It aroused great interest in abolitionist circles, and particularly among blacks. *The Colored American* carried accounts of the court actions and the lot of the prisoners and urged its readers to make cash contributions to help them.[109] Blacks shared in the joy of Cinque and his followers when, in March 1841, the Supreme Court ordered that they be freed.

In their hall of fame some blacks would enshrine those militants and resisters whose brave actions had received little or no public attention. Nominees in this unsung hero category came from Frederick Douglass and George T. Downing, a Newport, Rhode Island, caterer. Named by both was Margaret Garner, a runaway slave who killed one of her children and severely wounded two others to prevent them from being recaptured by the pursuing slave-catchers. Garner should "be honored as a benefactress," wrote Douglass.[110] Echoing this judgment, Downing would also endow the historical record with an even more obscure figure—a nameless Tennessee slave who was put to death after 700 lashes and his refusal to give the names of his co-conspirators in a plot to escape.[111]

Of a different stripe, but clearly falling within the domain of history-makers as interpreted by antebellum blacks, were those Afro-Americans who had been achievers in the more peaceful pursuits. Although not as highly revered as those whose fame had been won in the martial arts, they too were to be counted among the black vanguard. They included two eighteenth-century blacks of diverse talents, the poet Phillis Wheatley and the scientist Benjamin Banneker.

The second woman in British America to bring out a volume of poetry, Africa-born Phillis Wheatley won attention on both sides of the Atlantic in her day, her work, *Poems on Various Subjects, Religious and Moral,* going into five editions before 1800. Antebellum blacks would see to it that her name would not be forgotten. Addressing the New York African Society for Mutual Relief, William Hamilton praised her for having "some original ideas that would not disgrace the pen of the best of poets."[112] Her poems could be found in black periodicals, three such products appearing

---

[109]*The Colored American*, Nov. 28, 1840; Jan. 2, 1841.

[110]*Two Speeches by Frederick Douglass; one on West India Emancipation...,* *and the Other on the Dred Scott Decision* (Rochester, 1857), p. 22.

[111]Downing to Nell, Mar. 3, 1860, in *The Liberator*, Mar. 16, 1860.

[112]Hamilton, *An Address to the New York African Society for Mutual Relief, Delivered in the Universalist Church, Jan. 2, 1809* (New York, 1809), in Foner, ed., *Voice of Black America*, p. 35.

in *Frederick Douglass' Paper* for August 31, 1855. William G. Allen published five of her poems in his booklet *Wheatley, Banneker, and Horton.*[113] (George Moses Horton, like Wheatley at one time, was a slave poet.) Black publications also reproduced the letter sent to her by George Washington, dated February 28, 1776, speaking highly of her poetic talents, and inviting her to visit him if ever she happened to be near his Cambridge headquarters.[114] Upon reading Wheatley's volume of verse Charlotte Forten pronounced her a "wonderfully gifted woman," one whose character and genius afforded a telling refutation "that hers is an inferior race."[115]

Born in Maryland but not a slave, Benjamin Banneker was America's first black scientist of note. By 1791, when he sent a copy of one of his annual almanacs to Thomas Jefferson, he had a reputation as a mathematician and an astronomer. Seeking to keep his memory alive, antebellum blacks named literary societies after him, and black speakers recited his story in lectures on racial self-reliance and self-help.[116] Banneker had an especial appeal for black orators and writers because, as William G. Allen expressed it, "he excelled in the department of the intellect to which the colored man has usually been regarded as being illy adapted."[117]

Antebellum blacks would occasionally refer to contemporary well-known Europeans whose ancestry was partly black. Of these the most often mentioned was Alexandre Dumas, père, novelist and playwright, his father a French general, his mother a Negro. It was with the latter in mind that H. Ford Douglass numbered Dumas in the company of those who under adverse circumstances had elevated themselves "to the highest point of moral and intellectual greatness."[118] *The Anglo-African Magazine* was distressed with the editors of *Appleton's Encyclopedia* because they could "not find room" for Dumas in their 1856 edition.[119]

In summary, the history propounded by antebellum blacks was open to question in its documentation and tone. Their concept of history strong on the theoretically inferable, these black chroniclers

---

[113] William G. Allen, *Wheatley, Banneker, and Horton* (Boston, 1849), pp. 21–27.

[114] Delany, *The Condition . . . of the Colored People*, p. 71.

[115] Forten's diary, July 28, 1854, in Billington, ed., *Journal of Charlotte Forten*, p. 55.

[116] See, for example, William Still's glowing reference to Banneker in his lecture "Self-Improvement," delivered to the students of the Colored Evening School in Philadelphia on Mar. 2, 1860, in *Weekly Anglo-African*, Mar. 17, 1860.

[117] Allen, *Wheatley, Banneker, and Horton*, p. 7.

[118] *Anti-Slavery Bugle*, Aug. 31, 1850.

[119] *Anglo-African Magazine* (Jan. 1859), pp. 4–5.

did not, in general, deem it necessary to furnish their sources. Such a cavalier attitude toward documentation inevitably led to some unsupportable claims. In addition these black writers and speakers reflected the spread-eagle period in which they lived, with bombastic language the vogue. Chroniclers of the black past shared in this widespread penchant for overstatement, especially since they viewed Afro-American history as a form of shock therapy for whites.

Whatever the shortcomings of writers of black history they did not include an ignorance of the unusually formidable problems involved in such an undertaking. "He who understands well the history of the colored people, and writes it ... will be greater than he who leads an army to victorious battle," wrote William J. Wilson. "We constitute such a medley of incongruities. Such juxtapositions; so paradoxical! Without continuity, yet a life of continuity."[120] To study blacks properly, wrote James McCune Smith, required "an acuteness of vision and a patience in inquiry," along with "a freedom from prejudice, without which all efforts were vain."[121]

The pre–Civil War blacks produced no great historian, no outstanding single volume of history, no significant repository of records. Their communication with the past was imperfect, their soundings somewhat shallow. But if their grasp of history was fragmentary and partial, it was neither lacking in vision nor devoid of a core of essential truth. If faint at the time, black history's antebellum accents had a resonance that would not fade away.

Aware of their limitations, these early chroniclers of the Afro-American experience yet pointed the way for others. In the preface to his pioneer black history James W. C. Pennington caught something of this spirit of looking backward and forward simultaneously, a dual searching so characteristic of a minority group in the complementary quest of a more usable past and a more promising future. "The writer," said Pennington in the opening pages of *A Text Book of the Origin and History of Colored People,* "has attempted to do what he has so long desired to see performed by some abler pen; and so far as he has failed, he hopes yet to see the subject explored, and full justice done to it by someone more competent."[122]

[120]*Frederick Douglass' Paper,* Jan. 4, 1855.   [121]Ibid., Sept. 25, 1851.
[122]Pennington, *Text Book,* p. 3.

8. The Abduction of the *Planter*

O THE CONFEDERATE capital on a spring afternoon in the second year of the war came a one-sentence dispatch addressed to General R. E. Lee: "I have just learned by telegraph that [the] steamer 'Planter,' with five guns aboard, intended for the harbor, was stolen in Charleston this morning." Dated May 13, 1862, from the Savannah headquarters of the Department of South Carolina and Georgia, the terse report concluded with a "Very respectfully," and bore the name of the commanding officer, J. C. Pemberton.

Pemberton's dispatch referred to the "abduction" by a group of slaves of a Confederate vessel, a dramatic deed which made its instigator, Robert Smalls, "an object of interest in Dupont's fleet," as Admiral David D. Porter phrased it. The spectacular escape of Smalls and his party became one of the war's oft-told stories. Requiring careful planning and brilliant execution, the feat in truth was unparalleled in audacity. "I thought," said Smalls, as he delivered the vessel to the Union Navy, "that the 'Planter' might be of some use to Uncle Abe."

A native South Carolinian, Smalls was born in Beaufort in 1839. When he was twelve his master brought him to Charleston, where, after a succession of occupations, he finally became a rigger and began to learn boating and the twisting coastal waters. When the war came, the stockily built young slave was impressed into the Confederate service, and in March 1862, he was made a member of the crew of the *Planter*.

Formerly a cotton steamer plying the Pee Dee River and capable of carrying 1,400 bales, the *Planter* had been chartered by the war government and converted into a transport running from point to point in the Charleston harbor and the neighboring waters. Built of live oak and red cedar, the boat measured 150 feet in length, had a 30-foot beam, a depth of 7 feet 10 inches, and drew 3 feet 9 inches of water. As a Confederate dispatch boat, she mounted two guns for her own use, a 32-pounder pivot gun and a 24-pounder

135

howitzer. Attached to the engineering department at Charleston, the *Planter* carried a crew of eleven, of whom three were whites—captain, mate, and engineer—and the remainder slaves.

By far the ablest of the slave crew was Smalls. Determined to escape, Smalls hit upon the idea of making off with the *Planter*. Wherever the Union Navy extended its blockade along the southern seacoast, freedom-minded Negroes had sensed a new opportunity. By scow, oyster boat, barge, homemade canoe, or anything that would float, they made their way to the Union men-of-war. But no plan of escape was as imaginative and as daring as Small's.

The young wheelsman worked out the details in his mind. The escaping party would number sixteen, of whom half would be women and children, including Smalls's wife and their two young ones. The *Planter* would put out to sea casually, as though making a routine run to reconnoiter. Knowing they could expect little mercy if caught, Smalls bound the party to agree that if they were unable to make good their flight, they would blow up the vessel rather than be taken alive. Smalls's plan embraced one final but essential detail—all three white officers would have to remain ashore for the night. Such an absence would be contrary to standing general orders which stipulated that officers of light draft vessels were to remain "on board day and night" when their boat was docked at the wharf.

Finally came such a night as Smalls waited for—the night of May 12. Coincidentally, on the afternoon of that day, 200 pounds of ammunition and four guns—"a banded rifle 42, one 8-inch columbiad, one 8-inch seacoast howitzer, and one 32-pounder"—had been loaded on the *Planter* for transport to the harbor battery, Fort Ripley.

With the white officers ashore, Smalls began to put his plan into operation. The sixteen slaves got aboard in the crisp early morning, the women and children being led below deck in pin-drop quiet. Smalls broke into Captain C. J. Relyea's cabin and took the captain's hat. At 3:00 A.M. one of the fugitives struck a match and set the kindlings on fire under the boilers; twenty-five minutes later the hawsers which moored the boat to Southern Wharf were cast off. From the pilothouse Smalls sounded the wharf signal. The shore sentinel at his post some fifty yards distant noticed the ship gliding away but sensed nothing afoot; he "did not think it necessary to stop her, presuming that she was but pursuing her usual business," in the language of an official report issued later that day.

Now to run the many fortifications in the harbor. Bristling with sea defenses, the defiant city was ringed with forts and batteries on constant alert. But for the runaway slaves there was no turning back. Hoisting the ship's two flags, Confederate and Palmetto, Smalls eased into the inner channel. He geared the *Planter* to its customary pace, although not to dash at full speed required the utmost self-control.

The critical minutes of the great deception had arrived. Wearing the captain's hat and mimicking his gait, Smalls stood in the pilothouse with the cord in his hand. As the vessel passed Fort Johnson, he pulled the lanyard on the steam whistle and gave the proper salute. All went well.

Finally the abductors approached the last hurdle, historic Fort Sumter. Thirteen months ago it was here that the opening shots of the war had been fired, and at the identical morning hour. One of the four transport guns on the *Planter* belonged originally, as Smalls well knew, to Fort Sumter, having been struck on the muzzle during the bombardment of that bastion and now having been repaired because of the Confederacy's scarcity of heavy guns.

Abreast of Sumter, Smalls sounded the private signal, three shrill whistles followed by a hissing one. "The sentinel on the parapet called for the corporal of the guard and reported the guard-boat going out," stated the official report of Major Alfred Rhett. In turn, the corporal of the guard relayed the intelligence to the officer of the day, Captain David G. Fleming. The information had been passed along in routine fashion since it was, in Major Rhett's words, "by no means unusual for the guard-boat to run out at that hour." Then came the fateful order to permit the halted vessel to go on her way; by signal Sumter answered, "All right." The *Planter* had been taken for the guard boat and hence allowed to pass!

The slave-manned steamer moved in a southeasterly direction and entered the main ship channel, maintaining her leisurely pace until she had outdistanced the line of fire of the Confederate battery. Then she got up steam, lowered her guns, and ran up a white flag.

Not a minute too soon was the flag of truce hoisted. Off Charleston was a Union blockading fleet of ten warships, and the *Planter* had been spied by the lookout on the inside ship, *Onward*. The commander, J. F. Nickels, had ordered his ship swung around so as to train the maximum gunfire on the approaching craft. Just as the *Onward* succeeded in bringing her port guns to bear on the oncoming steamer, Commander Nickels caught sight of the white flag. The gunners relaxed.

Unmolested, the harbor boat drew up alongside the armed sailing vessel. A prize crew boarded the *Planter* and greeted its crew. Down came the white flag, and up went the American ensign. Then and there in the outer harbor the ownership of the captive boat was transferred from the Confederate States of America to the Union Navy.

Later that morning the senior officer commanding the blockading squadron off Charleston, E. G. Parrot, taking advantage of the good weather, ordered the prize crew to take the *Planter* and its captors to Port Royal, and there to report the incident to Flag Officer S. F. Du Pont. No order could have pleased Smalls and his companions more, most of them having originally come from the Sea Island region.

The *Planter* made the sixty-mile trip to Port Royal by way of St. Helena Sound and Broad River, reaching her destination shortly after ten in the evening. Word awaited Smalls that he was to report directly to Du Pont, and the next morning he was ushered aboard the flagship *Wabash*. There the elderly admiral, "that stately and courteous potentate, elegant as one's ideal French marquis," listened attentively as the ex-slave told his story.

Later that day, in a lengthy report to the Secretary of the Navy, Du Pont summed up the exploit: "The bringing out of this steamer, under all the circumstances, would have done credit to anyone." The admiral also jotted down another conclusion: "This man, Robert Smalls, is superior to any who have yet come into the lines, intelligent as many of them have been."

Back in Charleston the news was received with consternation not unmingled with disbelief. In a front-page story devoted to the "extraordinary occurrence," the *Courier* reported that "our community was intensely agitated Tuesday morning by the intelligence that the steamer 'Planter' . . . had been taken possession of by her colored crew, steamed up and boldly ran [*sic*] out to the blockaders." Added the daily, "The news was not at first credited." Another Charleston newspaper, the *Mercury,* concluded its descriptive story of the escape by explaining that "the run to Morris Island goes out a long way past the fort, and then turns. The 'Planter' did not turn."

Voicing the general indignation of Confederate South Carolina over the negligence of the white officers of the boat, the *Columbia Guardian* expressed a fervent wish that the "recreant parties will be brought to speedy justice, and the prompt penalty of the halter rigorously enforced." From army headquarters in Richmond came a dispatch to General Pemberton stating that General Lee had received the papers relative to the *Planter*'s escape and that "he very much regrets the circumstances, and hopes that necessary measures will be taken to prevent any repetition of a like misfortune."

News of Smalls's feat quickly spread throughout the North, and public sentiment became strong for awarding prize money to the *Planter*'s crew. Congress responded, moving with unusual speed. Two weeks from the day of the seizure, that body passed a bill ordering the Secretary of the Navy to have the vessel appraised and "when the value thereof shall be thus ascertained to cause an equitable apportionment of one-half of such value . . . to be made between Robert Smalls and his associates who assisted in rescuing her from the enemies of the Government." Within another week Lincoln had signed the bill.

Smalls turned out to be right in believing that the *Planter* might be of some use to the North. Admirably suited to the shallow waters of the Sea Island region, she was immediately equipped with musket-proof bulwarks and converted into a navy transport, carrying upwards of seventy men. Exactly one month after the abduction, Admiral Du Pont, in acknowledging two letters from naval officer A. C. Rhind, wrote that he was "glad that the 'Planter' has proved so useful a transport, and that we have again been able so materially to aid the army, especially at a critical time, when its generals were almost helpless for want of transports."

Early in September 1862, the *Planter* was sold to the army, which could make much better use of a wood-burner than could the sister service. The quartermaster's department welcomed the addition, "as we have comparatively no vessels of light draft." Until she was decommissioned and sold at Baltimore in September 1866, the *Planter* remained in military service, being used mainly as a troop transport, but seeing occasional service as a supply boat.

During most of its period of use by the armed forces, the *Planter* was piloted or commanded by Smalls. Over the four months the boat remained under navy supervision, the young Negro was employed as pilot. During the year 1863 and for the first two months in 1864, the army employed him in a like capacity, paying him $50 a month until September 30, 1863, then $75 a month from October 1 to November 30, 1863, and thenceforth $150 a month. On March 1, 1864, he was made captain.

The pilot was promoted to master as a reward for bravery under fire (before the war was over, Smalls had fought in seventeen engagements), but the appointment was merited on other grounds. For the fugitive slave brought much with him. His knowledge of the coastline of South Carolina and Georgia was intimate; few men were more familiar with the sinuous windings of those waters, and no hand was more skilled in their navigation. Indeed, "the accession of Smalls is deemed of more importance than the heavy guns of the 'Planter,' " wrote a reporter for the *Philadelphia Inquirer* (May 17, 1862), "as Smalls is thoroughly acquainted with all the intricacies of navigation in that region." Smalls also brought a knowledge of where the torpedoes had been planted to destroy the Union gunboats and where the masked batteries were located.

The intelligence he furnished was so valuable that the Secretary of the Navy, in his annual report to President Lincoln, made it a point to describe them:

From information derived chiefly from the contraband Pilot, Robert Smalls, who has escaped from Charleston, Flag Officer Du Pont, after proper reconnaissance, directed Commander Marchand to cross the bar with several gun-boats and occupy Stono. The river was occupied as far as Legarville, and examinations extended further to ascertain the position of the enemy's batteries. The seizure of Stono Inlet and river secured an important base for military operations, and was virtually a turning of the forces in the Charleston harbor.

At the war's end Smalls was among the thousands who witnessed the reraising of the American flag at Fort Sumter. This event had been scheduled for April 14, four years to the day after the one on which the Union forces had been forced to haul down the colors. Present at the flag-raising ceremonies was a distinguished roster of reformers and public notables, including William Lloyd Garrison, Judge Advocate General Joseph Holt, Supreme Court Justice N. H. Swayne, Senator Henry Wilson, and the chief speaker, Henry Ward Beecher. On hand also was Robert Anderson, brought back to Sumter to raise the very shot-pierced flag which the Southerners had forced him to lower four years previously. But perhaps the most symbolic figure present was Captain Robert Smalls, who that morning had left Charleston, Sumter bound, at the helm of the *Planter* profusely decorated with the Stars and Stripes and loaded down with hundreds "of the emancipated race."

After the war Smalls had fifty years to live, many of them spent in the public eye—as a member of the South Carolina legislature, a five-term United States Congressman, and Collector of the Port at Beaufort. But no moment of his eventful life could ever match that memorable dawn when he abducted the *Planter*.

Blacks in the Twentieth Century

9. The Morning Breaks: Black America, 1910–1935

I N BRINGING to a close his eloquent John Brown's Day address at Harpers Ferry on a mid-August afternoon in 1906, W.E.B. Du Bois expressed his faith in the future. "The morning breaks," he said, "and all across the skies sit signs of progress."

Looking backward at the notable career of Du Bois we know that he had the gift of social prophecy. At the time he delivered this eulogy to the memory of the martyred John Brown, however, the outlook for the Negro was particularly bleak. But just as "each age is a dream that is dying, or one that is coming to birth," the quarter of a century during which Du Bois edited *The Crisis*, 1910–34, would prove to have been a new day aborning. When that era opened the Negro's cause seemed almost hopeless; when the era ended there was a different story. Then the signs of progress that Du Bois had discerned had come to pass.

These signs were faint, however, when the new century began. To blacks the opening two decades of the 1900s seemed to have brought a rise in the level of white hostility. Jim Crow seemed more securely enthroned than ever, with residential segregation more widespread, and with the Supreme Court in 1908 upholding a Kentucky law which forbade interracial schools. The early years of the Woodrow Wilson presidency, beginning in 1913, witnessed the establishment of the color line in various departments of the federal government. The civil service began to require photographs of persons taking job examinations, a practice which lent itself to racial discrimination.

The widely prevalent idea of white superiority and black inferiority was starkly and vividly portrayed in the motion picture *Birth of a Nation*. Written in part and directed by D. W. Griffith, son of a Confederate soldier, and its scene the South just after the Civil War, the film depicted blacks in the worst possible light. They were pictured as ignorant, brutal, unprincipled, and with black males ridden by a consuming lust for white women. Despite spirited opposition by blacks and by white liberals, the film drew large crowds, in part because in technical brilliance "it was the nearest to fine art that the cinema had achieved" up to that time.

Birth of a Nation glorified the Ku Klux Klan of Reconstruction times and the year in which the film appeared, 1915, marked the birth of the new Ku Klux Klan. While extending its enemies list to include Catholics, Jews and foreigners, the reborn Klan retained the organization's historic concept of the black people as the nation's number one problem child and threat.

Like its predecessor the new Klan did not shun the use of violence. By no means, however, was the deeply rooted, historic pattern of interracial violence confined to the Klan, old Klan or new. Indeed the first major racial outbreak of the new century took place in 1906, nine years before the Klan's rebirth. This was the five-day riot which began in Atlanta on September 22 and which resulted in at least eleven deaths. "Atlanta Slays Black Citizens," ran a headline in the black weekly *New York Age*. This outbreak had been brought about in part by newspaper editors like the aristocratic John Temple Graves, whose *Atlanta Georgian* repeatedly proclaimed that the ultimate solution to the race problem was the deportation of all Negroes to Africa.

With the mass out-migration of southern Negroes during the World War I period, the pattern of race riots cut across geographic lines. The northern industrial cities to which the migrants had come now became the major centers of black-white strife, a long-simmering development which reached its boiling point in 1919. This bloodletting "red" summer witnessed more than twenty race riots, the worst of them breaking out in Chicago, where the dead numbered thirty-eight and the wounded ran to a total of 537.

During the same somber year, 1919, the number of blacks who were lynched rose to seventy-six, the highest in the decade. During the previous ten-year period, 1900–1910, there were 754 black lynchings, out of a total of 846.

The migration of blacks out of the South, one of the factors in the mounting racial tensions in the North, was not something new in black life. In 1879 Benjamin "Pap" Singleton, a Tennessee-born former slave, had led a campaign urging southern blacks to pack up their belongings and make their way to the Midwest. The black migrations of the early twentieth century, however, reached flood proportions undreamed of by the "exodusters" of Singleton's day.

The one million blacks in the North in 1910 had grown to a million and a half by 1920 and to two and a half million by 1930.

As the black newcomers from the South soon found out, however, the problem of racial discrimination was national rather than sectional. In the North, where the twin fears of social equality and black domination aroused less apprehension than in the rural South, the etiquette of Jim Crow was more relaxed. Wherever located, however, black Americans as a class bore the common marks of economic deprivation, political impotence and social stigma.

The black response to the mounting wave of anti-Negro sentiment took its basic form in 1910. Growing impatient with the gradualist, nonmilitant approach of Booker T. Washington, other black leaders and spokesmen, hitherto overshadowed by him, were in a position to try other methods. More outspoken than the "don't-rock-the-boat" Washington, these newer leaders held that new agencies, manned by new blood, were needed to tackle new problems and to cope with old problems grown worse. Reflecting the mass migrations to the cities, the character of Negro leadership underwent a change, with the spotlight falling mainly on urban-oriented leaders offering urban responses to urban problems.

The two major heralds of the new day in black life and black leadership were the National Association for the Advancement of Colored People and the National Urban League, both founded in New York City and within two years of each other, 1909–1911. The concerns and programs of the two organizations were broad and inclusive, with some inevitable overlap. The NAACP concentrated on civil rights, however, whereas the League's original and primary purpose was social work—the improvement of living conditions and the strengthening of family life.

The most prominent of the black leaders to emerge from the sprouting new organizations of the decade was the redoubtable W.E.B. Du Bois. As editor of The Crisis, a post he would retain for a quarter of a century, he quickly became the country's most articulate and influential black voice. Although The Crisis was the official organ of the NAACP, it was in essence "Du Bois's domain," bearing his stamp in tone and temper. He was an editor-columnist, with the pages of the monthly reflecting his moving and incisive literary style, his grasp of the plight and promise of black life, and his probing and well-stocked mind with its penchant for weighing and sifting a variety of data whether historical, sociological, political or economic.

Varied were the problems facing the new black leaders like Du

Bois and equally varied were their proposed solutions. Their basic response, however, was twofold: joining hands with sympathetic whites and picturing the Negro people as a proved national asset despite a long and continuing pattern of shameful racial discrimination.

The policy of "hands across the color line," of interracial goodwill, had long been practiced by Booker T. Washington. But the leaders after 1910, a different breed of blacks, sought a different type of whites, concentrating on those who were urban reformers, settlement house founders, social workers, and officials in such organizations as the young men's and young women's Christian associations. Whites of wealth and prominence were also welcomed, particularly in the early, struggling days of the new organizations. (William Monroe Trotter, the Harvard-trained militant loner, turned his back on the NAACP because of the prominence of whites in its founding and early operations. But his own organization, the Boston-based National Equal Rights League, had white members, if in small numbers.)

Interracial goodwill organizations were not confined to the North. With its headquarters in Atlanta, the Commission on Interracial Cooperation was founded in 1918, soon extending its operations and affiliates throughout the South. Black-white cooperation in that region took on a variety of forms, including a joint effort in Athens, Georgia, in 1910, to establish an industrial school to honor the memory of the "Old Black Mammies of the South."

This theme of a community of interests between blacks and whites found expression in 1917 with the entry of the United States in World War I. In an editorial, "Close Ranks," in the July 1918 issue of *The Crisis*, Du Bois voiced a sentiment widely shared in black circles: "Let us, while this war lasts, forget our special grievances and close our ranks shoulder to shoulder with our white fellow citizens." In similar vein P. B. Young, editor of the *Norfolk Journal and Guide,* advised blacks that if they "wanted to get something out of the war they would have to put something into it."

Blacks did put something into the war, more than 400,000 bearing arms, 40,000 seeing combat duty, and four of their regiments winning the Croix de Guerre for their bravery. Upon their return to civilian life, having discharged their obligation to "make the world safe for democracy," these black veterans were less likely to put up with racial discriminations in their own country. "We return from fighting," editorialized Du Bois. "We return fighting."

The homefront battle required allies, however, and a small number of blacks turned to such new befrienders as the socialists and the communists. Down to the turn of the century the former had devoted no major effort to woo blacks. But when a significant number of them began to migrate to the cities of the North, the bastions of socialist strength, the attitude of the party toward black membership changed from lukewarm acceptance to active recruitment.

The center of socialist strength was to be found in New York City, home of *The Messenger,* founded in 1917 and bearing the subtitle, "The Only Radical Negro Magazine in America." Its joint editors, A. Philip Randolph and Chandler Owen, were active in Socialist Party politics, Randolph running for state office as a socialist in 1920 and again in 1922. Despite their zeal, Randolph and Owen made few converts in black circles. In addition to their traditional loyalty to the Republicans, most black voters saw little point in supporting third-party candidates having little chance to win.

Like the socialists, the communists were unsuccessful in establishing a mass base among blacks. In capturing black attention, however, the communists overshadowed their rival Marxists. In the 1920s and 1930s they formed a succession of black-oriented organizations, beginning in 1925 with the American Negro Labor Congress, its broad aims including "the general liberation of the darker races," and "the abolition of all discrimination, persecution and exploitation of the Negro race and working people generally."

The communists made it a point to place blacks in conspicuous roles, the party nominating Georgia-born James W. Ford, who had witnessed the lynching of his grandfather, for the vice-presidency of the United States in the campaign of 1932. Later that year, as a demonstration of "the unity of Negro and white workers," the communist-controlled International Labor Defense named William L. Patterson as its national secretary. During the early 1930s the I.L.D. captured the attention of black America by its dramatic and spirited defense of the nine young blacks (the Scottsboro Boys) who were charged with raping two white women while on a freight train in Alabama on March 25, 1931. Despite their many-sided efforts, however, the communists made little sway in recruiting blacks, signing up only 1,300 in 1931 after a vigorous campaign.

The black working class, the special target of the communists, had long been rebuffed by the white labor unions. White workers regarded blacks as scabs and strikebreakers, undermining organized labor. Black-white cooperation on the labor front, however, took a significant turn for the better in the 1920s and 1930s. The great influx of blacks into the cities caused white labor officials to reappraise their attitudes toward recruiting Negro members and toward discriminating against those already in the fold.

The chief single portent of this new breakthrough in organized labor was the work of the Brotherhood of Sleeping Car Porters. Formed in 1925, with A. Philip Randolph as its general organizer, it worked not only to win better conditions for the Pullman porters and maids but also to overcome the hostility of blacks against the labor unions.

In the mid-1930s the Brotherhood won two notable victories— the receipt of an international charter from the American Federation of Labor and recognition by the Pullman Company as the bargaining agent for the porters and maids. "When the Brotherhood wins this fight," wrote Randolph to Du Bois (a staunch supporter) on May 24, 1935, "it will probably be the most significant economic victory the Negro has made in history."

The black leaders of the period, including Du Bois and Randolph, who believed in programs of interracial cooperation also believed that such a policy of working with whites must be accompanied by a campaign of public enlightenment about black people. To win whites to the cause it was necessary to correct the black image in their minds. Beyond an appeal to the conscience of whites, or to their democratic ideals, it was necessary to remove the misconceptions they held about blacks.

Certainly such a campaign of public enlightenment was in order. At the turn of the century the idea of black inferiority was held by whites in all walks of life, including eminent clergymen who evoked the curse of Cain. The notion of the Negro as "being a generous contributor to the common cultural core and a vital force in the formation of American civilization was a new approach to the race question," wrote James Weldon Johnson in 1917.

A new black history soon emerged, sparked by Carter G. Woodson, like Du Bois a scientifically trained historian. In 1915 Woodson founded a national historical society devoted to the black past, and a year later he brought forth the *Journal of Negro History*. Other early exponents of the new Afro-American history included the journalist-researcher J. A. Rogers and the bibliophile Arthur A. Schomburg, the latter pointing out that the Negro must "make history yield for him the same values that the treasured past of any people affords."

Whites were informed that "the gift of black folk" (to borrow

148

the title of a Du Bois book) embraced the broad range of art and music. And in these fields, as in others, a new readiness by black Americans to identify with Africa became apparent, with black artists turning to African motifs and black composers experimenting with African themes and cadences. Blacks also began to call attention to the cultural contributions of the unlettered folk Negro, pointing out that the blues and the spirituals were to be regarded as art forms rather than as manifestations of a culture lag.

White readers of black literature became aware of its steady undercurrent of racial pride. "Let us train ourselves to see beauty in black," wrote Du Bois in 1920. Echoing this swelling theme of racial self-worth, one black editor advised black parents that there was "no better way to start than by purchasing the child a black doll."

The most insistent of the voices proclaiming black pride was that of Marcus Garvey, an advocate of "race first." Coming from Jamaica in 1916 and settling in New York, Garvey would soon become the most widely known of the some 125,000 "African blacks" who entered the United States from 1900 to 1930, and whose viewpoints would not go unheard in Negro circles.

An exponent of "go-it-alone," Garvey did not seek the cooperation of whites. On the contrary, he preached racial separation and a return to Africa. "The Negro must have a country and a nation of his own," he said. Although black Americans had begun to take an increased pride in their African heritage, they were skeptical about Garvey's "Back-to-Africa" program, regarding it as unrealistic.

If Garvey had little success as a black Moses, such was not the case in the other major role he assumed—that of a herald of black pride. In stirring and eloquent language he summoned "blacks back to their blackness." "Up, you mighty race," ran his exhortation, as he held forth in his basic theme that blacks were a good people with a noble heritage. Having a mass following numbering in the millions, Garvey caused any number of blacks, particularly the rank and file, to rid themselves of feelings of inferiority and to take on a new sense of racial dignity and destiny. "He has constrained the Negro to think Negro, and that is a very great achievement," wrote T. Thomas Fortune, editor of *Negro World*, Garvey's weekly.

This deepened spirit of self-worth and new hope marked the Negro of the mid-1930s when Du Bois resigned as editor of *The Crisis*. There was an attitude of expectancy, a result of developments "along the color line" during the preceding twenty-five years. Blacks in 1910 had cooperated with whites in the forming of organizations for advancement and now these organizations had increasingly come under black leadership with whites less prominent at the top levels.

Now in 1935 the black worker was winning a power base in the major federation of organized labor. Now blacks were more conspicuous in political life, following their shift from the Republican Party to the Democratic Party in 1932 and having helped to elect a president who was committed to "a new deal" and to "the forgotten man." Now blacks had become more aware of the myriad ways in which their group had enriched the culture of the United States and they hoped that other Americans would come to share this knowledge before too long.

In bringing all this to pass no single figure loomed larger than W.E.B. Du Bois, and no single periodical was more in the thick of things than *The Crisis*. Du Bois and *The Crisis*, editor and journal— it had been a fruitful union, shaping its own times and influencing the shape of things to come.

10. A. Philip Randolph: Labor Leader at Large

AT THE TIME of his death in 1979, at the age of ninety, A. Philip Randolph had a reputation as the first national labor leader to emerge among black Americans and as a figure of major force in the mid-twentieth century civil rights movement. Randolph had become a dominant figure in black circles in 1937, when the Pullman Company grudgingly gave official recognition to the union that he organized and led, the Brotherhood of Sleeping Car Porters. Randolph's leadership image had been foreshadowed the preceding year, when he had prodded the American Federation of Labor (AFL) to grant an international charter to the Brotherhood, thereby making it equal to the other unions in the federation. From this double-barreled labor base Randolph had not only pressed insistently for further racial reforms in labor and industry but had joined in the battle against color discrimination on a broad-based front, whether in the armed services and the public schools or in government and politics.

Randolph's leadership was characterized by its receptive attitude toward new strategies in combating racial discrimination. In black circles he was a pioneer in the use of mass protest, a trail-blazing technique that he brought into play in the summer of 1941 on the eve of America's entry into World War II. Deeply concerned because black workers were denied an equal share in the newly created jobs in the production of defense and military equipment and supplies, Randolph called for a "March on Washington." Not caring to run the risk of a mass of protesters converging on the nation's capital, President Franklin D. Roosevelt issued an executive order establishing a committee to ensure fair employment practices. A breakthrough in enlisting the support of the federal government in striking at job discrimination, Roosevelt's decree was "the most significant executive action in the field of race relations since President Lincoln issued the Emancipation Proclamation."

151

Randolph's role as a black leader resulted from the pattern of race relations that prevailed during his formative years and, in equal measure, from his own qualities of mind and spirit. Born in 1889 in Crescent City, Florida, his father a struggling African Methodist minister, his mother a hard-working helpmate, Asa Philip Randolph grew up in a family marked by its respect for learning. Working at a variety of unskilled or semiskilled jobs during his teens, Randolph was graduated from the high school at Cookman Institute in Jacksonville.

In 1911, at age twenty-two, he left Florida, coming to New York City, his first and last migration. Taking odd jobs during the day, he attended City College during the evenings, his wide-ranging choice of courses embracing political science, philosophy, economics, and history. During the summer of 1914, Randolph married beautician Lucille Campbell Green, a most compatible union that lasted until her death in 1963.

The wedding of the Randolphs took place a few months after the outbreak of World War I, a development that brought a flood of southern blacks to northern cities like New York. Totaling nearly one-third of a million blacks during the decade 1910 to 1920, these migrations tended to raise the aspirations of urban northern blacks, old inhabitants as well as newcomers, leading them to press for equal rights in general and better job opportunities in particular. It was in the wake of this "northern fever" that swept the South that Randolph would seek his way, in the social and economic ferment of the war years and their aftermath that he would launch his career.

It was inevitable that Randolph would view the black working class as offering the greatest potential for an aspiring leader. Neither of the two existing major black betterment organizations, the National Association for the Advancement of Colored People nor the Urban League, had worked directly with laborers, nor had the black leadership in these organizations come from the working class. Considering the marked influx of blacks in the industrial labor market during World War I, there was much to be done in stimulating a labor consciousness among them, particularly in promoting labor unionism. To Randolph the trade union movement was the major remedy for the ills that beset blacks. In the labor movement lay the power to challenge the oppressors of the people.

Young Randolph's formulations of programs and strategies for blacks was typical of the analytical approach that would characterize his career. Unlike some black leaders, Randolph was not antitheoretical. A wide reader with a meditative turn of mind, he was at home in the world of ideas. Reflecting this somewhat scholarly temperament, his speeches and writings bore a steady note of high seriousness with few light or humorous touches. His rich vocabulary sometimes took on scriptural accents; a word like "verily" would not come unnaturally to one who had been a Bible reader since boyhood.

Randolph's readiness in diagnosis was matched by an equal penchant for prescription. To him theory and application were inseparable; vision must be linked to reality. As he pointed out in 1926, a reformer must go further than calling attention to social evils—he must also "indicate the cause and prescribe a remedy." A born organizer, Randolph would perpetually be trying to form unions of working people and coalitions of reformers to carry out the strategies he had conceived and publicized.

To the tasks he set for himself Randolph brought an array of leadership qualities. To begin with, he was never daunted by the thought of failure, never dismayed by the enormity of the odds against him. His struggle against the Pullman Company pitted him, as a contemporary put it, against "Pullman's millions of dollars when half the time he didn't have a dime in his pocket." According to George S. Schuyler, a staff worker on a monthly edited by Randolph in the 1920s, his employer was a man of unshakable aplomb "whether the rent was due and he did not have it, whether an unexpected donation failed to materialize, or whether the long-suffering printer in Brooklyn was demanding money." Of a silver-lining temperament, Randolph maintained an air of confidence however adverse the circumstances.

Another facet of Randolph's leadership was his integrity, a trait that endowed him with an air of moral authority. He could not be bought or bribed, easy money having no allure for him. His private life was likewise unassailable; a private, nonbusiness letter coming to his office from a woman trying to make his acquaintance would be routinely filed away and forgotten. Scandal-lovers and gossip columnists knew better than to waste their time on him.

Randolph's leadership qualities owed something to his bearing and manner, even though he conveyed more of an air of aloofness than any other twentieth-century black leader, including W. E. B. Du Bois. Never folksy or "down home," Randolph kept his distance. In a tête-à-tête he tended to speak as if addressing a public meeting. A visitor to his office would find, as in the case of Edwin R. Embree, president of the Julius Rosenwald Fund, that although

Randolph kept his eyes on his caller's face, they "seem focussed on far-distant places."

Randolph's formality, however, was mitigated by his innate graciousness and by a courtesy bordering on politeness. After forty years as his close friend and associate, Bayard Rustin said that he had never "once seen Mr. Randolph treat any human being with anything less than complete dignity and respect." Hence if Randolph seemed preoccupied, even remote, in his contacts with others, he certainly did not give them the impression that he looked down on them.

Randolph's leadership, however, did not rest in person-to-person negotiations behind closed doors. His strength rested more in addressing himself to the public. Bent on becoming a leader, he had schooled himself in the forms of public address. His deep bass voice had been trained by his courses in oratory at the College of the City of New York, by his study with a private tutor, and by his membership in Ye Friends of Shakespeare, an amateur group of thespians—when he first came to New York he had thought of becoming a stage actor. During these early years of leadership preparation Randolph acquired the so-called Harvard accent which his followers regarded not as an affectation but as another manifestation of his inherent dignity. And finally as to his image as a public figure, Randolph made an appeal to the eye as well as to the ear. His good looks and well-built physique were put to their best advantage by a carefully selected wardrobe.

Endowed with a combination of leadership qualities and confident he could acquire those he initially lacked, Randolph was ready by 1915 to take his first steps toward the making of a career that, he hoped, would give new meanings to the whole concept of black leadership in action. As it turned out, he did not underestimate himself. His impressive record as a mover and shaker for half a century might be illustrated by reviewing his activities as a socialist, a labor organizer, a proponent of mass action along a united front, a disciple of nonviolent protest, a shaper of black thought, and, however paradoxical it might appear, a consciously black leader whose outlook was not circumscribed by the color line.

Accepting an award at Carnegie Hall in 1944 from the Workers' Defense League, a socialist-oriented group that raised money for the legal defense of union workers, Randolph said that one of the fundamental forces that shaped his life was his study and reading in socialist philosophy and literature and his participation in the socialist movement. To this movement, he added, he owed his understanding of social forces, his awareness of the mission of the working class, and his world perspective.

Randolph's introduction to the tenets of socialism came from his courses at City College in 1912 and 1914 and from his contacts with campus activist groups. By 1917 when the United States entered World War I, Randolph had become a socialist, and his attitude toward this conflict and America's participation in it reflected the standard socialist theory that wars were brought about by the machinations of contending groups of capitalists and hence were of little concern to the workers of the world. After the United States entered the war, Randolph advised blacks to resist the draft and confine their fighting to the home front.

Fortunately for Randolph, his views about the war and on other issues could be expressed not only in personal appearances on tours to northern cities but also through the pages of the *Messenger,* a monthly magazine he edited in partnership with Chandler Owen, another black socialist. The duo worked well together, although Randolph was much the more influential of the two, his the more dominant voice. Moreover, Owen's participation would come to an end in 1923, when he left amicably to begin a new career in Chicago.

The *Messenger* drew much of its financial support from the predominantly white socialist-oriented needle trades and clothing unions, and it, in turn, favorably reported their activities and carried their advertisements. Asserting that blacks had been lulled into a false sense of security by the Booker T. Washington type of leader and by the gradualist approaches of the National Association for the Advancement of Colored People and the National Urban League, the *Messenger* called for a bold, black socialist leadership. Proudly announcing the magazine's radical orientation, its editors defined radicals as those who had the courage of their convictions, who sought "to get at the root of our social problems," in essence, seekers after truth.

Radicalism as interpreted by Randolph and Owen embraced the use of the strongest language and the open advocacy of the most controversial of causes. The *Messenger* did not hesitate to denounce those in the highest places, President Woodrow Wilson among them. In an article summarizing his two terms in the White House up to September 1919 the *Messenger* stated that "the chief beneficiaries of his public career are the combined manufacturers and capitalists and himself." Others, such as liberals, radicals, and Negroes, "would willingly witness the setting of his sun in public without grief. Unhonored, he will go down to the narrow, bigoted grave of private life from whence he sprang."

The *Messenger*'s boldness reached its peak in its support of the new regime in Russia. Coming at a time when the country was in the grip of a "red scare," the *Messenger*'s support of a government run by Communists inevitably drew fire. In a speech in the House of Representatives on August 15, 1919, James F. Byrnes charged that Randolph and Owen were "Bolsheviks." In a lengthy "Reply to Congressman James F. Byrnes of South Carolina," the accused editors stated that "they would be glad to see a Bolshevik government substituted in the South in place of your Bourbon, reactionary, vote-stolen, misrepresentative Democratic regime." Not to be silenced in the matter, the *Messenger*'s December 1919 issue, a so-called Thanksgiving issue, reported that among the things for which it was thankful was "the Russian Revolution, the greatest achievement of the twentieth century."

The prorevolutionary stance of the magazine had not escaped the attention of the Department of Justice, Randolph and Owen falling under its surveillance. While addressing a mass meeting in Cleveland on August 4, 1919, the two black socialists were arrested by an agent of the Department of Justice and spent two days in jail. Three months later the department submitted to the Senate Judiciary Committee a lengthy report dealing with radicalism in general and with due attention to its incidence among blacks. J. Edgar Hoover drafted this report, which characterized the *Messenger* as "the exponent of open defiance and sedition" and as "by long odds the most able and most dangerous of all the Negro publications." Almost half of the section of the report that concentrated on blacks was devoted to a reprinting of articles, editorials, and poems that had appeared in the *Messenger*. Additional censure and condemnation were visited upon the magazine by the New York state legislature through its Joint Committee Investigating Seditious Activities.

Although hailing the violent overthrow of the czarist regime in Russia, Randolph and Owen had in mind a more orderly socialist revolution for the United States. Their method was to unionize the workers and then get them to support the Socialist party. To this end Randolph and Owen formed a short-lived union of blacks who worked in hotels and apartments, the United Brotherhood of Elevator and Switchboard Operators. For a few months in 1917 the duo edited a trade journal published by the Headwaiters and Sidewaiters Society of New York, a monthly that went out of existence a few weeks before the birth of the *Messenger*. In 1919 Randolph and Owen served on the board of directors of the National Brotherhood Workers of America, an umbrella organization that tried to establish a national federation of labor but without success.

Undaunted by this succession of initial failures, Randolph and Owen in 1920 launched the Friends of Negro Freedom, an interracial but black-controlled organization whose overly ambitious program included the organizing of black laborers on an international scale. Almost simultaneously, however, the Randolph-Owen duo diluted the strength of the Friends by creating an overlapping organization, the National Association for the Promotion of Labor Unionism among Negroes. In 1923, after these two groups had become moribund, Randolph and Owen announced the formation of a United Negro Trades. Its objectives—to unionize and upgrade the black workers—were similar to those of its predecessors, and so was its fate.

Supplementing their efforts to unionize blacks, Randolph and Chandler, particularly the former, were active in Socialist party activities. Noting the Republican party's hold on Negroes, the *Messenger* asserted that inasmuch as blacks were workers they had nothing in common with a party dominated by capitalists and employers. "The Negro was a Republican and had been a Republican for fifty years because his father was a Republican and Abraham Lincoln was a Republican. But awake, old black brother Republican." As far as Negroes were concerned there was, said Randolph, no difference between the Republicans and the Democrats because "whichever wins, the people lose."

In 1917 Randolph and Chandler campaigned for the Socialist party candidate for mayor of New York, Morris Hillquit. In 1920, having served his apprenticeship, Randolph was nominated by the Socialists as their candidate for the state comptroller of New York, and two years later the party nominated him for the office of secretary of state of New York. (He would never run for public office again, graciously declining—"because of union duties"—an invitation in 1944 to become the Socialist party candidate for vice-president of the United States.)

For all his dedication to the Socialist cause Randolph could hardly have been surprised that he was able to make few converts among his fellow blacks. He may not have given sufficient weight to the class lines within the black community, but he was well aware of the strength of the Republican party therein. He knew, too, that most blacks and their leaders saw little point in voting for Socialist and other third-party candidates not likely to be elected.

In seeking to win blacks to socialism, however, Randolph tended to give insufficient consideration to certain race-related conditions. Holding that the black people needed allies, Randolph advocated working class solidarity across the line. Randolph himself worked smoothly with white Socialists, never seeking to establish a black wing of the group.

Interracial cooperation and harmony among Socialists, however, were not as simple as they might sound. Most white Socialists regarded race and color as incidental to the larger problem of class conflict. They did not sense that the black American was the victim not only of class oppression but also of race oppression. Hence, they did not think of the Negro question as one that required special approaches and remedies. It did not escape the notice of blacks that some white Socialists were prejudiced against them, and that in deference to its southern wing the party tended to gloss over the disfranchisement and lynching of Negroes in southern states. Hence, although the Socialists began a campaign to woo blacks during the years that Randolph was an active party member, the obstacles against them were formidable, the fruits were few.

Despite the Socialist party's lack of success in recruiting blacks, Randolph found much to be pleased with as a result of their work. The Socialists had, he claimed, succeeded in forcing black organizations to examine anew their programs and their leadership and in forcing the two major political parties to become more liberal in matters of race and color. The *Messenger* had broken new ground in organizing "the Radical Movement among Negroes in America" and in presenting "the Negro workers' question to the European workers, radicals and liberals." In an article published in *Opportunity* in January 1926 touching on Negro radicals, Randolph credited them with having shaped "a working class economic perspective in Negro thought." If any of his readers were ignorant of Randolph's own role in shaping this perspective, they certainly must have surmised it.

But by the time he wrote this article Randolph himself had become much less doctrinaire, having learned that blacks, even among the working masses, would not easily be converted to socialism. By the mid-1920s the *Messenger* had dropped its tone of ridicule as to black business and the black bourgeoisie and had begun to pay more attention to predominantly black issues and programs. During this period Randolph began to channel his energies into the practical and time-consuming work of trade-union organizing, with fewer precious moments to spare in holding forth on socialist theory and reformist doctrine.

The event that signaled Randolph's newer orientation and gave a whole new thrust was a mass meeting held in the Elks auditorium in Harlem on August 25, 1925, at which time Randolph accepted an offer to become the "general organizer" of the Brotherhood of Sleeping Car Porters. A newly formed organization, the Brotherhood sought to induce other porters to join them and to induce the Pullman Company to recognize it as the bargaining agent for the porters.

If the Brotherhood viewed the appointment of Randolph as advantageous, so did he. Its leaders had selected him because he had made a reputation as a forceful and well-informed public speaker; because he was not inexperienced as a labor organizer (although admittedly with little success thus far); and because he was not a porter and thus he was not subject to reprisals by the Pullman Company. Randolph, moreover, was editor of the *Messenger,* which, as he pointed out, "could be used to spread the propaganda of the organization," and which indeed became the Brotherhood's official organ, exchanging its more revolutionary accents for the less exciting tones of a trade journal.

Randolph, in turn, was pleased with the appointment, viewing it as an opportunity to test himself as a leader. Having schooled himself well in the theory of labor reform, he was now ready to tackle a job that would require more than a skill in dialectics. He must now face a more practical challenge, demonstrating the ability to cope with a formidable array of concrete problems, including the task of working cooperatively with a variety of other leaders and organizations. And nobody was more aware than he that blacks who attempted to form labor unions encountered peculiar difficulties, their color and marginal status making reprisals easier, not to mention their inequality before the law and their relative lack of personal security.

The most obvious and immediate problem confronting the new union and its general organizer was the economic plight of the Pullman porters. Their wages were low, making it necessary for them to depend upon tips, and out of their earnings they had to pay for their uniforms for the first ten years of service, for shoe polish, and for meals during runs. Porters averaged 400 hours a month on the job as contrasted with 240 hours for other train-service employees. Porters also wanted pay for preparatory time—

the time from which a porter reported for work rather than from the time the train pulled out of the station.

The Pullman Company's attitude toward the new union was predictably hostile. In 1920, in order to forestall an earlier effort at union organization by the porters and maids, Pullman had formed a company union, the Employees Representation Plan. To combat the Brotherhood the Pullman Company hired detectives to identify porters who were union members, and it threatened to replace Negro porters with Asians, particularly Filipinos. In its opposition to the union the company sought to enlist the support of blacks in all walks of life.

Such anti-Brotherhood blacks were not hard to find. Reflecting their middle-class orientation, most black professionals and intellectuals were cool toward organized labor. Some Pullman porters, too, according to Sterling D. Spero and Abraham Harris, contemporary authorities on black labor, "had all of the familiar middle-class prejudices of the white-collar worker and the upper servant," thus tending to identify with the rich and influential passengers who rode their cars.

With some notable exceptions, a majority of the black newspapers were against the Brotherhood. At its meeting in Atlanta in 1924 the National Negro Press Association went on record as "condemning all forms of Unionism and economic radicalism." Perry Howard, Republican national committeeman from Mississippi, charged that the Brotherhood was Communist-supported, but his criticism lost some of its force when it became known that he was a paid consultant to the Pullman Company. Opposition also came from the black clergy, particularly from those black congregations that depended upon white financial support. Reflecting their religious traditionalism, the more evangelical denominations were either antiunion or indifferent ("the greater the religiosity, the less the militancy," writes Preston Valien).

Randolph was quick to strike back at the Brotherhood's black critics. In January 1926 he charged two Chicago weeklies, the *Whip* and the *Defender,* with having surrendered to "gold and power." A month later, in a more sweeping indictment, he accused "hypocritical and corrupt Negro leaders" with having been "bought and paid with Pullman money. Like the dog before the gramaphone, they are listening to their master's voice, the Pullman Company."

Not able to count on the black church, Randolph sought assistance in other black quarters, soon enlisting the support of the NAACP and the Urban League. In early 1926 James Weldon Johnson, executive secretary of the NAACP, wrote public letters endorsing the Brotherhood, and in its April 1926 issue the *Crisis,* organ of the NAACP, carried an editorial by Du Bois condemning the Pullman Company for its machinations in trying "to block the belated effort of the Pullman porters to form a real and effective labor union." Randolph successfully wooed the influential black fraternal organization, the Improved and Benevolent Order of Elks of the World, winning its endorsement in 1928, not an inconsiderable feat inasmuch as the fraternity at its convention in 1925 had unanimously condemned organized labor. To no one's surprise, at its first national convention in 1929 in Chicago, the Brotherhood elected Randolph as president.

Whether coming in contact with him through the Brotherhood releases or from listening to him in public address, the porters were favorably impressed by their leader, viewing him as one who was whole-heartedly and single-mindedly devoted to their welfare. Warming to their high appraisal, Randolph exerted his spell, stirring them with words of hope and exhortation interspersed with snatches of fatherly advice. "A new Pullman porter is born," he informed them in the April 1926 issue of the *Messenger.* "He has caught a new vision. His creed is independence without insolence; courtesy without fawning; service without servility."

Randolph urged the porters to do their best on the job despite their multiple grievances. "The Brotherhood will not injure the Pullman Company," he wrote. "It does not counsel insubordination, but efficient discipline." Sounding like a latter-day Washington, Randolph preached the gospel of work and habits of industry. (In 1940, in the *Black Worker,* a Brotherhood periodical, Randolph would present to the porters a list of ten "Don'ts," beginning with "Don't drink on the job," and ending with "Don't annoy women.")

Viewing Randolph in terms of his external relationships to them and in the light of the public image he cast, the Brotherhood rank and file could hardly be aware of any leadership flaws with which his closer associates, the second echelon administrators, had to cope. On them fell the real task of organizing and operating the Brotherhood, Randolph showing little interest in administrative work or grasp of its content and perhaps not fully sensing its importance. At home in reading a treatise on theoretical economics on a global scale, Randolph found less satisfaction in scanning a Brotherhood balance sheet placed on his desk.

Fortunately for Randolph, throughout his long leadership of the Brotherhood he was able to develop a cordial relationship with one or another able subordinate who was willing to assume the major responsibilities for administrative operations. In the early years this role was admirably filled by Milton P. Webster, a former Pullman porter himself, who had come from Chicago, where he had been influential in black political and labor circles. Holding the rank of first vice-president of the Brotherhood, Webster was second only to Randolph in command. No "yes-man," Webster never hesitated to differ with "the Chief," vigorously defending his viewpoints but winning or losing with equal grace. Early in their relationships the two leaders had learned to respect and trust each other.

During the early years of the Brotherhood Randolph was equally successful in winning the strong personal loyalty of a countrywide network of dedicated lieutenants, whether in Oakland, Detroit, Pittsburgh, or St. Louis. Their dual devotion to Randolph and the Brotherhood was one of the major causes of the union's ultimate success.

After a twelve-year fight the persistence of Randolph and the patience of his followers was rewarded. The Railway Labor Act of 1934 outlawed company unions and granted railroad employees the right to organize without interference by the employer. Such legislative sanction of collective bargaining, a long-sought Randolph goal, was a significant victory for organized labor as a whole. The following year the Brotherhood, in an election contest with a union loyal to the Pullman Company (the Pullman Porters and Maids Protective Association), decisively won the right to represent the porters in collective bargaining. The Pullman Company held out for two more years, finally capitulating in August 1937 when it recognized the Brotherhood as the bargaining agent for the porters and maids, negotiating a contract covering wages, hours, and working rules.

The Randolph-led union had won an important victory. In a letter to Du Bois two years earlier (May 24, 1935) Randolph asserted that "when the Brotherhood wins this fight, it will probably be the most significant economic victory and stride of substantial and constructive progress the Negro has made in history." Randolph's evaluation was not without substance, if we grant that leaders as a class are entitled to a touch of hyperbole.

For indeed, the victory over the Pullman Company was a demonstration of the ability of blacks to organize and run a union despite a "sea of troubles." It made blacks more union-aware, decreasing their antilabor sentiment; it provided an organized group whose resources and leadership could be enlisted for service in other black causes, and it marked the beginning of black influence on national labor policy and in national labor circles.

The capitulation of the Pullman Company came at a propitious juncture in Randolph's fortunes, coming just when the AFL, growing weary of his continuous strictures, had considered ejecting the Brotherhood from the federation. In 1929 the Brotherhood had joined the AFL, although it had not received the kind of charter it sought. Randolph and his followers wanted an international charter that would make the Brotherhood equal with the other member unions, thereby wielding more influence in national labor circles and enabling it to operate independently in negotiating its own working conditions. Instead of receiving such autonomy the Brotherhood was placed under the direct jurisdiction of the president of the AFL, William Green, and its Executive Council. Randolph accepted this more limited "federal" charter because he deemed such a step as a temporary expedient, "establishing a beach-head," as he phrased it.

Randolph proceeded to use the annual conventions of the AFL as a forum, pressing for an international charter for the Brotherhood and sharply condemning the racial practices and policies of the member unions. He called for the elimination of the color clauses in their constitutions and the color pledges in their rituals, demanding the expulsion of "any union maintaining the color bar." In light of the deeply rooted patterns of racial exclusion and job discrimination so typical of its craft-union membership, the AFL could hardly deny Randolph's charges. At the annual meetings, however, Randolph's resolutions were generally referred to a committee which either pigeonholed them, recommended nonconcurrence, counseled patience, or expressed hopes for a more friendly spirit in the house of labor.

In 1936, however, upon the heels of the Brotherhood's decisive victory over the union sponsored by the Pullman Company, the AFL decided to grant Randolph's application for an international charter. The first predominantly black union to receive such a charter, the Brotherhood now became an autonomous unit, equal to other international units.

The organized labor movement would continue to discriminate against Negroes, and for more than one-third of a century Randolph would be a leader in the fight against such practices. But this recalcitrance on the part of white labor did not diminish the importance of the Brotherhood's feat in obtaining an international charter. However slow the organized labor movement might be in erasing the color line, its membership from top to bottom now became much more conscious of the Negro workers, their problems and possibilities.

Strengthened by its international union status and by its victory over the Pullman Company, the Brotherhood had become a dominant force in Negro circles by the late 1930s. Its cohesiveness and power enabled it to exert a major influence both in coming to the aid of other black unions and in assisting other black betterment movements and efforts. And, as a concomitant factor, Randolph himself now became a figure of consequence in black life. Girded by the power and prestige of the Brotherhood and by the accolades his leadership of the Brotherhood had brought him, he bore a new confidence and authority as he moved onto a wider stage.

Grounded in theory, Randolph knew something of black leadership as a type. In black life so little power was available that the competitive struggle for its exercise was bound to be intense, often ruthless. Randolph knew, too, that there was a multiplicity of black leaders and organizations, varying in strategy and tactics, and that no one of them spoke for all blacks. But if there were no universal leader, Randolph, by the late 1930s, was prepared to speak to and for an ever widening constituency, having already indicated his own broad social concerns and having already demonstrated his ability to work with other black leaders and other black protest and improvement organizations. In black leadership he aspired to exemplify the principle of collective action.

However inclusive his leadership outreach, Randolph spurned the overtures of one group, the Communists. Randolph had hailed the Russian Revolution of World War I years, but when the American socialists divided into right and left shortly after the war Randolph remained with the former. Hence, when the American Communist party was organized in 1921, he did not become a member.

To Randolph, the Communists imperiled all efforts toward joint action and interorganizational unity. From the year of its founding in 1925 Randolph denounced the American Negro Labor Congress, charging in September of that year that it was "not representative of the American Negro worker because its seat of control is Moscow." During the long struggle between the Pullman porters and the Pullman Company Randolph reiterated the point that the Brotherhood of Sleeping Car Porters was "not backed by Moscow, nor has it any Communistic connections." In a letter written in June

1928 he referred to the Communists as a "sinister and destructive crowd."

Randolph's highly critical appraisal of the Communists was heightened in the late 1930s as a result of his experience as president of the National Negro Congress. Organized in 1930, this was an umbrella-like combination of about twenty organizations, white and black, whose goal was racial advancement in general with emphasis on the problems of the black worker. To Randolph this seemed to be the kind of a "united front of all Negro organizations," which had become the dominant goal in his life. In his presidential address of 1936 (read in his absence) he opened by invoking "the spirit of Frederick Douglass and Nat Turner, of Gabriel and Denmark Vesey, of Harriet Tubman and Sojourner Truth—those noble rebels who struck out in the dark days of slavery that Negro men and women might be free." Randolph closed this initial presidential address by reminding the delegates that the ambitious program envisioned by the Congress would require the cooperation of various Negro organizations—"church, fraternal, civil, trade-union, farmer, professional, college and what not—into a framework of a united front, together with white groups of workers, lovers of liberty and those whose liberties are similarly menaced."

During its first four years, nearly half of its brief existence, the National Negro Congress did much to improve the lot of blacks, locally and nationally. But its significant accomplishments were obscured by the rising role and influence of the Communists within the organization. They had stayed in the background at first, but within two years it had become obvious that theirs was the dominant voice, theirs the source of funding. During these first years Randolph took little time in the operation of the Congress, his energies devoted to the Brotherhood's culminating struggles with the Pullman Company on one hand and the AFL on the other. Moreover, as in his leadership of the porters, Randolph showed little interest in administrative work. In the Brotherhood this shortcoming had been covered up by able and loyal subordinates, but in the Congress it emerged for all to see, thus diminishing his effectiveness.

The Congress did not convene in 1938 and 1939, and hence it was not until 1940 that the issue of Communist control reached its denouement. At that meeting Randolph resigned, charging that the Congress was Communist-dominated. "I quit the Congress because it was not truly a Negro Congress," he wrote in an article in the *Black Worker,* "Why I Would Not Stand for Re-election for President of the National Negro Congress." During his speech of resignation the Communists staged a demonstration, followed by a walkout.

The Communist party would not enroll many blacks. Not ideology-oriented, Negro Americans sought to improve the capitalist system rather than to liquidate it. Nonetheless the Communists had some success, in America and abroad, in dramatizing the grievances of black Americans, particularly of the black workers. Moreover, Randolph's own exposure to Marxist theory and practice had contributed to the tone and militance of his vocabulary and to his convictions as to the use of mass direct action techniques. But whatever their contribution to black advancement or to his own outlook or approaches, the Communists could only count Randolph as one of their most bitter black critics. In 1944 in proposing a "non-partisan political bloc," he called for their exclusion, asserting that "the Communist Party seeks only to rule or ruin a movement." In 1946, at the twenty-first anniversary celebration of the Brotherhood of Sleeping Car Porters, he characterized the Communists as "one of the greatest menaces to labor, the Negro, and other minorities."

Randolph's mindset about Communists was a factor in his decision to exclude all whites from participation in the "March on Washington" he scheduled for the summer of 1941. The possibility of Communist infiltration into this projected demonstration was, however, but one reason, and not the major reason, for Randolph's announced policy of racial exclusion. To white liberal groups and associates, such as the Fellowship of Reconciliation and its leader, A. J. Muste, who questioned this policy, Randolph had a ready answer. The proposed march, he explained, was "pro-Negro, not anti-white." Such an all-black movement would "create faith by Negroes in Negroes," developing "a sense of self-reliance with Negroes depending upon Negroes in vital matters."

Destined to be of major importance for its accomplishments and for its trail-blazing techniques in direct mass black pressure and action, the March on Washington Movement was a cooperative venture, with Randolph as its operating head. The movement grew out of the plight of the urban Negro worker on the eve of America's entry into World War II, black unemployment having reached 25 percent in 1940. The long-existent discriminatory practices in hiring, in on-the-job training, and in upgrading were more aggravating than ever to the Negro workers as they noted their country's eagerness to contrast the American creed of liberty and equality with the suppressions that characterized the Fascist nations, Hitler's Germany in particular. And although American industry was increasing its production to meet the needs of the national defense program, blacks were being turned away at the defense plant gates.

On September 27, 1940, Randolph and two other black spokesmen, Walter White of the NAACP and T. Arnold Hill of the National Urban League conferred with Roosevelt, but this White House meeting accomplished little, thus convincing Randolph that nothing short of mass action by blacks would suffice. Hence through the Negro newspapers (see, for example, the *Pittsburgh Courier,* January 25, 1941) he issued a call. Negro Americans, ran his summons, must bring their "power and pressure to bear upon the agencies and representatives of the Federal Government to exact their rights in National Defense employment and the armed forces of the country." He suggested that 10,000 Negroes march on Washington, their slogan, "We Loyal Negro American Citizens Demand the Right to Work and Fight for our Country."

Randolph's appeal exceeded even his characteristically optimistic expectations, drawing enthusiastic support throughout the black community, including the clergy, the press, and the rank and file. The leaders of other black organizations, including the Urban League and the NAACP, found themselves swept into the fold. However much Randolph's growing popularity might threaten their own leadership standing in black uplift, these spokesmen and spokeswomen could hardly stay on the sidelines, even though direct mass action of a marching kind took on a somewhat more confrontational style than some of them preferred. Their choice was predictable. "No Negro leader could risk the Uncle Tom label," explains Herbert Garfinkel in analyzing their uniformly affirmative response.

It would not be the last time that Randolph would put other black leaders in a position in which they felt themselves to be somewhat coerced into supporting a strategy he espoused. But it is to be noted that if Randolph made constant use of other organizations and their leaders, he in turn reciprocated in full measure. He was, for example, a longtime supporter of the NAACP's crusade against lynching.

Their groundwork laid, Randolph and seven other black leaders formed a March on Washington Committee, scheduling the march for July 1, 1941, and multiplying their projections as to the number of marchers. "Dear fellow Negro Americans," exhorted Randolph, with growing confidence, "be not dismayed in these terrible times. You possess power, great power. Our problem is to harness and hitch it up for action on the broadest, daring and most gigantic scale."

In early June the mushrooming march movement forced itself upon Roosevelt. Exercising his political skills, he tried to have the march called off, enlisting the services of his wife Eleanor, whose popularity among blacks was already legendary, and of New York's mayor, Fiorello H. La Guardia, also a favorite in black circles. The failure of such emissaries made it necessary to arrange a White House conference on June 18 with four black leaders, including Randolph. Calling the idea of a march "bad and unintelligent," Roosevelt strongly urged the leaders to cancel it. When it became evident that his plea was unacceptable without a quid pro quo, Roosevelt brought the thirty-minute conference to a close by appointing a committee of five high-ranking whites to meet with the black leaders in order to reach an agreement.

Following a quickly arranged series of meetings and telephone conversations, the two groups resolved their differences, and on June 25, one week after the White House conference, Roosevelt issued Executive Order 8802, decreeing that "there shall be no discrimination in the employment of workers in defense industries or government because of race, creed, color or national origin" and establishing a Committee on Fair Employment Practices (FEPC). Appointed on July 19, 1941, this six-member committee included Webster, vice-president of the Brotherhood, Randolph having declined an invitation to serve. In the meantime, in exchange for Roosevelt's order, Randolph called off the scheduled march, proceeding instead to form a new organization, the March on Washington Movement, to act as a watchdog over the FEPC, among other activities.

Randolph's success in persuading Roosevelt to issue Executive Order 8802 illustrated a technique familiar in black leadership circles for over a hundred years. This was the practice of operating from a relatively weak power base, but of making demands nonetheless, hoping to achieve the group's goal by the use of strong rhetoric along with the threat of a disruptive physical confrontation that would certainly reach the public eye, even if it failed to touch the public conscience. Bearing some semblance to the game of bluff, this technique sometimes failed, as in the Brotherhood's threat to strike against the Pullman Company in 1928. Keenly aware of the riskiness of this technique, Randolph also knew full well that a black leader does not enjoy a wide range of weapons.

A group, or coalition of groups, whose power was problematic faced another disheartening possibility, i.e., the victory they won might turn out to be less fruitful than they had expected. The aftermath of Randolph's march was a case in point. Despite its leader's vigorous efforts, the campaign for a permanent FEPC was unsuccessful, the wartime committee quietly expiring in the spring of 1946. Inadequately financed by the Congress and with little power to enforce its findings, the committee encountered bitter and unrelenting attacks. Malcolm Ross, its chairman beginning in October 1943, described it as the most hated agency in Washington, southern congressmen and their constituents regarding it as an attempt to impose social equality upon their states.

The National Council for a Permanent FEPC, established in 1943, had been unable to halt its demise, running completely out of funds in 1946 and facing internal dissension with a rift between co-chairman Randolph and executive secretary Anna Arnold Hedgeman. Nonetheless, the FEPC was important for its pioneering role—for "making the issue part of the national consciousness," as Hedgeman said later. In the some 10,000 cases it handled during its five-year existence, it met with some success in changing the discriminatory policies of employers and trade unions. Rather than face charges by the commission, some employers erased their color line, and others broadened their hiring policies.

Moreover, the existence of the FEPC meant that the federal government had now assumed a role in the elimination of Jim Crow practices in employment, that a precedent had been established for considering job discrimination a denial of one's civil rights. In addition the FEPC had its influence on the issuing of court decrees against job discrimination and on the establishment of state FEPC laws and of federal government contract compliance committees, the last-named capped by a committee on equal employment opportunity. And to Randolph, as to other black opinion-makers, no movement could be counted a failure that had succeeded in establishing among Negroes a greater sense of collective self-reliance.

Along with mass action and public demonstrations, Randolph made use of another technique that would foreshadow the civil rights revolution of the 1950s and 1960s, i.e., the Gandhian approach of nonviolent civil disobedience. During his *Messenger* days Randolph had been an exponent of retaliatory violence, but an older Randolph, under the influence of such pacifists as Rustin, then on the threshold of a long career in reformist causes, modified his views. At its founding in 1942 the Congress of Racial Equality named Randolph to its National Advisory Committee, well aware that he shared its philosophy of nonviolent direct action. At the annual meeting of the March on Washington Movement in 1943 in Detroit, Randolph challenged the 1,200 delegates "to adopt nonviolent, goodwill, direct action as organizational policy." Such an approach, as Randolph pointed out later that year, would require persons "who had undergone a rigid training and discipline to develop self-control and the requisite moral and spiritual resources to meet the most trying ordeal."

Randolph himself put this technique to the test in his campaign against segregation in the armed forces during the 1940s. During World War I Randolph had spoken out against discrimination in the armed forces, and he sounded a similar note on the eve of World War II. The White House meeting on September 14, 1940, between Roosevelt and the three black leaders, Randolph included, discussed the participation of Negroes not only in defense industries but in the military. The call to the March on Washington, issued in the spring of 1941, included a petition "for the integration of Negroes in the armed forces, such as the Air Corps, Navy, Army and Marine Corps of the Nation." To Randolph's disappointment, however, Roosevelt's Executive Order 8802 was confined to defense industries. Hence the abolition of Jim Crow policies in the armed services, including the Women's Auxiliary Army Corps and the Waves, became one of the major objectives of the March on Washington Movement.

The war ended but not the issue, the latter taking a new momentum in 1947 when a universal military training bill came before the Congress. A peacetime draft, it contained no antidiscrimination proviso. Responding to this omission, Randolph and Grant Reynolds, the black New York state commissioner of correction, established in November 1947 a Committee Against Jim Crow in Military Service and Training, a step that was hailed by blacks throughout the country.

The effort of this committee to persuade Congress to enact an antisegregation law for the armed services, or to persuade President Harry Truman to establish such a policy by executive decree, met with opposition from southern congressmen and from high army officials. Reflecting the mood of their constituents, a group of black leaders met with Truman late in March 1948, urging him to insist that the proposed draft law include an antisegregation amendment. Not mincing his words, Randolph reported that in his travels around the country he "found Negroes not wanting to shoulder a gun to fight for democracy abroad unless they get democracy at home." Following a further exchange of views between Truman and the black delegation, the meeting came to an inconclusive end.

In his testimony before the Senate Armed Services Committee nine days later, Randolph was just as frank as he had been at the White House. If Congress passed a "Jim Crow draft," he warned, he would advise blacks to resort to "mass civil disobedience" along the line of Gandhi's struggles against the British in India. Randolph openly pledged himself to counsel and assist young people, white and black, to "quarantine" a segregated "conscript system." When one senator raised the question of treason, Randolph replied that "we are serving a higher law than the law which applies to the act of treason."

When Congress, on June 22, 1948, passed a draft law that did not ban Jim Crow practices, Randolph announced the formation of a League for Non-Violent Civil Disobedience Against Military Segregation, which proposed to concentrate its efforts on persuading the president to alter the situation by executive order. The league called upon Truman to issue such an antidiscrimination order, stating that if such a step were not taken by August 16 (when the new draft law became operative), the league would conduct a campaign of noncompliance. Again making use of a technique that bore the earmarks of bluff, Randolph operated from no substantial base of power, and his willingness to go to jail in such a cause is open to question.

Truman, however, needed little further convincing. During his presidency he had grown more liberal on race issues, more concerned about civil rights. Moreover, in the presidential election to be held later that year, he needed the black vote, which had become increasingly important as the black population shifted from the South, where blacks could not vote, to the North, where they could. On July 26 Truman issued Executive Order 9981 declaring, as presidential policy, "that there shall be equality of treatment and opportunity for all persons in the armed services." A month later Randolph and Reynolds announced the termination of the league, the latter pointing out that the league had accomplished its mission "not in familiar legal or Constitutional terms" but in a program of noncompliance that had gone outside the traditionally accepted boundaries.

Randolph's crowning experience as an advocate of direct mass action by a coalition of reform-minded groups and agencies came in the summer of 1963 with the March on Washington for Jobs and Freedom. Publicly announced from Randolph's office in Harlem in February of that year, the idea for such a demonstration grew out of a conversation between Randolph and Rustin, his assistant, a few weeks earlier. Originally concentrating on black unemployment, the march soon broadened its scope to include the whole range of civil rights in response to the cry "Freedom Now!"—the slogan of blacks during the hundredth anniversary of the Emancipation Proclamation. Sponsors of the march sought to bring pressure on Congress to enact a civil rights bill, then dormant in the House Rules Committee. "Politicians," said Randolph, "don't move unless you move them."

A labor leader himself, it was natural for Randolph to have orginally thought of the proposed march as primarily a demonstration for jobs. But he had no quarrel with the slogan, "March on Washington for Jobs and Freedom," inasmuch as he held that economic freedom was the base of other freedoms, for, as he said, "Freedom requires a material foundation." But Randolph also knew that freedom had a protean quality, taking on a myriad of guises and fulfilling itself in many ways. Indeed, it was in quest of such an indivisible freedom that Randolph, now in his mid-seventies at the time of the march in 1963, had devoted his long career, as a moment of reflection would tend to indicate.

As to his sensitivity in the matter of jobs for blacks, Randolph stood above all other black leaders. During the twenty-five years between the granting of an international charter to the Brotherhood of Sleeping Car Porters and the proposed march on Washington in 1963, Randolph's devotion to the cause of the black workers had been unflagging and these workers needed such dedication. From his position as international president of the Brotherhood, Randolph raised an insistent voice for racial justice in the councils of the AFL. At its annual meetings in the 1940s and 1950s he proposed a series of resolutions, including those calling for the appointment of committees to investigate discriminatory practices among the member unions. As a rule the AFL reaffirmed its policy of opposition to Jim Crow practices but confessed itself without sufficient power to influence the autonomous individual unions. Randolph's own union, he noted, did not practice racial discrimination; of its 12,000 members in 1947 approximately 20 percent were whites, including Filipinos and Mexicans.

Randolph was hardly popular at the annual meetings of the AFL. Boos were not uncommon when he arose to speak, some delegates walking out and milling around in the halls until he took his seat. But Randolph was not to be silenced, winning the title, "the conscience of the AFL," and forcing the leaders to address themselves to the touchy questions of race and color.

In 1955 when the AFL merged with the Congress of Industrial Organizations (CIO) to form the AFL-CIO, the new federation named two blacks as vice-presidents, Randolph and Willard S. Townsend of the United Transport Service Employees. Founded in 1935, the CIO had made a strong effort to win the support of blacks. Organized along industrywide lines rather than the more restrictive craft lines, and forming new unions unburdened by a history of racial discrimination, the CIO's racial and social policies were broader than those of the AFL, even though Randolph had preferred to keep the Brotherhood in the latter. By the time of the merger, however, the CIO had become less vigorous in pressing for racial equality.

To Randolph's gratification the constitution of the new federation provided for a Civil Rights Committee, one pledged to "the effective implementation of the principle of non-discrimination." Randolph became disenchanted, however, at the union's failure to expel locals that were guilty of discriminatory racial practices. Randolph's insistent charges that the AFL-CIO's attack on color barriers was halfhearted became increasingly galling to George Meany, its president. Meany had grown impatient with Randolph, charging that his indictments were overdrawn and that he failed to give the federation any credit for its successes against segregation. The Meany-Randolph imbroglio came to a head in 1959 at the annual convention of the union. In a sharp exchange between the two, Meany gave way to his ire, saying to Randolph, "Who in hell appointed you as guardian of the Negro members in America?"

Bent on exerting pressure on the AFL-CIO, Randolph in 1960 founded the Negro American Labor Council, made up of black officials of existing unions. Representing the council as its president, Randolph presented to the AFL-CIO a list of grievances accompanied by suggested remedies. The federation leadership responded by denying the charges and sharply criticizing Randolph himself for causing "the gap that has been developed between organized labor and the Negro community." This rift in the Negro-labor alliance, however, was relatively short-lived, with Meany a featured speaker at the annual meeting of the Negro American Labor Council in 1962.

If the black worker and the organized labor movement were indebted to Randolph, the same was true, if to a lesser extent, of the civil rights movement as a whole. Randolph's social vision was broad. As president of the Brotherhood of Sleeping Car Porters, he reminded its membership of the necessity of supporting "progressive forces for the securing and maintaining of democratic institutions for the Negro." In 1957, at the request of Martin Luther King, Jr., Randolph became one of the sponsors of the Prayer Pilgrimage to Washington, an effort to prod the federal government to take further action on "the unresolved civil-rights issue." Randolph delivered a moving address to the some 20,000 gathered at the Lincoln Memorial on May 17, the third anniversary of the Supreme Court decree against segregation in the public schools.

To the seventy-four-year-old Randolph, therefore, a march was nothing new; "Mr. Randolph is a march man," observed Whitney M. Young, Jr., in 1963. "He's been marching since 1941." A march focusing on jobs and freedom was a fitting climax to a career such as his. It was Randolph, wrote King, who "proposed a March on Washington to unite in one luminous action all the forces along the far-flung front." It was Randolph who headed the march's organizing committee of six blacks and four whites, and it was Randolph's deputy director, Rustin, who planned and coordinated the operations, handled the complex details, and recruited the volunteers. Joining forces with Randolph in 1950, Rustin had soon become a trusted and efficient lieutenant, skilled as a troubleshooter.

To Randolph the 1963 march was the high point of his public life. Over 200,000 marchers took the mile-long walk from the Washington Monument to the Lincoln Memorial. At the more formal proceedings, held at the foot of the memorial, Randolph presided and also delivered the keynote address. The march "is not the climax of our struggle but a new beginning, not only for the Negro but for all Americans, for personal freedoms and a better life," he said. "The civil rights revolution is not confined to Negroes; nor is it confined to civil rights."

Randolph introduced the other nine speakers in turn, ending with King, whose address, "I Have a Dream Today," marked the high water mark in twentieth-century civil rights oratory. Orderly and inspiring, the march was characterized by a note of high seriousness from beginning to end. "The imposing dignity and patience of A.

Philip Randolph toned the whole affair," observed *Newsweek* columnist Kenneth Crawford.

Randolph counted the 1963 march as the most memorable day of his life, the crowning event associated with his leadership. And indeed the march was notable both as a symbol of past struggles and aspirations and, as Randolph had said, the herald of a new beginning.

There were, however, two aspects of the emergent black protest and activism of the 1960s that the aging Randolph found questionable, i.e., the cry of "black power" and the call for black separatism. Randolph held that although "black power" could be construed as "a valid and poetic 'cry for deliverance,' " its advocates had not succeeded in formulating a concrete program that was "applicable to the needs of practical political action." To Randolph, "black power was a slogan and slogans solve no problems."

Randolph did not believe that blacks should "go it alone," and thus he was out of tune with the position paper adopted in August 1966 by the Student Nonviolent Coordinating Committee: "If we are to proceed toward true liberation, we must cut ourselves off from whites." Forty years earlier Randolph had condemned the racially separatist tenets of the Marcus Garvey movement. Holding that antiwhite doctrines are dangerous and false, Randolph charged that Garveyism broadened the chasm between white workers and black workers and "engenders and fosters a virulent race prejudice." As for Garvey's cry that Negro Americans must establish an independent nation in Africa, Randolph replied that the liberation of Africa could come only "by allying the Negro liberation movement with the movements for the liberation of all the world's enslaved of all races, creeds and colors."

Randolph's attitude toward the black power militants of the 1960s was thus a reaffirmation of his essential ecumenism. Except for a brief spell while launching the 1941 March on Washington, Randolph's long leadership had consistently reflected a coalitionist bent. Randolph's concerns were global; for example, while most black leaders viewed World War II as an opportunity to win victory on the home front as well as victory over the Axis powers, Randolph viewed the conflict as an opportunity for a "Peoples' Revolution" that would "possess the fighting faith and crusading confidence of the masses of all colors and races," as he wrote in 1944. "The people can cause this war to usher in the Century of the Common Man."

Randolph's outlook embraced the generality of mankind. He

strove to "win a decent place in America" for blacks, but he sought to win it without "destroying the possibilities for mutual goodwill." Within black circles he stressed the commonalities that transcended the lines of class and occupation, among other dividers. Beyond the color line he sought the universals in the human experience.

It might be noted that Randolph's faith in the power of reason and his belief in people's common destiny led him at times to underestimate the tenacity of race and color prejudice in his native land. Devoid of such feelings himself, he did not gauge fully the status advantages to be derived from racial discrimination—that whites in labor unions, for example, were fearful not only of losing their economic benefits but also of jeopardizing their social standing if blacks were accorded job equality. Randolph does not seem to have fully weighed the social uses of racism, its role as a form of cultural taboo, its service as an ego-prop.

To the end Randolph believed that self-interest balanced by a concern for the common good would ultimately prevail, and that the enlightened, particularly those who were the victims of oppression, would make common cause. Working toward this goal was Randolph's essential contribution, and it received its most cogent expression from Rustin, his close friend and associate. Shortly after Randolph's death in 1979, Rustin listed what he had learned from his mentor, including nonviolent protest and the economic roots of racism. "But, above all," wrote Rustin, "I learned that the struggle for the freedom of black people is intertwined with the struggle to free all mankind."

Rustin was fortunate in having had the opportunity to learn such things firsthand. Others, however, would not go unendowed, the Randolph legacy having an outreaching quality, embracing in particular the seekers of social insight.

Note on Sources

The important manuscript source on Randolph is the papers of the Brotherhood of Sleeping Car Porters in the Manuscript Division of the Library of Congress and in the Manuscript Division of the Chicago Historical Society.

In the periodical literature, the most valuable single source is the *Messenger*, which was published in New York City from 1917 until its cessation in 1928. It is indispensable for Randolph's early career as a labor organizer and a socialist, and it describes his activities in laying the foundations for the Brotherhood and setting its course.

The secondary sources include one full-length study, Jervis B. Anderson's

A. Philip Randolph: A Biographical Portrait (New York: Harcourt Brace, and Jovanovich, 1973), in style, content, and insight an admirable introduction to the man. This work may be supplemented by a body of specialized studies of high caliber in which Randolph is the central figure. Listed according to their chronological coverage, the first is Theodore Kornweibel, Jr.'s *No Crystal Stair: Black Life and the Messenger, 1919–1928* (Westport, Conn.: Greenwood Press, 1975), a scholarly exposition and analysis of that journal's viewpoints. A similarly thorough volume, William H. Harris's *Keeping the Faith: A. Philip Randolph, Milton P. Webster, and the Brotherhood of Sleeping Car Porters, 1925–1937* (Urbana: University of Illinois Press, 1977), traces in detail the long battle between the Brotherhood and the Pullman Company, pointedly analyzing Randolph's leadership characteristics throughout. Harris holds that even though Randolph and his Brotherhood associates viewed themselves as path-breakers and innovators, "they functioned much in the tradition of other black leaders." The pioneer study of the Randolph-led union is Brailsford R. Brazeal's *The Brotherhood of Sleeping Car Porters: Its Origin and Development* (New York: Harper and Brothers, 1946), a solid work with an interpretive touch.

Works that deal with issues about which Randolph was concerned and his role therein including the following. Herbert Garfinkel's *When Negroes March: The March on Washington Movement in the Organizational Politics for FEPC* (Glencoe, Ill.: The Free Press, 1959) is skillfully organized and copiously documented, its conclusions soundly reasoned. Garfinkel may be supplemented by two additional studies that add to our understanding of that agency: Louis C. Kesselman's *The Social Politics of FEPC: A Study in Reform Pressure Movements* (Chapel Hill: University of North Carolina Press, 1948) and Louis Ruchames's *Race, Jobs and Politics: The Story of FEPC* (New York: Columbia University Press, 1953). The fight against Jim Crow practices in the services, with due attention to Randolph's role, is recounted in Richard M. Dalfiume's *Fighting on Two Fronts: Desegregation of the U.S. Armed Forces, 1939–1953* (Columbia: University of Missouri Press, 1969). Histories of black labor union movements of the twentieth century include Sterling D. Spero and Abram L. Harris's *The Black Worker: The Negro and the Labor Movement* (New York: Columbia University Press, 1931), which is somewhat critical of Randolph's leadership during the early years of the Brotherhood. One of the best of the studies that broadly and comprehensively covers the black worker is Philip S. Foner's *Organized Labor and the Black Worker, 1619–1973* (New York: Praeger Publishers, 1974), its index listing over forty references to Randolph.

Black History

11. Black History Unbound

UNTIL RECENT TIMES the role of the Afro-American in our national life was thought to be hardly worth considering. An intellectual "white flight" held sway; most writers in the social sciences and the humanities, whatever their individual specialties, assumed that they knew as much about blacks as they needed to know or as their readers cared to learn. With this static image, the black was considered something of an intruder, if not indeed an outsider. In many quarters he was regarded as an exotic, an offshoot, hardly "a peece of the Continent, a part of the maine." Certainly he was underplayed in American history and letters.

This situation has undergone considerable change in the past two decades. The stepped-up civil rights movement following the Supreme Court's public school desegregation decision in 1954 heightened black consciousness and sparked the demand for black power, thereby creating a larger audience for black expression in its various forms. The popularization of black history in the mass-circulation monthly, *Ebony,* particularly in the writings of its senior editor, Lerone Bennett, Jr., left a deep imprint on hundreds of thousands of readers hitherto unresponsive to the call of the past. Of considerable influence, too, in raising the level of black consciousness was the emergence of more than a score of black nations below the Sahara, whose newly acquired independence was at once a symbol and a reminder of a rich precolonial African heritage too long in limbo.

The colleges and universities have assumed a major role in this contemporary example of the present recreating the past. In predominantly white colleges, the proliferation of black studies owes much to pressures from black students, often supported by fellow students and faculty. The marked increase in the number of blacks attending these colleges in the sixties, combined with their search for personal identity and group solidarity, led to their demand for courses relating to the black experience, a demand often heading

the list designated as "nonnegotiable." Black colleges had long operated precursor programs in black studies, but in the 1960s they
considerably increased their offerings.

Although such black-oriented programs, quite unlike other college offerings, made their way into the curriculum as a result of
student pressures, the colleges soon realized that the newly introduced disciplines were worthy of inclusion. Black history might
well have healing in its wings, but it also had an intrinsic importance
much broader than its therapeutic value.

Black studies, despite their tender years, can no longer be regarded
as a controversial academic innovation, though coming-of-age ceremonies would certainly be premature at this "growing pains"
stage. It is impossible for American society to be properly appraised
if blacks are left out of the picture. "We cannot," writes Columbia
historian Walter Metzger, "understand America without the help
of those studies now called 'black.' " John W. Blassingame of Yale
concurs, pointing out that "no American can truly understand his
own society and culture without a knowledge of the roles Negroes
have played in them." The black looms large in American letters,
writes Jean Fagan Yellin: "His dark figure is ubiquitous in our
fiction; the American imagination was as obsessed in the nineteenth
century by the black as it is today." Since Jamestown, black-white
relationships have been a central attribute of our national culture.
The experiences of blacks and whites, though profoundly different,
have always been intertwined and complementary, even symbiotic
on occasion, however much whites may have monopolized the process and substance of power. Hence American studies, properly
perceived, must be viewed through a multiracial lens.

The role of blacks in America—what they have done and what
has been done to them—illuminates the past and informs the present. The father of black historiography, Carter G. Woodson (1875–
1950), and his associates and successors have told us much about
the constructive role played by blacks in the making of America.
But for all his scholarship and perception, Woodson did not fully
sense the dimensions of what had been done to blacks. He was, of
course, familiar with the well-known U. B. Phillips contention, advanced in 1928, that the central theme in Southern history was that
the South was and should remain a white man's country. But Woodson and his black-oriented contemporaries could hardly have been
fully aware of the extent of racism in America, a topic which has
only recently been given the type of probing scrutiny found, for

example, in Winthrop D. Jordan,[1] who feels that, without the blacks, the early whites would have experienced an identity crisis. As Joanna E. Schneider and Robert L. Zangrando have pointed out, one of the ways in which the American past must be reappraised is in terms of the interactions of the dominant whites with red, black, and yellow peoples. "Unless we fully comprehend the role of racism in this society, we can never truly know America," they observe, adding that black history "offers us an indispensable opportunity" to do so.[2]

If coming to grips with this component of our national experience confronts us with some of our more sober realities, ironies, and paradoxes, it will also revitalize inquiry. Any loss of innocence should be more than balanced by the virtues of a viewpoint more broadly humanistic in its outreach. Black literature, for example, may offer new insights into classic American literature. William W. Nichols has compared Frederick Douglass's statements in *My Bondage and My Freedom,* written in 1855, with Thoreau's in *Walden,*[3] viewing both as seekers after freedom. Similarly, Leonard J. Deutsch, in an article entitled, "Ralph Waldo Ellison and Ralph Waldo Emerson: A Shared Moral Vision,"[4] sees points of correspondence between the two men of letters despite differences in their exteriors, not to mention in their times and manners. New awareness of the interactions of whites and blacks is making it necessary for many branches of learning to redefine themselves.

Black studies, however, are more than a prelude to cross-cultural understanding; they celebrate ethnic pluralism as a fact in our national life. More and more we are beginning to see America as a multiculture. This heightened ethnic consciousness is not confined to color alone, but embraces non-Anglo-Saxon whites as well. To these people not of the "old stock," the idea of cultural assimilation has lost much of its appeal. In part this has stemmed from a sense of disillusionment. "Are we living the dream our grandparents dreamed when on creaking decks they stood silent, afraid, hopeful

[1] Winthrop D. Jordan *White Over Black: American Attitudes Toward the Negro, 1550–1812* (Chapel Hill, N.C.: University of North Carolina Press, 1968).
[2] Joanna E. Schneider and Robert L. Zangrando, "Black History in the College Curriculum," *Rocky Mountain Social Science Journal* 6 (October 1969): 134–42.
[3] William M. Nichols, "Individualism and Autobiographical Art: Frederick Douglass and Henry Thoreau," *College Language Association Journal* 16 (December 1972): 145–58.
[4] Leonard J. Deutsch, "Ralph Waldo Ellison and Ralph Waldo Emerson: A Shared Moral Vision," *College Language Association Journal* 16 (December 1972): 159–78.

at the sight of the Statue of Liberty?" Michael Novak asked in 1972. "Will we ever find that secret relief, that door, that hidden entrance?"[5] But the essential feeling behind the rise of white ethnic consciousness comes not from a sense of social acceptance withheld, but rather from a realization that assimilation means "Anglo-assimilation," that minority groups wishing to enter the mainstream must first divest themselves of their own values and traditions. Hence, the thrust by blacks has legitimated cultural diversity, and the push for black studies has served as a spur to studies of women, white ethnic groups, and other minorities.[6] White ethnic groups, while still priding themselves on their true-blue Americanism, no longer feel that they must surrender whatever distinctive Old World ties or traits they still retain. The immigrant past is no longer considered "fringe" history.

This polycultural concept of our country and its past, to which black studies have contributed so markedly, holds that America's diversity is one of her richest national endowments. It says unmistakably, if by inference, that the northern European types were not the only ones who brought gifts to their new land. And, it might be added, this new acceptance of pluralism by no means connotes a rise in racial antagonisms. We are not unmindful of the admonition of William Dean Howells: "Inequality is as dear to the heart of America as liberty," nor do we forget that many Americans, black and white, forge their identity around the concept of color. A genuine ethnic pluralism, however, would tend less to polarize tension among groups than to reaffirm their mutuality.

Views of Black History

Although black Americans are no longer regarded as an out-group with a blank past, the field of black history is attended by ongoing problems—in the attitudes of its chroniclers, the sources available, and the changes in interpretations.

In the last two decades black history has attained a growing

[5] Michael Novak, *The Rise of the Unmeltable Ethnics: Politics and Culture in the Seventies* (New York: Macmillan, 1972).

[6] In higher education in the academic year 1973–74 an estimated 2,000 courses designed to expand the study and understanding of women were offered in America, a manyfold increase from the handful of such courses in the late 1960s. Cheryl M. Fields, "Women's Studies Gain; 2,000 Courses Offered this Year," *Chronicle of Higher Education* 8 (December 17, 1973): 6. It may be noted that in 1972, Sarah Lawrence College began a master's degree in women's history (if this is not a contradiction in terms).

acceptance in learned quarters. White historians could hardly escape noting such statements as those of Robert I. Rotberg that "the existence of African history has, in recent years, achieved scholarly recognition," and of C. Vann Woodward that "so far as their culture is concerned, all Americans are part Negro," and as a consequence, "American history, the white man's version, could profit from an infusion of 'soul.' " If white historians still think of themselves as the custodians of the word and the gate-keepers of the citadel, they are no longer so set on viewing the Negro as a stranger, if not a barbarian at the gates. They now deal more circumspectly with blacks, hoping to avoid what logicians call the "fallacy of initial predication."

However, although they may have succeeded in ridding themselves of preconceptions and opening their minds to reassessing their sources, they are still subject to some nagging doubts. Many historians have a built-in skepticism concerning innovation, particularly when it comes to a new field of inquiry or a new viewpoint about a low-status minority. The instinct for disciplinary tidiness can be especially strong in a field that is preoccupied with the past.

Still gripped by the genteel tradition of the eighteenth and nineteenth centuries, some historians almost unconsciously believe that society was and is characterized by a high culture and a low culture, and the less said about the latter the better. If a lady (Clio) had her dubious off-moments (mayhap an underworld connection or two), the well-bred and well-trained (the Ph.D.'s) hardly care to call attention to them. And for many historians, despite all their avowed devotion to the canons of objectivity, the mystique of kith and kin still remains strong, making it difficult for them to do full justice to those they regard as beyond the pale. Obviously, too, there are honest differences of opinion among historians; an event that one regards as a watershed may be regarded by another as little more than water under the dam.

Despite assurances from recognized fellow practitioners, many white historians also believe that the whole corpus of black studies is more topical than anything else, a congeries of pressure-group accretions with very little content and a primarily political function. These guardians of the portals see black history as the current faddishness in the profession, its chief result for the discipline a decline in the quality of documentation. Some historians who acquired their basic knowledge and skills when the material available concerning blacks was indeed limited and distorted, feel that new material about blacks must also lack intellectual objectivity and fail to meet valid academic standards. The culture-bound character of their research tools enveloped them in an atmosphere which was nonblack to the extent that black issues were not discussed, and antiblack to the extent that they were. To white scholars, as to whites in general, black history is painful since it forces them to shed the notion that American society is open and fluid, a land where everyone has an equal chance for place and power. As a group, furthermore, blacks have been have-nots and, as Jesse Lemisch points out, "The history of the powerless, the inarticulate, the poor, has not yet begun to be written because they have been treated no more fairly by historians than they have been treated by their contemporaries."

Black chroniclers are not color blind, but they too have their blind spots. The blacks who write history are, in the main, in search of truth, the great canon of the discipline, its very elusiveness making it all the more of a challenge. The search for truth has an intrinsic value, liberating the mind and the spirit. But like many whites in the field, many black historians have "a magnet in their mind," to use Herbert Butterfield's perceptive phrase. There is no magic in skin color, and black historians too sometimes engage in adversary proceedings, with racial vindication the paramount consideration.

Black writers of history for the masses often reflect "the great man" theory of history, presenting a gallery of heroic men and women pushing on to victory against great odds. The black bibliographer, A. A. Schomburg, characterized these glorifiers as "glibly trying to prove that half of the world's geniuses have been Negroes and to trace the pedigree of nineteenth century Americans from the Queen of Sheba." Most writers in this school of "Claim-the-World Negro History" were not as able as J. A. Rogers, the black biographer who died in 1966. That Rogers was an indefatigable researcher on an intercontinental scale is attested to by his wide-ranging *World's Great Men of Color*.[7] Operating from the premise that "the story of contacts of whites and blacks is usually told from the white angle," Rogers designed his capsule biographies as a source of inspiration to the young, particularly to those who were black. But in his desire to project a heroic black image, he was sometimes carried away and his sketches of historical figures are shot through with hyperbole and panegyric.

Another group who view the past from a special angle are the revolutionary black nationalists. They do not feel that history

[7] J. A. Rogers, *World's Great Men of Color*, 2 vol., ed. John Hendrick Clarke (New York: Macmillan, 1972).

should be hero worship. "Black history does not seek to highlight the outstanding contributions of special black people to the life and times of America," writes Vincent Harding, the eloquent director of the Institute of the Black World in Atlanta. "Rather our emphasis is on exposure, disclosure, or reinterpretation of the entire American past. We want to know America at its depths, now that invitations to its life are besieging us." The revolutionary black nationalists are exponents of functional research, issue laden and action oriented. Not addressing themselves to pure, theoretical, knowledge-for-its-own-sake investigation, they do not propose to scale the mountain simply because it is there. They hold that black studies, including history, should be a catalyst for the new day a-coming. To Nathan Hare, editor of *The Black Scholar*, "a black studies program which is not revolutionary and nationalist is, accordingly, quite profoundly irrelevant." Scorning objectivity as a species of ivory-towerism, the revolutionary nationalists hold that ideology and intellectualism are not incompatible, and that a person who has leaned too long in one direction may, for a time, have to lean in the other if he is to achieve balance.

Essentially these nationalist intellectuals share many of the beliefs of the sociologist-psychiatrist, Frantz Fanon of Martinique, who held that "African-Negro" culture would develop not around songs, poems, and folklore, but around the struggles of the people. "White America," he said, was "an organized imperialist force holding black people in colonial bondage." The black revolutionaries address themselves to the task of decolonizing America, including her history. Fanon also held that for "the wretched of the earth" the way out was physical confrontation. He thus gave to violence an aura of romance, suggesting that it had a cleansing, releasing effect. Thus disdaining the doctrine of reconciliation and determined not to forget white America's massive assault upon the humanity of blacks, the revolutionary nationalists consciously choose to imprison themselves in the castle of color. The construct of the White Man dominates their thinking, much as the Devil was once the central figure in some Christian theologies.

Nevertheless, we dismiss the black revolutionary nationalists at our intellectual and social peril. Even though we might not share their fondness for rhetorical flourishes and threatening hyperbole, their demand for heretical history must be carefully weighed, especially as they bring to their reflections a tunnel vision so often characteristic of the powerless people whose cause they proclaim. "Let us not decide to imitate Europe," urged Fanon. "Let us try to create the whole man, whom Europe has been incapable of bringing to triumphant birth." The revolutionary black nationalist interpretation of the black experience is somewhat new in American thought, although the nationalist point of view is not.[8]

The Problem of Materials

An old and recurring phenomenon in black history writing is the paucity of sources, the lack of hard data. Many questions must remain unanswered because there are no sources from which to formulate a trustworthy response. Negro sources are not easy to come by; documents, more often than not, are not readily accessible. The formal record is often thin, for most blacks were not articulate in a literary sense. John Chavis, director of behavioral science research at Tuskegee Institute's Carver Research Foundation, has posed the problem of the investigator: "Where are the diaries, the family Bibles, the correspondence in fancy script tied in bundles? These are not, in most instances, part of the Negro past. Where are the silver services, the porringers, the samplers, the furniture dark and glossy, the oil portraits of awesome ancestors?" Even when Negro memorabilia do exist, they are often hidden away in a basement or an attic, prey to fire or other loss. Such privately held material is invariably unprocessed. All too often even in major research libraries, particularly those of state and local historical societies, Negro-related holdings have never been catalogued.

Fortunately, the available sources are now being more widely publicized than ever before, and depositories are calling attention to their black-oriented materials, including early black newspapers and magazines on microfilm. The *Quarterly Journal of the Library of Congress,* for example, has devoted a special issue to its African materials.[9] In the extent of its black documents, the Library of Congress is rivaled by a sister federal agency, the National Archives. In June 1973, more than 150 scholars and interested parties attended a two-day "National Archives Conference on Federal Archives as Sources for Research on Afro-Americans," a meeting which addressed itself to the agency's Negro-related materials (a number of them audiovisuals), including the originals of the well-

---

[8] See, for example, the twenty-four-page introduction to Sterling Stuckey, ed., *The Ideological Origins of Black Nationalism* (Boston: Beacon Press, 1972).

[9] *Quarterly Journal of the Library of Congress* 27 (July 1970). See also John McDonough, "Manuscript Sources for the Study of Negro Life and History," *Quarterly Journal of the Library of Congress* 26 (July 1969): 126–48, a description of the library's extensive holdings on black Americans.

known Emancipation Proclamation and the Civil War amend-
ments.[10] Historical societies have also begun to furnish guides to
their Negro-related holdings.[11] This itself is a hopeful sign inasmuch
as research libraries, like museums and art galleries, are selective
in their acquisitions; they do not buy or accept and certainly do
not publicize anything they feel will have too low a yield in public
or professional interest and prestige.

During the past decade black source materials have profited from
an infusion of oral history, created by interviewing selected persons
of note and tape-recording and transcribing their remarks. What

[10] A quarter of a century earlier, in 1947, the Committee on Negro Studies of
the American Council of Learned Societies published its path-breaking and still
available "Guide to the Documents in the National Archives: For Negro Studies"
(Washington, D.C.: American Council of Learned Societies).

[11] For a joint catalogue of the black historical materials—manuscripts, pamphlets
and books—in the Library Company of Philadelphia and the adjacent Historical
Society of Pennsylvania, see Edward Wolf, ed., *Negro History, 1553–1973* (Philadelphia: Library Company of Philadelphia). For a list of the black history collections
in the Maryland Historical Society, see Nancy G. Boles (curator of manuscripts),
"Notes on Maryland Historical Society Manuscript Collections: Black History Collections," *Maryland Historical Magazine* 106 (Spring 1971): 72–78; for useful hints
on the search for black genealogy, see Mary K. Meyer's, "Genealogical Notes," 79–
81, in the same issue. See also John Slonaker, *The United States Army and the
Negro* (Carlisle Barracks, Pa.: U.S. Army Military History Research Collection,
1971); Joyce B. Schneider, *Selected List of Periodicals Relating to Negroes, with
Holdings in the Libraries of Yale University* (New Haven: Yale University Library,
1970); Earle H. West, *A Bibliography of Doctoral Research on the Negro, 1933–
1966* (New York: Xerox Company, 1969). The most comprehensive early-twentieth-
century bibliography is Monroe N. Work, *Bibliography of the Negro in Africa and
America* (New York: H. W. Wilson Company, 1928). For the 1950s/1960s the most
serviceable of the various annual compilations is the one published by G. K. Hall,
Boston, successively titled, *Index to Selected Negro Periodicals, Index to Selected
Periodicals,* and *Index to Periodical Articles By and About Negroes.* For excellent
recent bibliographies see James M. McPherson et al., *Blacks in America: Biblio-
graphical Essays* (Garden City, New York: Doubleday, 1971); Louis Harlan, *The
Negro in American History* (Washington: American Historical Association, 1965);
Elizabeth W. Miller and Mary L. Fisher, *The Negro in America* (Cambridge: Harvard
University Press, 1970); Darwin T. Turner, *Afro-American Writers* (New York:
Appleton-Century Crofts, 1970); and Dorothy B. Porter, *The Negro in the United
States: A Selected Bibliography* (Washington, D.C.: Library of Congress, 1970), a
work with a detailed index and 1,781 entries, among them eighty-one describing
other reference sources. Dorothy B. Porter, librarian of the Moorland-Springarn
Collection at Howard University, a treasure house of materials on black Americans,
has also edited seventy-two selections written by early blacks: *Early Negro Writing,
1760–1837* (Boston: Beacon Press, 1971). For a model example of a bibliographical
study which focuses on one state, see *New Jersey and the Negro: A Bibliography,
1715–1966* (Trenton: The New Jersey Library Association, 1967), an excellent work
which lists 1,016 entries, divided into twenty-eight headings, and dealing not only
with Negro life in New Jersey but also with New Jersey's role in black history plus
the racial attitudes of white New Jerseyites. Finally, the black quarterly, *Freedom-
ways,* features annotated bibliographical surveys written by Ernest Kaiser of the
staff of the Schomburg Collection in New York.

189

is, in essence, a memory bank of formal oral history was inaugurated a quarter of a century ago at Columbia University by Allan Nevins. In the first two decades of Columbia's Oral History Collection, of 200 interviewees only three were black—W.E.B. Du Bois, journalist George S. Schuyler, and Roy Wilkins. In orders received for micro-published copies of the memoirs, however, the top best seller as of April 1973 was that of W.E.B. Du Bois, and the third-ranking best seller was that of Roy Wilkins.

In recent years other oral history collections have sought Negro-related materials.[12] The largest collection which concentrates on blacks is the Civil Rights Documentation Project at Howard University, dealing with black protest expression since 1954.[13] Currently it includes 703 tape-recorded interviews, sixty conference tapes, and 800 transcripts. In Alabama, seven predominantly black colleges have launched a Statewide Oral History Project "to document the personal experiences of black Alabamians in their attempts to cope with racial prejudice and in their struggle to achieve racial equality."[14]

The mounting number of black research materials has led black librarians to seek ways to work cooperatively in providing reliable information on Afro-American bibliography. With an initial grant in June 1971 from the U.S. Office of Education, the North Carolina Central University School of Library Science began a project to identify and coordinate all African-American materials in six southeastern states. A year earlier, a group of librarians and scholars, meeting in Philadelphia, formed the Association of African-American Bibliography, one of whose announced aims was the establishment of "a Black Union Catalog on a regional and national basis."

By far the most urgent need in black history (and in black studies in general) is for just such a massive, comprehensive bibliography of black source materials, modeled along the lines of the National Union Catalog, compiled by the Library of Congress. Such a compilation might take a dual form, providing a catalogue of printed works and another of manuscripts. It would serve many interests. Although scholars would be the immediate beneficiaries, the aca-

---

[12] Gary L. Shumway, *Oral History in the United States: A Directory* (New York: The Oral History Association, 1971).

[13] Directed from its beginning in 1967 by Vincent J. Browne, this project was sponsored and funded by the Ford Foundation which, in 1973, chose Howard University as the recipient of the collection.

[14] The Fisk University Library, in Nashville, has a Black Oral History Program which proposes "to bridge gaps in black history and culture."

190

demic community in general would profit. People in public life and in the media would benefit from the availability of a trustworthy guide to materials on black citizens and black-white relationships. Such a tool would also lead reformist groups to the data they need.

Although publicizing the existing data would be a major step forward in black historiography, it should be accompanied by a reexamination of what is considered historical evidence and an inclination to ask new questions of the data. In fields other than the natural sciences, basic theoretical frameworks have not been staked out, and in an evolving field like black history the play of flexibility and innovation has a special place. With no vested interest in one type of documentation, the researcher in black history can be eclectic in his selection of ways and means. In order to ferret out the true dimensions of the black past he may have to run some methodological risks. Certainly, this is not the place for watertight compartmentalization. Those who work in black studies must be prepared to "stay loose," opening their minds to new approaches while subjecting the familiar ones to constant scrutiny.

Traditional source materials on blacks are in particularly short supply for the periods preceding the Civil War. The African background of the New World blacks is, for example, very difficult to document, and illustrates the need for less traditional methodological approaches. The belief that black Africa had no history has a twofold origin. With the coming of the European powers, Africa passed into a stage of colonialism. African history was not taught; indeed, the rulers assumed that no such history existed, it being one of their cardinal premises that the history of their subjects dated from their own arrival. Once determined to exploit Africa's human resources, Europeans, as men of conscience and religion, had to convince themselves of the innate inferiority of the natives. Furthermore, written records about West Africa prior to the coming of the Europeans are limited, and thus historical reconstruction is difficult and requires a number of technical skills. Hence, even a historian like Arnold Toynbee was led to believe that the black race was the only one that had made no creative contribution to any of the world's civilizations. Toynbee was careful to disavow the factor of race and color in accounting for the existence of advanced civilizations, but he did tend to make the error common to historians—that of overvaluing peoples for whom written records are abundant and underrating those for whom written records are relatively scarce. In contrast, however, L.S.B. Leakey has pointed out that "men of science today are, with few exceptions, satisfied that Africa was the birthplace of man himself, and that for many hundreds of centuries thereafter Africa was in the forefront of all world progress."[15] As could be expected, the late Dr. Leakey was a social anthropologist.

"The most spectacular feature of the new post-war boom in African history," writes Philip D. Curtin, "has been the development of new techniques for investigation, and the application of older techniques to the African past." In a perceptive booklet,[16] Curtin describes some of the fields which are throwing light on early Africa, including archaeology, botanical evidence, linguistic studies, and the oral tradition. The oral tradition is particularly important because most precolonial African civilizations were "oral civilizations" documentable in no other way.[17]

Although the main emphasis in American history writing has traditionally been political and intellectual, areas in which the disadvantaged and anonymous masses did not have much direct impact, other facets of history, whose influence is now growing, take much greater notice of minorities. Social history, for example, views society as a whole, taking into account ordinary people and their patterns of living, and giving attention also to the phenomena of social protest.[18]

The urbanization of black Americans in the twentieth century has had a profound effect not only on blacks themselves but also on America's cities and on the country more generally. A number of excellent books have been written on the daily experiences of ordinary people in American cities.[19] David M. Katzman has illustrated the use of the concept of caste in black urban history.[20] The National Urban League, an agency that has been on the cutting edge of the unprecedented cityward migration in the twentieth century, has been described and assessed by Guichard Parris and Lester Brooks in a book which deals with other major black institutions

[15] L. S. B. Leakey, *The Progress and Evolution of Man in Africa* (New York: New York University Press, 1961).

[16] Philip D. Curtin, *African History* (New York: Macmillan, 1964).

[17] Jan Vansina, "Once Upon a Time: Oral Traditions as History in Africa," *Daedalus* 100 (Spring 1971).

[18] Gilberto Freyre, *The Masters and the Slaves: A Study in the Development of Brazilian Civilization* (New York: Knopf, 1946).

[19] Gilbert Osofsky, *Harlem: The Making of a Ghetto: New York, 1890–1930* (New York: Harper and Row, 1966); Allen H. Spear, *Black Chicago: The Making of a Negro Ghetto, 1890–1920* (Chicago: University of Chicago Press, 1967); and St. Clair Drake and Horace R. Clayton, *Black Metropolis: A Study of Negro Life in a Northern City* (New York: Harcourt, Brace, 1945).

[20] David M. Katzman, *Before the Ghetto: Black Detroit in the Nineteenth Century* (Urbana: University of Illinois Press, 1973).

as well, including the church and the press.[21] Black businesses, small and short-lived as a rule, have not attracted many researchers, but the distinct possibilities in black entrepreneurial history become clearly evident in a meticulous and interpretive study of the North Carolina Mutual Life by Walter Weare.[22] Urban-based reform movements likewise constitute a fruitful line of investigation. August Meier and Elliot Rudwick, one trained in history and the other in sociology, have written a model study of CORE which suggests the desirability of collaborative efforts in black history.[23] The broadening of the kinds of evidence now considered historical is also indicated by new quarterlies like *Ethnohistory,* with its emphasis on general culture, and the *Journal of Interdisciplinary History,* whose avowed purpose, as set forth in its first issue in the autumn of 1970, is to "stimulate historians to examine their own subjects in a new light, whether they be derived from psychology, physics, or paleontology."

Psychohistory, a field of particular importance for minorities, is attracting new attention. This relatively unknown field includes group psychopathology, which touches on the fantasy life and self-image of minorities and on the positive aspects of their differences. It encompasses the best-selling work, *Black Rage,* in which psychiatrists Charles Grier and Price M. Cobbs describe the impact of prejudice on Negro personality patterns. The newest historical periodical is *History of Childhood Quarterly: The Journal of Psychohistory,* which first appeared in the summer of 1973. Earle E. Thorpe, himself black like Grier and Cobbs, holds that "black history always has been cut more from the psychohistory mold than has been the case with modern white Occidental history." In two case studies of Southern life, he challenges the "hate-and-conflict" image of black-white relationships in the antebellum South, holding instead that interracial responses and attitudes were characterized in part by intimacy and affection.[24] Slave-born John Roy Lynch, congressman from Mississippi during Reconstruction, concurred in this viewpoint, taking note of "the bond of sympathy between the

---

[21] Guichard Parris and Lester Brooks, *Blacks in the City: A History of the National Urban League* (Boston: Little Brown, 1971).

[22] Walter Weare, *Black Business in the New South* (Urbana, Ill.: University of Illinois Press, 1973).

[23] August Meier and Elliott Rudwick, *CORE: A Study in the Civil Rights Movement, 1942–1968* (New York: Oxford University Press, 1973).

[24] Earle E. Thorpe, *Eros and Freedom in Southern Life and Thought* (Durham, N.C.: Seaman Printery, 1967); and *The Old South: A Psychohistory* (Durham, N.C.: Seaman Printery, 1972).

masses of the two races in the South." Thorpe's viewpoints and procedures are stimulating and suggestive. Nevertheless, it is historical revisionism of no mean proportions to view racial relationships below the Potomac as a web of mutuality.

In the less traditional branches of history, particularly those concerned with social behavior and action, investigators of the black experience are turning for information to lesser-mined ores, including church and police records, census publications, city directories, housing and unemployment files, local tax lists, popular culture materials (such as black discography), and legal documents. Court records form the base of historian Letitia Woods Brown's study, *Free Negroes in the District of Columbia, 1790–1846.*[25] Black history stands to gain as more scholars receive training in demographic and family history and in the use of quantitative techniques, including computerized data processing.

New Emphases in Black History

The increasing receptivity to new types of source material for black history has brought about new analyses of familiar topics, such as slavery, and the concept of black uniformity. If, as Staughton Lynd asserts, slavery is "a key to the meaning of our national experience," then we should have as balanced a portrayal of it as possible. Until recently, however, the standard view of slavery tended to reflect the attitudes of the master class. As Henry Steele Commager has pointed out: "The slave-owner was literate and articulate, the Negro slave was illiterate and inarticulate; it was, until recently, the slave-owner's version of slavery which came down to us and which was widely accepted as history." The portrait of slavery that came down from the past was fashioned in the big house and not in slave row. Thus a historian like U. B. Phillips, using sources that represented the views of the masters, tended to depict the slave as contented and his surroundings as pleasant. According to Phillips, plantation life was punctuated by such congenial pastimes as "the dance in the sugarhouse, the bonfire in the quarters with contests in clog dances and cakewalks, the baptizing in the creek with demonstrations from the sisters as they came dripping out, the rabbit hunt, the log-rolling, the house-raising, the husking bee, the quilting party, and the crap game."[26]

[25] Letitia Woods Brown, *Free Negroes in the District of Columbia, 1790–1846* (New York: Oxford University Press, 1972).

[26] U. B. Phillips, *Life and Labor in the Old South* (Boston: Little Brown, 1929).

Today scholars interested in slavery give more prominence to the slave himself and take little stock in the theory of his total powerlessness. "Any history of slavery must be written in large part from the standpoint of the slave," wrote Richard Hofstadter in 1944. Hitherto consigned to a position as a pawn, the slave is now regarded as a role player, and we are having second thoughts about the allegation that his nature and mentality were servile. We now realize that everybody on the plantation made history, the slave as well as the master.

Something of the slave's experiential world and internal life may be gathered from an examination of his literature—his songs and narratives about bondage and freedom, written or oral. Mark Miles Fisher has opened our eyes to the subtle "this-worldly" character of the ostensibly "other-worldly" religious songs heard along slave row.[27] Sterling Stuckey uses folk songs and folk tales to document his assertion that slaves were able to fashion a life style and set of values of their own.[28] In efforts to reconstruct the slave's world, contemporary slave literature was, of course, a valuable historical source.[29] In addition, the early decades of the twentieth century witnessed a number of efforts to interview ex-slaves and record their impressions. The most comprehensive was conducted by the Federal Writers' Project of the Works Project Administration during the years 1936 to 1938, and resulted in 2,300 recorded interviews, over two-thirds with people over eighty years old.[30]

Used with proper professional safeguards, such nontraditional sources, helped by a fresh glance at the more conventional sources, tell us that slaves found many outlets for their creative energies and social instincts, outlets often hidden from, or unnoted by, their masters. We are now finding that a slave often took as his models of behavior and authority not his master alone, as Stanley Elkins has suggested, but blacks like himself—the sage, the preacher, the

[27] Mark Miles Fisher, *Negro Slave Songs in the United States* (Ithaca, N.Y.: Cornell University Press, 1953).

[28] Sterling Stuckey, "Through the Prism of Folklore; the Black Ethos in Slavery," *Massachusetts Review* 9 (Summer 1968): 417–37.

[29] John W. Blassingame, *The Slave Community: Plantation Life in the Ante-Bellum South* (New York: Oxford University Press, 1972). This book includes a "Critical Essay on Sources," which justifies the use of slave literature and comments on some of the major secondary works on slavery.

[30] The materials from this federal project, along with two collections assembled by Fisk University and issued in mimeographed form in 1945, were published in nineteen volumes in 1972: George P. Rawick, ed., *The American Slave: A Composite Autobiography* (Westport, Conn.: Greenwood Publishing Company). See also Norman R. Yetman, *Voices From Slavery* (New York: Holt, Rinehart and Winston, 1970).

bold and defiant, the trickster slave so beloved in black folklore who was adept at "puttin' on ole massa," and even the driver who enforced the dictates of the white overseer. The range of options open to slaves was wider than we had believed, and we are now learning of the myriad ways in which they maintained considerable group solidarity despite the formidable odds against it.

A second example of the many changes in black history is the increased emphasis on the concept that the black is not monolithic, a concept amply illustrated in the rich field of biography and autobiography. In the eyes of others, black Americans often take on a massively uniform quality; if they are not viewed as looking alike, they are thought of as at least thinking and acting alike. This misleading impression stems in part from a tendency to lump all blacks together—to typecast them—and in part from their understandably united and standard response to color discrimination. Blacks, for example, often vote as a bloc against a prejudiced or racially obtuse politician.

Aside from their common cause against an adversary and a shared sense of having been wronged, however, American blacks have been marked historically by diversity. Within themselves, they fall into a congeries of groups reflective of a typically American individualism. They have always had their own class lines. In antebellum America, the free black thought of himself as inhabiting a niche considerably above that of the slave. And within the free black group there were further distinctions, including those based on skin color, occupation, schooling, and free ancestry. Slave society also had gradations. House servants had the most prestige; below them came the skilled laborers; and bringing up the rear were the field hands. In the quarter century following the Civil War, skin color (light or dark) loomed even larger as a status determinant; since 1900, however, in line with the national pattern, money has been the most important determinant of rank in the black American's unofficial who's who.

With regard to religious affiliations and political party ties, as in other areas, blacks have had varied preferences. Since they have had no universally held dogmas, they have never had an official spokesman; even Booker T. Washington, although he exercised great influence among prominent whites, could never speak for more than a fraction of his fellow blacks. The Communists made a strong bid for colored membership in the 1930s, but found that they could make little headway against the black American's dislike for regimentation and for thinking in lockstep. Indeed, even in fighting discrimination, blacks have never agreed upon one approach or strategy, but have made proposals ranging from going back to Africa to setting aside a portion of the United States for black occupation. Blacks are persons as well as types. There is no such thing as a universally held black ideology or point of view. In America, land of individualism, there is no end to the number of ways of being black.

The field of life-writing bears this out, revealing a multiplicity of disparate personalities. Slave narratives aside, black biography received its first great thrust with the publication, in 1887, of *Men of Mark: Eminent, Progressive and Rising*, by William J. Simmons. A former slave who had become a clergyman and educator, Simmons consistently sounded an inspirational, eulogistic note in the 178 sketches he assembled.[31] Simmons included no women in the hope, which proved vain, that he would be able to publish a companion volume devoted to them. From 1912 to 1952, sketches of black notables were carried in the *Negro Yearbook and Annual Encyclopedia of the Negro*.[32] In more recent years a number of professionally trained historians have published black collective biographies.[33] There are also a number of black biography series in the field, most notably those of the University of Chicago[34] and the Oxford University Press.[35] In addition three of the most prom-

---

[31] Although Simmons admitted he was no scholar, *Men of Mark* "is still the basic text in black biography," in the words of Lerone Bennett, Jr. in his foreword to the 1970 edition of the over 800-page volume, published by the Johnson Publishing Company, Chicago.

[32] *Negro Yearbook and Annual Encyclopedia of the Negro* (Tuskegee, Ala.: Department of Records and Research, Tuskegee Institute, 1912–52). This was the brainchild of Monroe N. Work, for thirty years director of the department of records and research at Tuskegee Institute.

[33] For a panorama of black notables from Crispus Attucks to Ralph Bunche, etched against a backdrop of three time spans, see Richard Bardolph, *The Negro Vanguard* (New York: Rhinehart, 1959). See also Edgar A. Toppin, *A Biographical History of Blacks in America Since 1528* (New York: David McKay, 1971), half of which is devoted to vignettes of 145 black achievers. Wilhemina S. Robinson, in *Historical Negro Biographies (New York: Publishers Company, Inc., 1967), includes blacks from Africa and the other Americas. Projected for publication in 1974 is a Dictionary of American Negro Biography*, ed. Rayford W. Logan and Michael R. Winston.

[34] Edited by John Hope Franklin, this series includes biographies of such varying contemporaries as the journalist T. Thomas Fortune (by Emma Lou Thornbrough) and painter Henry Ossawa Tanner (by Marcia M. Matthews).

[35] This series, edited by Hollis R. Lynch, is devoted to "distinguished Black Americans and Black Africans." In the first of its published studies Okon E. Uya portrayed the career of Robert Smalls, Civil War hero and congressman from South Carolina; a more recent study by Carol V. R. George focused on the influence of Richard Allen, the slave-born pioneer black bishop.

inent of all American blacks, Frederick Douglass, W.E.B. Du Bois and Booker T. Washington, are now coming under fuller study and investigation as efforts proceed to publish their papers.[36]

The Periodical Literature

Afro-American History: A Bibliography, edited by Dwight L. Smith,[37] is a compendium of 2,900 abstracts on the black experience, compiled by combing the periodical literature from 1954 to 1971, a period in which awareness of the presence of blacks reached new heights, spurring a vast outpouring of articles. Better than any other single work, *Afro-American History* helps illuminate the new kinds of concerns that have become paramount; it tells much about the kinds of materials that are being used, the questions that are being raised, and the interpretations that are becoming common.

The focus of the bibliography is the United States, but other countries are not ignored and many of the articles come from foreign language periodicals. One abstract gives a sketch of American blacks in czarist Russia, including the famed Shakespearean actor, Ira Aldridge; another suggests that in Italy the stage version of *Uncle Tom's Cabin* has always been a great favorite, particularly in times of political crisis.

Many of the abstracts carry a concluding sentence on the source materials used; one has only to take a random sample of these to sense their richness. Even when conventional sources, such as diaries and letters, are used, it is edifying to learn, for example, that George A. Matson, who operated as a barber, schoolmaster, and clergyman in Lincoln, Nebraska, kept a diary from 1901 to 1903; or that the former slave, Taylor Thistle, while studying theology in Nashville, sent seven letters to his benefactors. Photographs, electoral maps, church and regimental records—conventional though they be— have importance, particularly when they shed light on Negro experience. The family Bible, with its record of births, marriages, and deaths, has its uses, particularly where, as in the case of blacks, other records of vital statistics are in short supply. Nonliterary sources appear infrequently, although some of the authors urge

---

[36] Yale University has projected a Frederick Douglass Papers Project, under the editorship of John W. Blassingame. The W.E.B. Du Bois papers, recently acquired by the University of Massachusetts, are being edited by Du Bois's literary executor, Herbert Aptheker. The Washington Papers, like the others a multivolumed undertaking, are being edited by Louis R. Harlan of the University of Maryland.

[37] Dwight L. Smith, ed., *Afro-American History: A Bibliography* (Santa Barbara, Ca.: American Bibliographical Center, 1974).

others to make use of them. Certain of the articles are highly personal, essentially exercises in self-discovery.

As David B. Davis makes clear elsewhere, slavery remains a prime subject of study, and recent literature suggests that the Reconstruction period also retains its fascination. If, on the one hand, we are reminded anew that there was no such thing as black rule and that many carpetbaggers were men of probity, we are also reminded increasingly of the political mind of the Negro, and of men like Richard Allen and Matt Gaines in the Texas legislature, who promoted state and regional measures beneficial to all. We learn of black-on-black political intimidation, with black Republicans using strong-arm tactics on black Democrats. The historiography of the period is still the "dark and bloody ground" that Bernard Weisberger found it fifteen years ago.

Afro-American History includes a number of articles on the age-old question as to whether the mean differences in intelligence scores between white and black children stem from environmental or genetic factors, and, although proponents of the latter have grown more defensive in recent years, they have not left the field.

Contemporary periodical literature indicates an increase in studies comparing blacks with other groups. One author, comparing the Negro with the immigrant, concludes that the factor of race was crucial; the immigrant faced the problem of assimilation, to be sure, but he did not face the insurmountable wall of caste. Tackling the question of why Japanese-Americans have fared better than black Americans, one observer points to the former's smaller numbers and higher educational level. Another writer sees parallels in the relationships between Jews and peasants in prewar Eastern Europe and between Jews and Negroes in modern America; in each instance, he points out, the Jews regarded the other group as violence-prone and lacking in culture.

White-black violence is the topic of a great number of articles. Urban racial unrest, including its precipitants and underlying causes, receives its full share of attention. Blacks viewed these disturbances as protests against racial discrimination, whereas whites saw them as conspiracies masterminded by Communists and outside Negroes. A race riot, even when viewed in retrospect, is a sobering experience. Yet, seen in a broader context, it is consistent not only with the nation's history in race relations but with the fact that Americans are a violence-prone people even where the factor of race is not present.[38]

[38] Those proposing to scrutinize the anatomy of black-white outbreaks might

Among the topics which received little scholarly attention is the role of black women. Historically, women were hardly in the public eye; an article on the early history of Negro women in journalism, for example, yielded few names until the appearance of the militant Ida Wells Barnett of Memphis and Chicago at the turn of the twentieth century. As for the women's liberation movement of our own day, this is hardly a matter that attracts blacks or their chroniclers. To black men and women, the battle of the sexes seems almost a diversion in light of the whole range of problems they have in common because of their color.

On the other hand, recent black-oriented periodical literature has devoted considerable attention to the discipline of black studies, a constellation of fields in college curriculum offerings in which history is the largest single component. Supplementing his use of this voluminous literature with visits to more than a hundred colleges, Nick Aaron Ford published *Black Studies: Threat or Challenge* in 1973.[39] Professor Ford holds that while badly conceived black studies programs pose a threat to effective education, well-conceived programs "are a threat to false and distorted scholarship." Black studies generally are a challenge, calling upon "the national educational establishment" to reexamine "moribund concepts and outmoded methods."

Mirroring the new awareness of Negro history, the literature has put historians themselves under scrutiny, noting their changing images of blacks. There are scores of articles on the treatment of blacks by historians. Some are broadly based; others deal with a particular historian, period, or event. Some indicate topics and themes that are deserving of further research.

In American historiography blacks have sometimes been victimized more by being ignored than by overt prejudice; omission can of course be construed as a form of prejudice. This, however, is no longer a major problem. Although it may be premature to proclaim the full arrival of blacks in American history, they are at least now listed in the cast of characters; if their roles are still too often indeterminate, at least their names are now likely to be spelled correctly.

---

gain insight and perspective by first noting the volume by Hugh Davis Graham and Ted Robert Furr, *Violence in America: Historical and Comparative Perspectives— A Staff Report to the National Commission on the Causes and Prevention of Violence* (Washington, D.C.: U.S. Government Printing Office, 1969).

[39] Nick Aaron Ford, *Black Studies: Threat or Challenge?* (Port Washington, N.Y.: Kennicat Press, 1973).

In fine, this is a day of unusual ferment in black history—in its substantiative outreach and in its documentation. In their quest for a usable past, blacks have done two things. They have helped re-shape our assessment of "what has actually happened," spurring the use of long-muted evidence. And they have helped alert us to the possibilities of alternate methodologies within the discipline itself. The concept of history "from the bottom up," now so prev-alent, is certainly not new, but a good portion of its present sweep and momentum unquestionably stems from the marked upturn of interest by scholars and laymen in the historic role played by Amer-icans from Africa.

In his thoughtful and imaginative book, *The Future as History,* Robert L. Heilbroner bids us not despair as we face the years that seem to loom so ominously before us, but instead to take heart, drawing upon a sense of historical identity and awareness. History does indeed remain the great synthesizing discipline, and Heilbroner is most persuasive in elucidating the grand dynamic of its forces. We must, however, proceed with due caution. A valid projection of the future as history, for all its importance, requires a fresh look at the past as history. "No fact has ever been wholly ascertained, but a fact may be progressively ascertained," observes R. G. Coll-ingwood; "as the labour of historians goes forward, they come to more and more facts, and to reject with greater and greater con-fidence a number of mistaken accounts of them."[40]

[40] Robert L. Heilbroner, *The Future as History* (New York: Harper and Brothers, 1959); R. G. Collingwood, *Essays in the Philosophy of History,* William Debbins, ed. (Austin: University of Texas Press, 1965).

12. Black History's Diversified Clientele

LONG WITH many other denials since he arrived on these shores, the black American has until recently been denied a past. The consequent damage to his psyche can hardly be imagined. In a poem entitled "Negro History," appearing in the volume *From the Ashes: Voices of Watts* (Budd Schulberg, editor), young Jimmie Sherman depicts the past as his grandfather viewed it:

> A ship
> A chain
> A distant land
> A whip
> A pain
> A white man's hand
> A sack
> A field
> of cotton balls—
> The only things
> Grandpa recalls.

Such an outlook on the past has a stultifying effect, making for apathy and despair. Hence black leaders since the birth of the republic have been advocates of Negro history, obviously envisioning a far broader coverage of it than Jimmie Sherman's grandpa had come to know. Black scholars, led by Carter G. Woodson in 1915, began to remove the layers of ignorance and distortion that had encrusted the Afro-American past. One of these scholars, W. E. B. Du Bois, in the closing line of his autobiography, written during his last months, bespoke anew his lifelong devotion to history: "Teach us, Forever Dead, there is no Dream but Deed, there is no Deed but Memory." A quarter of a century earlier Du Bois fired back a sharp rejoinder to a magazine editor who had rejected a Du Bois essay because it had touched upon the past. "Don't you understand," Du Bois wrote, "that the past is present; that without what was, nothing is."

During the past decade the cry for black history has been stronger than ever before. Numbered among the proponents of such history are the newer black militants. "We Blacks," writes Imamu Amiri Baraka (LeRoi Jones), "must learn our collective past in order to design a collective destiny." Of his period of confinement at the Norfolk (Massachusetts) Prison Colony, Malcolm X wrote: "I began first telling my Black brother inmates about the glorious history of the Black man—things they had never dreamed." On another occasion he referred to history as "a people's memory" without which "man is demoted to the lower animals." In his assessment of the past, Malcolm X did not ignore the less glorious aspects of the black pilgrimage in America. Speaking to a ghetto audience in Detroit in 1953 he evoked a deep response with the words: "We didn't land on Plymouth Rock, my brothers and sisters—Plymouth Rock landed on *us!*"

Eldridge Cleaver, who, like Malcolm X, became a serious student of history while serving time in prison, spoke its praises. In his essay "To All Black Women, From All Black Men," in *Soul on Ice*, he writes:

Be convinced, Sable Sister, that the past is no forbidden vista upon which we dare not look, out of a phantom fear of being, as the wife of Lot, turned into pillars of salt. Rather the past is an omniscient mirror: we gaze and see reflected there ourselves and each other—what we used to be and what we are today, how we got this way, and what we are becoming. To decline to look into the Mirror of Then, my heart, is to refuse to view the face of Now.

One of the sable sisters who has needed no convincing about history's role is poet Sarah Webster Fabio, who writes:

> Now at all costs, we must heal our history.
> Or else our future rots in the disease of our past.

Although black history is now coming into its own as never before, not all of its proponents are in pursuit of the same goal. Indeed, today black history is being called upon to serve an increasing variety of publics, four of whom we may scrutinize briefly. These are the black rank and file, the black revolutionary nationalists, the black academicians, and the white world, both scholarly and lay. Not mutually exclusive, these groups often overlap. But this fourfold typology enables us to illustrate the major contemporary uses of black history. We may take these in turn, first describing their aims and then noting their general content and style.

For the black rank and file, the man in the street, the laity, black history's main objective is to create a sense of racial pride and personal worth. To the rank and file the new black history is good therapy, its end result an improved self-image. In a world that has traditionally equated blackness with inferiority, black history serves as a balm to make the wounded whole. In a world that has traditionally equated blackness with low aim, black history serves as a stimulus to success. To a black person seeking to resolve an identity crisis, black history is ego-soothing; it places one in the thick of things, thereby diminishing his sense of alienation, of rootlessness. Black history is a search for the values and the strengths imbedded in the black subculture. Black history strikes at the black American's legacy of self-rejection, the burden of shame that he had been taught was his to bear going back to the curse of Cain. "I always wanted to be somebody," runs the title of the autobiography of a black tennis champion. Black history tells the black reader that he is somebody, however vicariously.

In its content black history for the masses reflects somewhat "the great man" theory of history. White or black, the typical American, himself individualistic, conceives of his country's past as the achievements of a group of outstanding characters, pushing on against Herculean odds. History is a tableau of heroes set in bold relief. To the generality of blacks their men of mark constitute their history, the bulk of their attention falling upon individual achievers— an underground railroad conductor like Harriet Tubman, a dedicated bishop like Daniel E. Payne, an educator like Mary McLeod Bethune, a sports celebrity like prize fighter Peter Jackson or jockey Isaac Murphy, and a singer like Elizabeth Taylor Greenfield (the "Black Swan") or Bessie Smith. The list is endless, ranging from an early African king to a present-day ghetto leader.

Upbeat and achievement-oriented, black history for the rank and file stresses victories—the peak that was scaled, the foe that was vanquished, the deep river that was crossed. Moreover, to the masses, youth makes a special appeal, the younger Frederick Douglass arousing more interest than the Sage of Anacostia. Local black historical figures likewise meet with a readier response than out-of-staters, however more nationally important the latter may be. Moreover, history designed for the laity will of necessity devote as much attention to popular culture and the lively arts as to the more traditional staples, politics and economics, particularly since the black stamp on the former is more readily discernible.

The emphasis on the lively arts and popular culture lends itself to the mass media. Hence black history for laymen has found a natural ally in television, commercial as well as educational, but obviously of far greater proportions in the latter. Radio, too, especially in the Folkways recordings, lends itself to black cultural history. Other mass media such as newspapers and magazines are increasingly carrying black history articles, biographical sketches, and pictorial materials. Sensing the growing interest in black history, commercial firms have brought out coloring books, alphabet books, black history games, and black history in comic-book format.

History as hero worship is hardly the kind of history espoused by the second black group under survey—the black revolutionary nationalists. This group focuses upon exploiters and oppressors, a case study in man's inhumanity to man. This group views history as grievance collecting, a looking back in anger. Black nationalist history is essentially the story of a powerful white majority imposing its will upon a defenseless black minority. Black nationalists hold that American society needs to be reconstructed and that black history is, or should be, a means of ideological indoctrination in the revolutionary cause of black liberation.

Black nationalist history is not without its traces of paranoid thinking, one which holds that the forces of evil are banded in an eternal conspiracy to maintain their oppressive sway. Of very ancient origin, this devil theory of history is deeply rooted in the human psyche and hence should occasion no surprise when met in any of its multiple guises.

Like so much else in American life, black nationalism has, as it has always had, a variety of forms—cultural, religious, and economic, among others. Revolutionary nationalism moves a step beyond the others in its goals and does not rule out violence in achieving them. Revolutionary black nationalists, having carefully examined the almost unbelievable pervasiveness of color prejudice in our society, have, in essence, given up on America. Estranged from the land of their birth, they ponder its dismantlement.

As to content, revolutionary black history is not as interested in historical spadework as in providing new interpretations of that which is already known. Black nationalist history emphasizes racial contrast, physical and cultural. It propounds a black aesthetic and implies a black mystique. It bespeaks the essential kinship of black people on whatever continent they be located or in whatever walk of life. Its central theme is oppression, slavery in one guise or another. Rebelliousness against the oppressor likewise looms large in nationalist lore.

A compound of black rage and white guilt, revolutionary black history makes much of the analogy of colonialism, holding that black Americans live in a state of vassalage to white Americans. Black America is a semicolony of white America.

Going further, the revolutionary school of thought stresses separatism, insisting that black Americans have always constituted a nation. To those who hold these views, black history has one overriding purpose; namely, to promote nation-building.

In tone, black revolutionary history is judgmental, with overtones of recrimination, moral condemnation, and prophetic warning. Apocalyptic and polemical in temper, it scorns objectivity, which it equates with a defense of the status quo. Revolutionary black history may, on occasion, read like social commentary, sometimes taking on a man-the-barricades urgency.

Selective in content, black revolutionary history ignores as irrelevant those aspects of the past which do not relate to its philosophy. As will be noted in just a moment, however, this tendency to pick and choose is nothing new in the historical profession.

The third group under survey are the black academicians—the intellectually sophisticated, the college and university trained, the well-read. Like the revolutionary nationalists, they operate on a more studious level. They would concur with the revolutionary nationalists in holding that history is a weapon in the warfare. But to the academically oriented mind the basic foe is ignorance, be it willful or otherwise. It hardly need be added that ignorance is a somewhat impersonal foe and hence less easily pinpointed, less starkly isolated.

To the black academician, history is a discipline, an attempt to recapture and mirror the past as accurately as possible. Admittedly this is a tall order, considering the nature of the evidence and the unreliability of so many of the witnesses. Black academicians hardly need to be reminded that history, as we know it, is not neutral, not value-free. Who can tell the black academician anything new about the insensitivity of past generations of white scholars, of their neglect or distortion of the role of black peoples? But the black academician would question the viewpoint that prejudiced history must be met with prejudiced history; he would doubt that the best way to strike at the mythmakers of history is to imitate them. In *The Fire Next Time,* James Baldwin has observed that "an invented past can never be used; it cracks and crumbles under the pressures of life like clay in a season of drought." As we have noted, however, white Americans have made some use of an invented past. But black Americans must realize that a powerful majority may for a time be able to afford the luxury of fantasy. Such indulgence on the part of a minority is a species of living beyond its means, a minority having to husband carefully its limited resources.

Like the layman and the nationalist, the black academician finds in black history a deepening sense of racial worth and of peoplehood. He, too, reads black history with pride. The black academician views America as a civilization upon which his ancestors have left their stamp. Hence he does not regard America as a white civilization exclusively; to him it also has its black, red, and yellow components. The black academician holds that his forebears helped to build America, and this being the case no one should sensibly expect him to pack his belongings and leave for other shores.

In addition to personal and racial gratification the black academician reads black history because he feels that it will contribute to his knowledge and understanding of mankind, of his fellow travelers in time and space.

For academicians, the content of black history would be more selective than for the laymen, in an attempt to avoid the obvious or the well known. Black history for the academician would deal less with persons and more with processes, less with general black history than with selected topics in black history. It would include comparative studies and pose methodological problems. On the grounds that academicians do not shy away from the unpleasant, black history for them would not ignore the less glorious aspects of the black past—the African tribesmen who engaged in the slave trade, the slave drivers on the Southern plantations, the black informers who divulged the slave conspiracies or those who revealed the hiding place of a runaway slave. History has its share of those blacks who turned out to be all too human.

The academician would grant that, more often than not, the truth makes one sick. But he believes the New Testament adage about truth also making one free. The academician holds that truth, including the search for it, has a liberating effect. To be truly free is to be free first and foremost in the great franchise of the mind. To a group like black Americans, who have been subjected to so much falsehood by others, it would seem that the quest for truth should be held in high favor, having a relevance never failing.

Black history written for the academic fraternity will in the main take on a reflective, judicial tone, taking its cue from the careful winnowing and sifting that preceded it. The style will be sober, the rhetoric restrained. Passionate and deeply emotional language is highly necessary and desirable in human affairs, but such expression is more the province of the poet, the orator, and the charismatic leader than of the professional historian. An orator may give full vent to his innermost feelings, and to the innermost feelings of his audience, but a social scientist works in a discipline which has imperatives of its own, imperatives which may point to conclusions that run counter to his private wishes.

The codes of his discipline bring the black academician face to face with one of the major problems confronting every social scientist, namely, whether his citizen role should overshadow his professional role, whether he should give priority to social action or to scientific inquiry. Should an academician strive for competence in his discipline or should he seek primarily to become personally involved and relevant? To the black academician this dilemma takes on an unusual urgency inasmuch as he is fully aware of the long-standing discriminations against black people in the American social order. Addressing himself to this question of citizenship role versus professional role, sociologist Ernest Q. Campbell comes to the conclusion that "there is no intrinsic reason why the roles of scientific inquirer and staunch advocate are incompatible" ("Negroes, Education, and the Southern States," *Social Forces*, March 1969). But to play these two roles simultaneously would seem to require unusual abilities and energies. In their absence each black academician must come to some hard choices as to his own major commitment.

To the final audience under survey, the white community—academic and lay—black history has an important message. Black history should not be confined to blacks alone—this would be like confining the Gospel to those already converted, to use a familiar figure. Black history, like other phases of black studies, is no longer a matter of limited concern. Whites need to know black history. As Theodore Draper points out in *The Rediscovery of Black Nationalism* (New York, 1970), "In the interest of the entire society, white students need Black Studies as much or even more than black students." At a meeting of the Organization of American Historians in 1969, C. Vann Woodward voiced much the same sentiment in his presidential address, "Clio with Soul." Woodward spoke of black history as being "too important to be left entirely to Negro historians."

To begin with, whites should realize that the major reason for the long neglect of black history falls upon the historical guild itself. As Carl Becker has pointed out, "The historian selects from a number of particular facts certain facts which he considers most important to be known." Historians, continues Becker, "unconsciously read the objective facts of the past in the light of their own purposes, or the preoccupations of their own age." To point out that written history has a subjective element is certainly nothing new—Becker's observations were made in 1910. But to mention this matter at the outset makes for the open-mindedness so essential to a proper perspective on the black American. Whites who read history should know by now that white historians have until recently dealt with the American past in such a way as to ignore the black presence or to minimize its importance in the making of America.

The aim of black history for white readers is twofold: first to eliminate the myth that our country's past was rosy and romantic, a new Eden "with liberty and justice for all," and second, to illustrate the centrality of the black American in our national experience. White historians have until recently tended to play down the somber aspects of black-white relationships in America—the deeply ingrained sense of white superiority dating back to Jamestown and Plymouth, the brutality of slavery, the mockery of post-Reconstruction, and the twentieth-century offshoots of these persistent pathologies. The American past has a tragic component which cannot be brushed away. White Americans must take a second thought as they sing the familiar lines, "Thine alabaster cities gleam,/Undimmed by human tears."

Black history would enable whites to more realistically appraise some of our country's boasted achievements and some of its acclaimed public figures. For example, whites generally view the age of Andrew Jackson as one in which the right to vote was extended to the common man. But whites need to know that it was during this period that states like North Carolina and Pennsylvania were explicitly prohibiting blacks from exercising this privilege. White readers of American history have thought highly of Woodrow Wilson for his espousal of the "New Freedom" and for his doctrine of "making the world safe for democracy." But white readers need to know that during Wilson's presidency, and with his acquiescence, black federal workers in the District of Columbia were systematically segregated and were given inferior working conditions and restroom facilities such as had not existed up to this time in the federal government.

Black history would be remiss if it did not call attention to these sobering aspects of the American past. But black history does not consist solely of white denial and discrimination. Hence black history for whites would indicate the myriad ways in which this country's history and culture would have been different without the presence of the black man. Many of these ways—economic, political, constitutional, and military—are more quickly spotted than others. In some fields—art, literature, music, the dance, and popular culture in general—the black contribution centers in the common core, making its stamp more difficult to isolate. But whether obvious or subtle, the black man's gifts to America have been freely received if slowly acknowledged. To this extent all Americans are part black in their cultural patrimony. Blacks in general would concur in the sentiment expressed by a stanza from James Weldon Johnson ("Fifty Years, 1863–1913," in his *Fifty Years and Other Poems,* Boston, 1921):

> This land is ours by right of birth,
> This land is ours by right of toil;
> We helped to turn its virgin earth,
> Our sweat is in its fruitful soil.

The acceptance of black history by whites has been greatly facilitated by the current emphasis on social history. "It is a good moment to be a social historian" writes E. J. Hobsbawn *(Daedalus,* Winter 1971), history professor at the University of London. This branch of history pays particular attention to the anonymous common man and to the manners and customs of everyday life. And even more importantly for a black orientation, this branch of history emphasizes social movements and the phenomena of social protest.

For the white reader of black history the content would, at least initially, suggest the centrality of the Negro American and his identification with this country's great, professed goals. Therefore such history would comprise a general presentation of the American past with the black component interwoven throughout, appearing at its proper chronological juncture and not separately, somewhat like a disjointed subtheme for the curious, Clio's underworld.

In style and technique black history for whites would differentiate between the white layman and the white intellectual. For the white layman the approach would be much the same as for his black counterpart, that is, an emphasis on biographical sketches and on the lively arts and popular culture, including sports. Again, as for the black layman, books would be greatly supplemented by the mass media. Indeed, of course, the mass media outlets used to reach black people will inevitably reach many whites.

For the white academician the approach to black history might be broader than the biographical and less fearful of the recipient's short attention span. Black studies for white intellectuals would back assertion with documentation, presenting proof and citing authorities. A footnote is not an end unto itself. But those of an academic bent have been trained to look for the hard evidence; to them a statement must be intellectually tenable, its sources as trustworthy as possible. For the open-minded scholar—the seeker after truth—the will to believe is not an acceptable substitute for the data that corroborates.

We have dealt with black history for four different audiences. But in written history the use of different approaches and viewpoints need come as no surprise. No one category of events, no single interpretation, can furnish the cloth for that seamless garment we call history. There is no single compass by which to unravel the course of historical causation. Written history, in form and content, is manysided, however much this may disconcert the doctrinaire types.

This short excursion into black history has taken note of varying viewpoints as to its function. Although varied, these approaches are often complementary rather than contradictory. More than anything else they demonstrate that there are alternate ways of looking at the past. The viewpoints of the revolutionary nationalist and the academic historian are not necessarily antagonistic. The academician, for example, may disavow an activist role and say that he is dealing with ideas for their own sake. But ideas are weapons and, as a rule, action is germinated by ideas.

In the formation of the new black history the academician—the traditionalist—will continue to be of major importance. But if black history is to come of age, revolutionary black nationalists will also have much to contribute. The nationalist historians will force a reexamination of the historic patterns of color prejudice in America, not only in its grosser, more obvious manifestations, but in its manifold subtle forms, its protective coloration, one might say. The nationalists will bring into purview the blacks of the so-called Third World, comparing and contrasting them with their counterparts in America. The tone of moral outrage that characterizes the nationalist school has its value, too, a healthy anger often acting as a social catalyst.

And finally the revolutionary black nationalist has made it clear that to properly assess the black past we need newer, nontraditional techniques. A multidisciplinary approach is called for, one not relying so largely on written records. Historical inquiry is already profiting from the methodology of the behavioral sciences—sociology, anthropology, and psychology. Interdisciplinary history opens vistas across and beyond the traditional chronological and geographic boundaries. These widening approaches to appraising the past have led to such newer periodicals as the *Journal of Interdisciplinary History,* its first issue appearing in the autumn of 1970 and its avowed purpose to "stimulate historians to examine their own subjects in a new light, whether they be derived from psychology, physics, or paleontology."

This is the age of ideological cross-fertilization. It is to be noted, for example, that today in the study of early man on this planet no fewer than twelve different special skills are necessary—six field skills and six laboratory skills. In properly assessing the black role in American history a comparable if less numerous list of skills is needed. Without the use of these newer tools the past will remain an incompleted past. In fine, historians of the black past must take into consideration "the changing character of historical evidence, the development of new techniques and concepts in related disciplines, and the growing body of research by non-historians into historical problems," to borrow a phrase from David S. Landes and Charles Tilly ("History as Social Science," in Social Science Research Council *Items,* March 1971).

The newer black history, looking afresh down the corridors of time, has a revolutionary potential of its own. For blacks it is a new way to see themselves. For whites it furnishes a new version of American history, one that especially challenges our national sense of smugness and self-righteousness and our avowal of fair play. Beyond this the new black history summons the entire historical guild—writers, teachers, and learners—to higher levels of expectation and performance. History, as all of its disciples know, is both continuity and change. Change stems from our readiness to challenge the current order, using the best tools of our trade. A new black history would revitalize education, quickening whatever it touches.

In 1925 in the foreword to his pathbreaking volume *The New Negro,* Alain Locke, one of the many illustrious Howard University scholar-humanists, said many things that have a contemporary ring: "Negro life is not only establishing new contacts and founding new centers, it is finding a new soul. There is a fresh spiritual and cultural focusing. . . . There is a renewed race-spirit that consciously and proudly sets itself apart." Locke, of course, was speaking primarily of creative expression in the arts, but his words aptly characterize the current black thrust in history. In its work of restoring history's lost boundaries, the black history of today is establishing new contacts and finding a new soul.

Chapters in this book were previously published in the following journals and collections and are reprinted by permission.

"The Colonial Militia and Negro Manpower," *Mississippi Valley Historical Review* 45, no. 4 (March 1959): 643–52. © 1959 by Organization of American Historians.

"Lord Dunmore as Liberator," *William and Mary Quarterly* 15, no. 4 (October 1958): 494–507. © 1958 by the Institute of Early American History and Culture.

"The Revolutionary War as a Black Declaration of Independence," in *Slavery and Freedom in the Age of the American Revolution*, ed. Ira Berlin and Ronald Hoffman (Charlottesville: University Press of Virginia, 1983).

"Sources of Abolitionist Income," *Mississippi Valley Historical Review* 32, no. 1 (June 1945): 63–76.

"Ministers without Portfolio," *Journal of Negro History*, January 1954, pp. 27–42.

"Antebellum Free Blacks and the 'Spirit of '76,'" *Journal of Negro History*, July 1976, pp. 229–42.

"Black History's Antebellum Origins," *Proceedings of the American Antiquarian Society* 89, part 1 (April 1979): 116–22. © 1979 by American Antiquarian Society.

"The Abduction of the *Planter*," *Civil War History* 4 (March 1958): 5–10. © 1958 by Kent State University Press.

"The Morning Breaks: Black America, 1910–1935," *The Crisis*, November 1980, pp. 333–37.

"A. Philip Randolph: Labor Leader at Large," in *Black Leaders of the Twentieth Century*, ed. John Hope Franklin and August Meier (Urbana: University of Illinois Press, 1982). © 1982 by the Board of Trustees of the University of Illinois.

"Black History Unbound," *Daedalus*, Journal of the American Academy of Arts and Sciences, Spring 1974, pp. 163–78. © 1974 by The American Academy of Arts and Sciences.

"Black History's Diversified Clientele," in *Africa and the Afro-American Experience: Eight Essays*, ed. Lorraine A. Williams (Washington: Howard University Press, 1977). © 1971 by Howard University Department of History.

The introduction by August Meier was originally published as "Benjamin Quarles and the Historiography of Black America," *Civil War History* 26, no. 2 (1980): 101–16. © 1980 by Kent State University Press. It has been revised specifically for this volume.

973.0496 Quarles, Benjamin.
QUA
        Black mosaic.

                                    29430
$12.95

DATE			
FEB 23 20??			